Demystifying Globalization

Globalization and Governance

Published in association with POLSIS, University of Birmingham

General Editors: **Colin Hay** and **David Marsh**

Globalization has become the buzzword of the age. It conjures an ever-growing set of associations, connotations and mythologies.

This series will engage in a critical interrogation, unpacking and disaggregation of the often underdeveloped, undertheorised and unduly homogeneous concept of globalization that pervades much of the existing literature and debate.

In examining the complex and multiple processes that constitute the dynamics of globalization, the series aims to contribute to the demystifying of the concept, challenging its logic of inevitability by putting the political back into the analysis of globalization.

The spirit of the series is international and interdisciplinary. It assesses the practices and processes of globalization in the cultural, political, social and economic spheres, examining the empirical evidence for the phenomenon, unpacking the ideological underpinnings of its discourse and discussing the prospects for its governance.

Titles include:

Colin Hay and David Marsh (*editors*)
DEMYSTIFYING GLOBALIZATION

Colin Hay (*editor*)
GLOBALIZATION, WELFARE RETRENCHMENT AND THE STATE

Globalization and Governance Series
Series Standing Order ISBN 0–333–79238–6 hardcover
(*outside North America only*)

You can receive future titles in this series as they are published by placing a standing order. Please contact your bookseller or, in case of difficulty, write to us at the address below with your name and address, the title of the series and the ISBN quoted above.

Customer Services Department, Macmillan Distribution Ltd, Houndmills, Basingstoke, Hampshire RG21 6XS, England

---

Demystifying Globalization

Edited by

Colin Hay

and

David Marsh

in association with
POLSIS, University of Birmingham

First published in hardcover 2000

First published in paperback 2001 by
PALGRAVE
Houndmills, Basingstoke, Hampshire RG21 6XS and
175 Fifth Avenue, New York, N.Y. 10010
Companies and representatives throughout the world

PALGRAVE is the new global academic imprint of
St. Martin's Press LLC Scholarly and Reference Division and
Palgrave Publishers Ltd (formerly Macmillan Press Ltd).

ISBN 0–333–77895–2 hardback (*outside North America*)
ISBN 0–312–23027–3 hardback (*in North America*)
ISBN 0–333–96857–3 paperback (*worldwide*)

This book is printed on paper suitable for recycling and
made from fully managed and sustained forest sources.

A catalogue record for this book is available
from the British Library.

10   9   8   7   6   5   4   3   2   1
10   09   08   07   06   05   04   03   02   01

Printed and bound in Great Britain by
Antony Rowe Ltd, Chippenham, Wiltshire

Contents

Acknowledgements

The present volume arises out of a series of papers presented at a conference on *Globalization: Critical Perspectives* held at the University of Birmingham 14–16, March 1997. This conference was jointly funded by the Political Sociology Research Group of the Department of Political Science and International Studies and the School of Commerce and Social Sciences whose support we gratefully acknowledge. We would also like to thank Suzy Kennedy and Matthew Watson for their help in organising the conference and Sunder Katwala for the original suggestion for the series, of which this is the first volume, and for successive rounds of editorial encouragement.

Finally, and more formally, we would like to acknowledge the support of the ESRC for our research on 'Globalization, European Integration and the European Social Model' (L213252043).

Notes on the Editors

Colin Hay is Senior Lecturer in the Department of Political Science and International Studies at the University of Birmingham. When this book was written he was a visiting fellow of the Department of Political Science at MIT and a research affiliate of the Center for European Studies at Harvard University. He is the author of *Re-Stating Social and Political Change* (1996), winner of the Philip Abrams Memorial Prize, and *The Political Economy of New Labour: Labouring under False Pretences* (1999), co-author of *Postwar British Politics in Perspective* (1999) and co-editor of a number of volumes, most recently *Theorizing Modernity* (1998, with Martin O'Brien and Sue Penna). He is on the Editorial Board of *Sociology* and, with David Marsh, is series editor of *Globalization and Governance*.

David Marsh is Professor of Political Science and Head of Department in the Department of the Political Science and International Studies at the University of Birmingham. He is the author or editor of numerous books and articles. His latest books include *Marxism and Social Science* (1999, co-edited with Andrew Gamble and Tony Tant), *Comparing Policy Networks* (1998) and *Postwar British Politics in Perspective* (1999). He is currently working on books on the changing political culture of Whitehall and on political behaviour in the context of the structure/agency debate. He is the editor of *the British Journal of Politics and International Relations* and, with Colin Hay, is series editor of *Globalization and Governance*.

Notes on the Contributors

Attila Ágh is the Head of the Political Science Department of the Budapest University of Economics and Director of the Hungarian Centre for Democracy Studies. In the 1980s he was the Director of the Hungarian Institute for International Relations.

Andreas Busch is a Lecturer in the Political Science Department of Heidelberg University. His research interests are primarily in the fields of comparative politics and political economy. He is the author of *Neokonservative Wirtschaftspolitik in Großbritannien* (1989) and *Preisstabilitätspolitik. Politik und Inflationsraten im internationalen Vergleich* (1995). Besides that, he has published in journals such as *West European Politics*, *Government and Opposition* and *Politische Vierteljahresschrift* as well as contributing to several edited volumes. He is presently working on a project titled 'The state's capacity to act under conditions of globalization – the case of banking regulation'. In 1997/98, he was John F. Kennedy Memorial Fellow at the Center for European Studies at Harvard University.

John Clammer is Professor of Comparative Sociology and Asian Studies at Sophia University, Tokyo and has previously taught or researched at a number of universities in Asia, Europe and Australia including the National University of Singapore, Hull, Kent and Murdoch. His interests are primarily in the sociology of culture, the study of social inequality and ethnicity and in the relationships between contemporary social theory and Asian societies. His most recent book is *Contemporary Urban Japan: A Sociology of Consumption* (1997).

Ngai-Ling Sum is Simon Research Fellow at the International Centre for Labour Studies, Manchester University. She has research interests in the trans-border regions, the political economy of East Asian newly-industrializing countries, and the relationship between political economy and identity politics. She is on the Editorial Board of the *Pacific Review*. Her most recent publications include articles in *Economy and Society*, *New Political Economy* and *Emergo*. She has also contributed to edited volumes including *Fragmented Asia* (1996), *Regionalism and World Order* (Macmillan 1996), *Beyond Markets and Hierarchy* (1997) and *Dynamic*

Asia (1998). She is currently working on a book on *Capitalism in East Asian Newly-Industrializing Countries: A Regulationist Perspective.*

Peter J. Taylor is Professor of Geography at the University of Loughborough. A political geographer with a particular interest in world-systems analysis, he is founding editor of *Political Geography* and member of the Gulbenkian Commission on the Restructuring of the Social Sciences. His recent books are *The Way the Modern World Works: World Hegemony to World Impasse* (1996), *Modernities: a Geohistorical Interpretation* (1998) and *Political Geography: World-Economy, Nation-State, Locality* (4th edn, 1999).

Nigel Thrift is Professor and Head of the School of Geographical Sciences at Bristol University. His research is in a number of areas including social and cultural theory, technological cultures, time and the nature of contemporary capitalism. His recent books include *Mapping the Subject* (coedited with Steve Pile), *Spatial Formations, Money/Space* (with Andrew Leyshon), and *Shopping, Place and Identity* (with Danny Miller, Peter Jackson and Beverley Holbrook and Mike Rowlands).

Daniel Wincott is Senior Lecturer in the Department of Political Science and International Studies of the Unviersity of Birmingham, having previously worked at the Universities of Leicester and Warwick. His main areas of research interest are Comparative Political Economy and European integration, particularly the theorization of European law, on which he has published in a range of journals. He is an editor of the *British Journal of Politics and International Studies*.

1
Introduction: Demystifying Globalization

Colin Hay and David Marsh

The realm of politics – of agency, imagination, of demonic and heroic intent – matters in creating the structures which then limit human possibilities. (Piven 1995: 114)

The untrammelled hegemony of Anglo-American ideological premises is one of the most salient forces shaping the specific character of the current global economy, including the extent to which globalization is viewed as entailing the eclipse of the state. (Evans 1997: 64)

Globalization has, within academic, political and business circles alike, become the buzz-word of the 1990s, conjuring an ever-growing diversity of associations, connotations and attendant mythologies. Given the sheer scope and diversity of this literature, together with its (ever-) gathering prominence (both academic and political), it is perhaps unsurprising that it has come to resolve itself into often jealously guarded and distinct 'disciplinary discourses' (on which see Robertson and Khondker 1998). Thus, economists debate the extent to which we now inhabit a global free market characterised by heightened and, in some accounts, perfect mobility of goods, labour and capital (investment and financial) – a condition summoned by deregulation, financial liberalization and the information technology 'revolution'. Relatedly, political economists assess (and increasing contest) the extent to which such economic processes engender a 'withering of the state' rather more abrupt even than that envisioned by Marx. Heightened capital mobility and the punitive discipline of the financial markets, it is argued, weaken the authority of the state in the spheres of fiscal and (especially) monetary policy, driving a seemingly inexorable process of (neo-liberal) convergence, so-called 'institutional isomorphism' and state retrenchment (though

1

see Berger and Dore 1996; Garrett 1998). Meanwhile, political scientists, normative political theorists and scholars of international relations, often impressed by such claims about the obsolescence of the nation-state in an era of globalization, ponder the desirability and, in some accounts, the claimed 'reality' of global governance, a world political system and an emergent post-national *cosmopolis* (see for instance Bobbio 1984; Falk 1995; Hoffman 1995; Luard 1990; Zolo 1997). Paralleling such concerns, sociologists debate the extent to which one can posit the existence of a more or less homogeneous global civil society as the world has become united, variously, by political struggle and patterns of mobilization which transcend the boundaries of the national, by Westernization, McDonaldization, Coca-Colonisation and American cultural imperialism, by heightened or 'reflexive modernisation', post-modernization or neo-Medievalism (see, for instance, Albrow 1996; Beck et al. 1994; Giddens 1990; Latouche 1996; Maffesoli 1995; Meyer 1980; Ritzer 1992; Shaw 1994; Tomlinson 1991; Waterman 1993). Finally, and perhaps most consistently, a diverse group of cultural theorists, literary critics and anthropologists tracing their lineage to McLuhan's reflections on the 'global village' in the 1960s, have debated the nature, depth and indeed the very existence, of a global culture that is post-nationalist, postcolonial, postmodern and cosmopolitan (see, for instance, Appadurai 1996; Bhabha 1994; Cheah and Robbins 1998; Featherstone 1990, 1995; McLuhan 1964; Wilson and Dissanayake 1996).

What these literatures share is a common emphasis upon flows – whether of capital (financial or industrial), labour, information, technology, culture, images, or even people in the form of cosmopolitan 'post-tourists' (MacCannell 1992). Such flows give rise to a profusion of fluid, irregularly shaped, variously textured and constantly changing landscapes or '-scapes'. In a path-breaking analysis, Appadurai identifies five inter-related yet nonetheless distinguishable dimensions to such global flows: *ethnoscapes* – the moving landscape of tourists, immigrants, refugees, exiles, trans-national commuters and so forth; *technoscapes* – relating to flows of technology and information across boundaries; *finanscapes* – a virtual landscape configured by currency markets, financial innovations and currency speculations; *mediascapes* – the dissemination and proliferation of images; and *ideoscapes* – the political and strategic diffusion of images by states and oppositional movements (Appadurai 1996: 33–7). This establishes the (often virtual) terrain of globalization and the focus of our concerns.

In what follows, our aim is to cast a critical and in large part sceptical gaze over some of the often wildly exaggerated and wilfully extrapolated claims made in the name of globalization, whilst seeking to transcend the disciplinary shackles that have come to characterise, as they have come to limit, our understanding of the dynamic processes and mechanisms of globalization. In so doing we echo what, following Kofman and Youngs, we will identify as the 'second wave' literature on globalization (1996). Our purpose, however, both for the present volume and for the series as a whole, is to contribute further towards the development of a more integrated, indeed post-disciplinary, 'third wave' literature. Such a perspective, still very much in its infancy, seeks to develop a multidimensional approach to the various processes that interact – often in highly complex and contingent ways – to produce the phenomena variously referred to as economic, political, social and cultural globalization (as well as the chapters in Kofman and Youngs 1996, see also Lash and Urry 1994; Scott 1997; Thrift 1996). It is important, however, that we clarify this project at the outset. For, in positing an inter-disciplinary, indeed post-disciplinary, approach to globalization we do not wish to imply that there is a singular process of cultural, political or economic globalization, nor that globalization itself constitutes a singular process or dynamic. Rather, our claim is that there are multiple processes of globalization, that these interact in specific and contingent ways, that such processes are unevenly developed over space and time, are complex and often resisted and, moreover, that they are simultaneously social, cultural, political and economic. Accordingly, an account which privileges (empirically or, worse still, causally) one 'moment' (whether social, cultural, political or economic) can but only fail to capture the complexity and contingency of contemporary change. Thus, as Robertson and Khondker note, 'particularly in the vast field of global studies, the necessity is to display as fully as possible the extent of the complexity before we begin to engage in practices of simplification . . . we should begin with the task of complexification before we engage in the task of simplification' (1998: 27).

In sum then, the purpose of this volume, and the broader series of which it forms a part, is to unpack and expose to critical scrutiny the concept of globalization. In so doing, our aim is to assess the extent to which the various processes appealed to in the notion of globalization imply a qualitative, indeed, epochal shift in the contours of contemporary societies, to evaluate the constraints and opportunities that such a confluence of globalizing tendencies implies and, above all, to emphasize the complex, contested, contingent and deeply political character of such processes considered separately and, hence, of the overall dynamic itself. Our abiding ambition is that, by so doing, we might contribute further to the demystification of globalization and the 'logics of inevitability' it is variously held to conjure (on which see Hay 1998; Hay and Watson 1998).[1] As such and in its related concern to advance a post-disciplinary perspective to global dynamics, we see this volume as part of an emerging and distinctive 'third-wave' of writings on globalization.

Surfing the Tides of Globalization

The first wave can be characterised (without too much licence) by its appeal to a series of often overblown, distorted, uncritical and seldom defended assertions about the inexorable and immutable globalization of capital, culture and communications alike. This has, or is in the process, of laying waste the nation-state, the welfare state and distinct civil societies themselves, thereby marking a qualitative and quantitative shift of epochal proportions. Or thus we are entreated. Such a view is still extremely influential amongst the self-styled media gurus of the 'information age' as it is amongst political and business elites and, indeed, amongst certain sections of the academic left. It is tirelessly rehearsed in the editorial columns and business pages of the financial, tabloid and broadsheet media alike and is often associated with a certain neo-liberal triumphalism and the view (rather more widely held) that there is simply no alternative to neo-liberalism within the contours of the new global political economy (Levitt 1983; Ohmae 1990, 1995; Reich 1992; Sachs and Warner 1995; see also Barnet and Cavanagh 1994; Barnet and Müller 1974). Empirically, as a growing number of political economists and political scientists have demonstrated in recent years in often meticulous detail (see, for instance, Bairoch 1996; Hirst and Thompson 1996; Watson 1999a; Zysman 1996), there is little or no substance to this exaggerated parody of, and wild extrapolation from, contemporary developments. Indeed, as Andreas Busch reveals in his contribution to this collection, the first-wave literature is marked as it is marred by 'casual empiricism'. For it is only the unscrupulous and/or selective use of evidence (where evidence is appealed to at all) that can sustain the image often depicted in this 'business globalization' literature of the withering away of the state at the hands of footloose multinational corporations and capital.

The sceptical and critical response to, and rejection of, this crude 'business globalization' literature has stimulated a distinctive and rather more rigorous 'second-wave'. This has been mirrored by similar developments which challenge the notion of a homogeneous global culture or society – the global-babble of the infotech revolution. Here, for brevity, we concentrate on the former literature. A number of authors in recent years have come to challenge the received wisdom that during the 1980s and 1990s (if not before)[2] we have witnessed an inexorable, accelerating and homogenizing tide of globalization, levelling a once differentiated and contoured terrain to reveal the flat expanse of a 'borderless world' supported and sustained by a genuinely global market place. This second-wave and largely secondary literature has pointed to a number of factors, each of which, taken on their own, puncture fairly convincingly such a global mythology. Taken together they constitute a devastating refutation of the business globalization thesis. Among these factors, we might usefully identify the following: (i) the apparently positive (and, in fact, ever stronger) correlation between 'stateness' (reflected in higher levels of social expenditure) and both 'openness' and competitive advantage within the international political economy (Evans 1997: 68–9; Garrett 1995; 1998; Rodrik 1996);[3] (ii) the rather exaggerated claims made about the hyper-mobility of, particularly, foreign direct investors and productive capital in the 'first wave' literature (Hirst and Thompson 1996; Watson 1998); (iii) the seeming lack of convergence in macroeconomic indicators and policy across national boundaries despite globalization's supposedly 'homogenizing' effect (Berger and Dore 1996; Watson 1999b); (iv) the empirical fact that domestic consumption demands continue overwhelmingly to be satisfied via the domestic circuit of capital and, moreover, that these domestic producers remain predominantly domestically owned (Epstein 1996: 213; Hay and Watson 1998; Obstfeld 1995: 35; Piven 1995); (v) the fact that international flows of capital (such as foreign direct investment, FDI) tend to be extremely concentrated within the core 'triad' (of Europe, North America and Pacific Asia) providing evidence of regionalization, 'triadization' or internationalization but hardly of globalization (Allen and Thompson 1997; Frankel 1997; Hirst and Thompson 1996); (vi) that when expressed as a proportion of GDP, today's flow of FDI are merely comparable with those of the pre-First World War period (Bairoch 1996: 188); and, finally, (vii) that far from inhabiting a world defined purely by global economic relations, productive capitals continue to act primarily within the more familiar confines of national economic spaces, suggesting in turn that national economic regulation is very far from obsolete (Hay and Watson 1998; Wade 1996; Weiss 1996).

As the above paragraph would perhaps suggest, this second-wave literature has contributed enormously to our understanding of the complex, contingent and unevenly developed processes and practices of globalization. The result is a much more nuanced and differentiated view, yet one which is still essentially derivative (albeit in a very negative sense) of the initial tide of 'globaloney' (to adopt Ellen Meiksins Wood's memorable phrase)[4] that characterized the 'first-wave'.

Whilst in no sense seeking to detract from the very considerable accomplishments of those who pioneered the much-needed, indeed long overdue, critique of the business globalization literature and its political logic of no alternative, in this series our aim is to contribute to the development of a distinct 'third-wave' literature. This, we suggest, must build on the foundations laid by the critique of earlier, more cavalier, appeals to the notion of globalization, to further unpack and demystify this 'process without a subject'. The challenge which such a literature must address – a challenge that, as series editors we posed to the contributors to this volume as we pose it to future contributors to the series – is to view globalization not so much as a process or end-state, but (as in Peter Taylor's contribution to this volume) as a *tendency* to which there are *counter-tendencies*. Moreover, once viewed as merely tendential, the challenge is to reveal the dynamic and contingent articulation of processes in certain spatial contexts at certain moments in time to yield effects which might be understood as evidence of globalization.[5]

In this sense, then, we reverse the conventional direction of causality appealed to in the literature on globalization. *We ask not what globalization (as a process without a subject) might explain, but how the insertion of subjects into processes might help to explain the phenomena widely identified as 'globalization'.* Globalization (in so far as it can be identified as a tendency) becomes then for us not so much 'that doing the explaining' (the *explanans*) as 'that to be explained' (the *explanandum*).

Recast in this way, there is no need to make essentialising and reifying assumptions about the effects, consequences, or even the very existence, of globalization. For, in so far as globalization can be identified, it is understood as the contingent (and only ever tendential) outcome of a confluence of specific processes that are themselves likely to be limited in space and time. Globalized outcomes and effects might then be the product of very different, indeed entirely independent, mechanisms and processes of causation that can only be obscured by appeal to a generic (and causal) logic of globalization. Whilst problematizing and interrogating the processes which underpin globalizing tendencies, then, we resist the temptation to appeal to globalization itself as a causal factor or process working, apparently independently of the actions, intentions and motivations of real subjects. It is precisely this appeal to causal processes *without subjects* that summons the logic of necessity and inevitability so often associated with the notion of globalization. In so doing it serves to render the otherwise contingent necessary (on which see Hay and Watson 1998). If we are then to demystify globalization, we must ensure that in making what we think are causal arguments, we can identify the actors involved, thus giving due attention to the 'structuration' of globalizing tendencies whilst rejecting structuralist or functionalist 'logics' operating over the heads or independently of social subjects (see Daniel Wincott's discussion of 'structuralist bias' in the final chapter of this volume).

It is only by paying careful attention to the problem of structure and agency in this way, dismissing accounts which privilege either structure or (far less frequently in analyses of globalization) agency in the determination of outcomes, that the notion of globalization might be used to open up and not merely to obfuscate the analysis of social, political and economic change.

Demystifying Globalization: In the Wake of the Second Wave

Having said this, however, the present volume, in its concern to demystify globalization and in the context of the above challenge, lies somewhere between the second and third waves of the globalization debate. Its principal aim is to review and take stock of existing approaches to the analysis of globalization, establishing a basis from which to respond to the challenge of the third wave taken up more explicitly and positively in the second, third and subsequent volumes of this series (Hay and Marsh 2000a, 2000b). Nonetheless, its novelty and consistency as a collection of essays lies in a series of theoretical innovations (at least within the literature on globalization) which might serve to differentiate it from the existing approaches more characteristic of the second wave. They might also serve as a point of departure for further research prepared to take up the challenge of scrutinising and interrogating the complex, contingent and heavily mediated processes of change that tend to be subsumed and obscured by appeal to the blanket label 'globalization'.

By way of introduction to the chapters which follow, then, it will perhaps prove instructive to reflect upon such points of theoretical and analytical convergence. Though numerous others can, no doubt, be identified, we will here concentrate merely on four: (i) the emphasis placed upon the discourse and ideology of globalization and on discursive and ideational processes in the mediation of globalizing tendencies;

(ii) the emphasis placed upon the identification of mechanisms and processes of change in the development of a diachronic and processual analysis of globalizing tendencies and counter-tendencies; (iii) the related need to unpack abstract, universal and homogenizing concepts like globalization to reveal the specificity of inter-regional, inter-national, regional, national and local dynamics which may, or may not, contribute to globalizing tendencies; and (iv) the identification of linkages between cultural and economic processes of transformation at a variety of spatial scales.

The discourse of globalization

Despite the above suggestion that we invert the conventional causal logic and conceive of globalization as the independent rather than the dependent variable, there is at least one sense in which we must regard globalization as itself a causal factor. This, as Daniel Wincott notes in his perceptive and provocative chapter, is when it is the *discourse* of globalization that yields material effects. Examples are legion and are appealed to by a number of authors in this collection. Thus, Attila Ágh points to the often regressive consequences of what he terms the 'global ideology of globalization' precisely by virtue of its failure to grasp the complex realities of political and economic change. Similarly, Andreas Busch notes, citing Keohane and Milner, that even although there is little evidence for the much-vaunted hyper-mobility of capital, the *perceived* potential for capital flight in response to changing interest rates may, nonetheless, exert significant pressures on incumbent administrations 'even if no capital movements actually take place' (1996: 3). More generally, as John Clammer argues, the effects of globalization in specific national contexts (he focuses upon Japan) are often made manifest in terms of the responses they engender. Yet these responses are not so much responses to globalization (or even to globalizing tendencies) *per se*, but to particular understandings and constructions of globalization. However reluctant we may be to ascribe a causal role to globalization itself, then, it seems imperative that we consider the independent role that ideas about globalization may have in shaping the social, political and economic contexts we inhabit (see also Douglas 1997).

At the same time, however, we should be wary of an overemphasis upon, and privileging of, the discursive. Our concern should be with the relationship between ideas held about globalization on the one hand and the processes such ideas purport to describe on the other. Whilst the contributors and editors of this volume vary over the precise extent to which social, political and economic contexts constrain, circumscribe and delimit the ideas held about them and the related extent to which ideas mediate, condition and circumscribe the realm of social, political and economic intervention, they agree on the need to understand this relationship dynamically and historically. The material does not determine the discursive, just as the discursive does not determine the material.[6]

Nonetheless, and somewhat ironically, the very discourse and rhetoric of globalization may serve to summon precisely the effects that such a discourse attributes to globalization itself. This is a key theme of Wincott's chapter. For instance, a belief that expansionary measures may precipitate a flurry of capital flight may well be sufficient to ensure a persistent deflationary bias that may bear no relation to real economic processes. Yet such a bias may in turn serve further to entrench the impression that reflation is impossible and that there is no alternative to neo-liberal economics in a context of heightened capital mobility. Moreover, for such a view to produce such an effect requires no evidence of capital mobility, though its very existence is likely to be taken as a further indication of precisely such a logic (for a further development of this argument see Hay 1997; Hay and Watson 1998).

A sensitivity to the role of ideational factors in the production of effects generally attributed to the 'invisible hand of globalization', however, does not exhaust the concern in this volume with the discursive. Drawing upon the pioneering work of Edward Said on 'Orientalism', Ngai-Ling Sum develops an important and theoretically innovative account of the role of trade-competitiveness-development discourses in mediating social and economic relations and developmental trajectories in the Asian Pacific. Similarly, though in a more explicitly Foucauldian manner, Nigel Thrift examines the global diffusion of new 'pastoral' forms of regulation associated with the rise of new systems of expertise (such as new managerial theory) and their dissemination on an international stage. In both of these chapters, the constitutive role of the discursive is emphasised as, respectively, a series of 'new Orientalisms' and a new managerialist 'power-knowledge regime' are seen both to condition and simultaneously to constrain the strategic resources of the state.

Finally, Peter J. Taylor, in an important and innovative chapter, problematizes the very language with which we have tended to approach questions of epochal international or global change – namely that of '-izations'. 'Izations', he warns us 'invite obfuscation' in their conflation of process and end-state, becoming and being, and hence in their invocation of inevitability. Accordingly, if we are to continue deploying the terminology of Americanization, modernization, globalization, and so forth, it is imperative that where we do, we expose such linguistic devices to critical scrutiny, retaining at least the capacity to disentangle being and becoming. Whilst demystifying globalization then, we must also constantly demystify our very appeal to such a notion.

The unpacking of causal processes

If, as Peter Taylor demonstrates, the very language of globalization implies and invites a conflation of being and becoming, process and outcome, then it is important that in demystifying globalization we unpack and reveal the underlying processes that the term itself tends to mask. For, as Attila Ágh, Peter J. Taylor and Daniel Wincott all note in their chapters, where globalization is appealed to as a singular process it obscures more than it clarifies. This is a central theme of the present collection. Once again, it is taken up by almost all contributors.

As the above discussion would suggest, appeal to the concept of globalization may give the impression of explanation, but it cannot in itself explain anything. It is in fact merely to redescribe, and to redescribe in the most imprecise and obscurantist terms at that, the object of our attentions. It is in short a redescription masquerading as an explanation. As such, our critical hackles should be raised whenever globalization is appealed to as a causal factor. Accordingly, wherever we hear reference to globalization's 'imperatives', we should perhaps join with Will Hutton in blowing a big collective raspberry (1996).[7] Yet cathartic though this might be, it is no substitute for the precise analysis of process, causality and outcome which rarely accompanies the concept of globalization yet which forms a unifying theme of the present collection.

Despite the diversity of their empirical concerns and objects of analysis, the present contributors are united by their refusal to deploy globalization as a ubiquitous and often omnipotent causal factor that can be used to account for almost anything, according to it in so doing a certain air of stature and inevitability. More positively, they are united by a common concern with 'process-tracing'. In problematizing and thereby demystifying globalization as they do, they cut through the causal haze that tends to surround the concept, offering rigorous and precise accounts both of globalizing tendencies and of de-globalizing counter-tendencies as and when they can be identified. What this serves to reveal is the highly complex, contested, contingent and political nature of global social, political and economic dynamics as well as the paucity of undifferentiated accounts couched at the level of the global system. A couple of examples will perhaps suffice.

First, Attila Ágh in his chapter examines the complex relationship between globalizing and democratising dynamics, concentrating in particular upon the experience of Eastern Central Europe in recent years. By way of a subtle and nuanced analysis of the specific processes involved and of the interplay of such processes with the institutional and cultural environments upon which they impinged and impinge, he is able to expose the crass distortions of generalised analyses of globalization's democratising embrace.

Similarly, Ngai-Ling Sum's chapter details the complex dialectic of regionalisation and globalization in the Asia Pacific region, demonstrating how this is mediated discursively and institutionally. She too points to the theoretical, analytical and empirical poverty of accounts couched at the level of global trends which identify globalization simply with the 're-making of the world' in the image of the neo-liberal 'Washington Consensus'.

Heterogeneity and the specificity of globalizing dynamics

It is perhaps unremarkable that the concern for process-tracing exhibited by the contributors to this volume should lead them also to a common emphasis upon heterogeneity rather than homogeneity, difference rather than singularity, divergence rather than convergence, and specificity rather than generality (on the question of homogeneity/heterogeneity see also Robertson 1992: 12, 1996). In this respect, as in many others, the present volume builds upon the work of the second-wave literature on globalization (see, for instance, Appadurai 1996; Berger and Dore 1996; Keohane and Milner 1996; Zysman 1996).

Once the absence of simple, homogeneous and general (indeed universal) globalizing dynamics and processes is revealed, and attention is focused instead upon the confluence of processes that underpin globalizing tendencies, it is not surprising that heterogeneity and specificity should be emphasised. For, as the various chapters of this volume attest, it is often very different processes (operating at a variety of different spatial scales and over wildly divergent time-horizons) that interact to produce different and distinctive globalizing tendencies in different contexts. What is required, then, is not so much generic accounts and theories of globalization *per se*, but differentiated analyses capable of reflecting the specificity of such processes and their complex interaction in different institutional and cultural environments.

This point is made in a variety of different ways in the different chapters, yet, once again, it is a theme addressed by all contributors. Andreas Busch notes that in so far as there are convergent tendencies in the global political economy these are exhibited at the regional and certainly not at the global level, necessitating a disaggregated analysis of regionalizing-globalizing dynamics. This, too, is the message of Ngai-Ling Sum and Daniel Wincott's chapters, both of which point to the uneven spatial development of globalization and globalizing tendencies, identifying clear regional and 'triadic' patterns of response and counter-response. Sum take this one step further, emphasising with Attila Ágh the specificity of national and local responses to globalizing and regionalising tendencies and developments. This motif is taken up and developed by John Clammer for the Japanese case which is highly distinctive in almost all respects. Common to both Attila Ágh and Daniel Wincott's chapters is a rejection of the generalising and distorting political narratives of globalization which, however politically expedient and proscriptive, tend to be characterised by crass distortions and inaccuracies. Agh stresses the significance of institutional and cultural mediations and legacies, while Wincott emphasises the path-dependent character of complex institutional change. Finally, Nigel Thrift notes that despite the existence of new modes of expertise and strategies of governmentality that are genuinely global in their reach, these are differently appropriated and assimilated at the national level, requiring, once again, differentiated and institutionally- and culturally-sensitive analyses.

Cultural–economic linkages

A final theme common to a number of the chapters in this collection is the linkage between cultural and economic dynamics, suggesting perhaps the need for a rather more interdisciplinary (even post-disciplinary) analysis of globalizing tendencies and dynamics. This suggestive, if still tentative, idea is most explicitly raised by Ngai-Ling Sum, who posits the need for a new 'cultural political economy' sensitive to the complex and dialectical interplay between discursive-cultural dynamics on the one hand and economic-institutional factors on the other (for a more detailed exposition of this see Sum 2000). Such an approach has clear affinities with Nigel Thrift's identification of what he terms the 'cultural circuit of capitalism' and his more general emphasis upon the role of the social organization of knowledge, intelligence and expertise in the regulation of capitalist economic relations across space and time. The benefits of a dialogue between, and potential synthesis of, the existing (second-wave) literatures on economic and cultural globalization are further revealed in Peter J. Taylor's chapter. Specifically, he suggests that analyses of the political economy of globalization might benefit from the concern of the cultural globalization literature with globalization as a field of struggle and with the contested nature of socio-cultural dynamics. His rehabilitation of a Gramscian conception of hegemony within international political economy is also suggestive of possibilities for a new 'cultural political economy' (cf. Gill 1993). Finally, John Clammer's chapter on the specificity of Japanese attitudes and responses to 'globalization' demonstrates yet again that economic processes must be situated in cultural contexts and understood in terms of cultural specificity, since the process of change resides neither in one moment (the economic) nor the other (the cultural), but in the articulation of the two.

Bringing the Subject Back In

As we indicated earlier, although we see the need to initiate a break with the second-wave globalization literature reviewed at the outset, we do not regard the present volume as unambiguously pioneering this third wave. Indeed, we see it as inhabiting a potentially rather ambiguous liminal zone between waves. We do hope, however, that the above discussion of points of theoretical convergence between the chapters might provide some indication of the central themes that will need to be taken up if a third wave is to develop, whilst indicating the distinctiveness of the present volume.

In so far as it is unified by a single theme cutting across the issues discussed in the previous section, that is the 'bringing of the subject back in' to the analysis of globalization. This, as we have argued, requires an inversion of the conventional lines of causality which run from globalization to a variety of assumed outcomes and effects (the withering of the state, macroeconomic convergence, welfare retrenchment, cultural homogenization, a new cosmopolitanism and so forth). In so far as globalization can be identified as a process (and, we argue, it is far more usefully conceived of as a tendency to which there are, and will continue to be, counter-tendencies), it is a process without a subject. Our concern, and the concern of this volume and series, is to identify processes with subjects. As Frances Fox Piven notes in the quote with which we began this introduction, 'the realm of politics – of agency, imagination, of demonic and heroic intent – matters in creating the structures which then limit human possibilities' (Piven 1995: 114). This is as true of globalization as it is of any other social, political and economic phenomenon. Globalization is the product of human interaction, the product of subjects making history, but not in circumstances of their own choosing (to paraphrase Marx's famous aphorism). It is to the structuration of globalization, then, that we must turn if we are to rediscover the capacity (that the rhetoric of globalization so frequently denies us) of shaping, steering and ultimately transforming the globalized world that we have made and which we must now inhabit.

Notes

1. For representative samples of the now growing literature sceptical of the heroic claims often made in the name of globalization, see in particular Berger and Dore (1996), Boyer and Drache (1996), Garrett (1998), Hirst and Thompson (1996), Keohane and Milner (1996) and Mittelman (1997).
2. This in itself raises an interesting and perplexing issue and one which massively polarises the existing literature on globalization – that of timing. When does globalization begin? If the conventional view in comparative and international political economy is that globalization is initiated by the ending of the Bretton Woods system and the liberalization of financial markets from the early 1970s, accelerating rapidly in the 1980s, then for world systems theorists such a Wallerstein, globalization, as reflected in the existence of a world economic system, can be traced at least to the late fifteenth and early sixteenth century (Wallerstein 1974). Robertson goes further still, arguing that 'overall processes of globalization (and deglobalization) are at least as old as the rise of the so-called world religions two thousand and more years ago' (1992: 6–7). Others, still, pinpoint the moment of globalization as the very second when the first images of the earth as a globe were received from space. Suffice it to say that there is little agreement about either when globalization began (if indeed we suggest it has) or in what it consists. We should perhaps be content to speak of different modes of globalization, unevenly developed spatially – a 'multi-speed globalization' tendency exhibiting 'variable geometries'. We are indebted to Matthew Watson for suggesting this line of analysis to us.
3. In noting this strengthening correlation, these authors draw on the earlier pioneering work of Cameron (1978) and Katzenstein (1985).
4. See Wood (1997). Wood in fact attributes the term to Doug Henwood, who in turn claims he borrowed if from Bob Fitch. We thus extend further a global yet virtual nexus!
5. To be fair, this is a challenge that has already been taken up by some contributors to the second-wave literature – particularly those who seek to interrogate the political authoring of globalization. See for instance Cox (1996), Hay and Watson (1998), Helleiner (1994; 1996), Watson (1999a; 1999b).
6. For a further elaboration of this position see Hay and Marsh (1999).
7. Again, we are indebted to Matthew Watson for bringing this reference to our attention.

Bibliography

Albrow, M. (1996) *The Global Age: State and Society Beyond Modernity*, Cambridge: Polity.
Allen, J. and G. Thompson (1997) 'Think Globally, Then Think Again: Economic Globalisation in Context', *Area*, 29 (3), 213–27.

Appadurai, A. (1996) *Modernity at Large: Cultural Dimensions of Globalization*, Minneapolis, MN: University of Minnesota Press.

Bairoch, P. (1996) 'Globalization Myths and Realities: One Century of External Trade and Foreign Investment', in Boyer and Drache eds, *States Against Markets*.

Barnet, R. J. and J. Cavanagh (1994) *Global Dreams: Imperial Corporations and the New World Order*, New York: Simon and Schuster.

Barnet, R. J. and R. E. Müller (1974) *Global Reach: The Power of the Multinational Corporations*, New York: Simon and Schuster.

Beck, U., Giddens, A. and S. Lash (1994) *Reflexive Modernisation*, Cambridge: Polity.

Berger, S. and R. Dore (eds) (1996) *National Diversity and Global Capitalism*, Ithaca, NY: Cornell University Press.

Bhabha, H. K. (1994) *The Location of Culture*, London: Routledge.

Bobbio, N. (1984) 'Democrazia e sistema internazionale', in *Il futuro della democrazia*, Turin: Einaudi.

Boyer, R. and D. Drache (eds) (1996) *States Against Markets: The Limits of Globalisation*, London: Routledge.

Cameron, D. R. (1978) 'The Expansion of the Public Economy: A Comparative Analysis', *American Political Science Review*, 72 (4), 1243–61.

Cheah, P. and B. Robbins (eds) (1998) *Cosmopolitics: Thinking and Feeling Beyond the Nation*, Minneapolis, MN: University of Minnesota Press.

Cox, R. (1996) 'A Perspective on Globalization', in Mittelman, (ed.) *Globalization: Critical Reflections*.

Douglas, I. R. (1997) 'Globalisation and the End of the State?', *New Political Economy*, 2 (1), 165–79.

Epstein, G. (1996) 'International Capital Mobility and the Scope for National Economic Management', in Boyer and Drache, (eds) *States Against Markets*.

Evans, P. (1997) 'The Eclipse of the State? Reflections on Statenss in an Era of Globalization', *World Politics*, 50 (1), 62–87.

Falk, J. (1995) *On Humane Governance: Towards a New Global Politics*, Cambridge: Polity.

Featherstone, M. (ed.) (1990) *Global Culture*, London: Sage.

Feathersone, M. (1995) *Undoing Culture: Globalization, Postmodernism and Identity*, London: Sage.

Frankel, J. A. (1997) *Regional Trading Blocs in the World Economic System*, Washington, DC: Institute for International Economics.

Garrett, G. (1995) 'Capital Mobility, Trade and the Domestic Politics of Economic Policy', *International Organization*, 49 (4), 657–87.

Garrett, G. (1998) *Partisan Politics in the Global Economy*, Cambridge: Cambridge University Press.

Giddens, A. (1990) *The Consequences of Modernity*, Cambridge: Polity.

Gill, S. (ed.) (1993) *Gramsci, Historical Materialism and International Relations*, Cambridge: Cambridge University Press.

Hay, C. (1997) 'Anticipating Accommodations, Accommodating Anticipations: The Appeasement of Capital in the Modernisation of the British Labour Party, 1987–92', *Politics and Society*, 25 (2), 234–56.

Hay, C. (1998) 'Globalization, Welfare Retrenchment and the Logic of No Alternative: Why Second-Best Won't Do', *Journal of Social Policy*, 27 (4), 525–32

Hay, C. and D. Marsh (1999) 'In Conclusion: Analysing and Explaining Postwar British Political Development', in Marsh, D. et al. (1999) *Postwar British Politics in Pespective*, Cambridge: Polity.

Hay, C. and D. Marsh (eds) (2000a) *Globalization, Welfare Retrenchment and the State*, London: Macmillan.

Hay, C. and D. Marsh (eds) (2000b) *Globalization and Governance: Discourse, Processes and Practices*, London: Macmillan.

Hay, C. and M. Watson (1998) 'The Discourse of Globalization and the Logic of No Alternative: Rendering the Contingent Necessary in the Downsizing of New Labour's Aspirations for Government', paper presented at the PSA Annual Conference, University of Keele, April; reprinted in abbreviated form in Dobson, A. and J. Stanyer (eds) (1998) *Contemporary Political Science 1998*, Oxford: Blackwell/PSA.

Helleiner, E. (1994) *States and the Reemergence of Global Finance: From Bretton Woods to the 1990s*, Ithaca: Cornell University Press.

Helleiner, E. (1996) 'Post-Globalization and Financial Markets: Is the Financial Liberalisation Trend Likely to Be Reversed?', in Boyer and Drache (eds) *States Against Markets*.

Hirst, P. and Thompson, G. (1996) *Globalisation in Question*, Cambridge: Polity.

Hoffman, J. (1995) *Beyond the State*, Cambridge: Polity.

Hutton, W. (1996) *The Observer*, 17 November.

Katzenstein, P. (1985) *Small States in World Markets: Industrial Policy in Europe*, Ithaca: Cornell University Press.

Keohane, R. O. and H. V. Milner (eds) (1996) *Internationalisation and Domestic Politics*, Cambridge: Cambridge University Press.

Kofman, E. and G. Youngs (eds) (1996) *Globalization: Theory and Practice*, London: Pinter.

Lash, S. and Urry, J. (1994) *Economies of Signs and Space*, London: Sage.

Latouche, S. (1996) *The Westernization of the World*, Cambridge: Polity.

Levitt, T. (1983) 'The Globalisation of Markets', *Harvard Business Review*, May–June, 101.

Luard, E. (1990) *The Globalization of Politics: The Changed Focus of Political Action in the Modern World*, London: Macmillan.

McLuhan, M. (1964) *Understanding Media: The Extensions of Man*, Cambridge, MA: MIT Press.

MacCannell, D. (1992) *Empty Meeting Grounds: Tourist Papers*, London: Routledge.

Maffesoli, M. (1995) *The Time of the Tribes*, London: Sage.

Meyer, J. W. (1980) 'The World Polity and the Autority of the Nation-State', in A. Bergeson (ed.) *Studies of the Modern World System*, New York: Academic Press.

Mittelman, J. H. (ed.) (1997) *Globalisation: Critical Reflections*, Boulder, CO: Lynne Rienner, 1997.

Obstfeld, M. (1995) 'International Capital Mobility in the 1990s', in Kenen, P. B., ed., *Understanding Interdependence: The Macroeconomics of the Open Economy*, Princeton, NJ: Princeton University Press.

Ohmae, K. (1990) *The Borderless World: Power and Strategy in the Interlinked Economy*, London: Collins.

Ohmae, K. (1996) *The End of the Nation State: The Rise of Regional Economies*, New York: Free Press

Piven, F. F. (1995) 'Is It Global Economics or Neo-Laissez Faire?', *New Left Review*, 213, 107–14.

Reich, R. (1992) *The Work of Nations*, New York: Vintage Books.

Ritzer, G. (1992) *The McDonaldization of Society*, London: Sage.

Robertson, R. (1992) *Globalization: Social Theory and Global Culture*, London: Sage.

Robertson, R. and H. H. Khondker (1998) 'Discourses of Globalization: Preliminary Considerations', *International Sociology*, 13 (1), 25–40.

Rodrik, D. (1996) 'Why do More Open Economies Have Bigger Governments?', *NBER Working Paper* No. 5537, April.

Sachs, J. D. and A. Warner (1995) 'Economic Reform and the Process of Global Integration', *Brookings Papers on Economic Activity*, 1995, vol. 1, 1–118.

Scott, A. (ed.) (1997) *The Limits of Globalization: Causes and Arguments*, London: Routledge.

Shaw, M. (1994) *Global Society and International Relations*, Cambridge: Polity.

Sum, N-L. (2000) '"Cultural Political Economy" in the Making: Reconciling with the "Narrative Turn"', *New Political Economy*, forthcoming.

Thrift, N. (1996) *Spatial Formations*, London: Sage.

Tomlinson, J. (1991) *Cultural Imperialism*, London: Pinter.

Wade, R. (1996) 'Globalisation and Its Limits: Reports of the Death of the National Economy Are Greatly Exaggerated', in Berger and Dore (eds) *National Diversity and Global Capitalism*.

Wallerstein, I. (1974) *The Modern World-System*, Cambridge: Cambridge University Press.

Waterman, P. (1993) *Globalization, Civil Society, Solidarity: The Politics and Ethics of a World Both Real and Universal*, Institute of Social Sciences Working Paper No. 147, The Hague: Institute of Social Sciences.

Watson, M. (1999a) 'Globalization and the Development of the British Political Economy', in Marsh, D. et al. (1999) *Postwar British Politics in Pespective*, Cambridge: Polity.

Watson, M. (1999b) 'Rethinking Capital Mobility: Putting a Different Kind of "P" into Financial Market Regulation', *Putting the 'P' Back into IPE*, special issue of *New Political Economy*, 4 (1), 55–75.

Weiss, L. (1997) 'Globalisation and the Myth of a Powerless State', *New Left Review*, 225, 3–27.

Wilson, R. and W. Dissanayake (eds) (1996) *Global/Local: Cultural Production and the Transnational Imaginary*, Durham, NC: Duke University Press.

Wood, E. M. (1997) 'Globalization or Globaloney? A Reply to A. Sivanandan', *Monthly Review*, 48 (9), 21–31.

Zolo, D. (1997) *Cosmopolis: Prospects for World Government*, Cambridge: Polity.

Zysman, J. (1996) 'The Myth of a "Global" Economy: Enduring National and Emerging Regional Realities', *New Political Economy*, 1 (2), 157–84.

Part I
What Is Globalization?

2
Unpacking the Globalization Debate: Approaches, Evidence and Data

Andreas Busch

Introduction[1]

Globalization[2] has become a very popular term for analysing the present political condition.[3] It has been suggested that 'globalization may be *the* concept of the 1990s, a key idea by which we understand the transition of human society into the third millennium.' (Waters 1995: 1). But at the same time it has also been criticized as 'largely a myth'. (Hirst and Thompson 1996: 2). As students of globalization will quickly note, there is no universally accepted definition of the term. Rather it is a 'shifting concept' (Wiesenthal 1996: 1). Some definitions may therefore serve to illustrate the great variety of senses of globalization, ranging from the narrowly economical to the truly, well, global:

> Globalization refers to a world in which, after allowing for exchange rate and default risk, there is a single international rate of interest. (Brittan 1996)

> ... globalization means the partial erasure of the distinctions separating national currency areas and national systems of financial regulation. (Strange 1995: 294)

> Term for the emergence of world-wide financial markets for bonds, money and currencies as well as credit, favoured by new information and communications technology as well as financial innovations. (Brockhaus-Enzyklopädie 1989, vol. 8: 597)

> Globalization refers to the multiplicity of linkages and interconnections between the states and societies which make up the modern

world system. It describes the process by which events, decisions, and activities in one part of the world can come to have significant consequences for individuals and communities in quite distant parts of the globe. (McGrew 1992: 23)

Globalization of industry refers to an evolving pattern of crossborder activities of firms involving international investment, trade and collaboration for purposes of product development, production and sourcing, and marketing. These international activities enable firms to enter new markets, exploit their technological and organisational advantages, and reduce business costs and risks. Underlying the international expansion of firms, and in part driven by it, are technological advances, the liberalisation of markets and increased mobility of production factors. (OECD 1996: 9)

A social process in which the contraints of geography on social and cultural arrangements recede and in which people become increasingly aware that they are receding. (Waters 1995: 3)

Globalization is 'action at distance'. (Giddens 1994: 4)

Globalization therefore means a lot of different things to a lot of different people and has, small wonder, also met fierce criticism. Susan Strange has called it 'a term used by a lot of woolly thinkers who lump together all sorts of superficially converging trends in popular tastes for food and drink, clothes, music, sports and entertainment with underlying changes in the provision of financial services and the directions of scientific research, and call it all globalization without trying to distinguish what is important from what is trivial, either in causes or in consequences' (Strange 1995: 293). Similarly, R. J. Barry Jones notes: 'Globalization will [...] be seen to be a seriously simplistic conception of an international political economy that is, in reality, composed of multiple layers of differing patterns of action and interaction' (Jones 1995: 15).

The word 'globalization' has been in use since the early 1960s. According to the Oxford English Dictionary, *The Spectator* concluded as early as 1962 that 'globalization is, indeed, a staggering concept'. Academic use of the word only began in the early 1980s, but has taken off enormously in recent years. Whatever one may think of the merits of the debate, globalization is unquestionably an academic growth industry. As Figure 1 shows, publications on globalization started to appear in the first half of the 1980s, at a rate of one to three per year[4] In the late

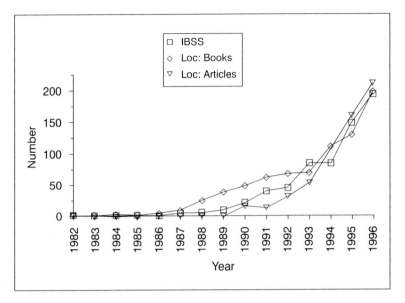

Figure 1. Publications on Globalization, 1982–96

1980s there was strong growth in books dealing with globalization, nearly doubling in number over three successive years. In the 1990s, growth was strongest in the number of articles published, with the yearly output growing by a factor of more that four in the course of only three years. In 1996, the publication of 200 books and 213 articles dealing with globalization were registered by the Library of Congress. And this, it should be stressed, only counts publications that explicitly carry the word in its title.

This wealth of publications can partly be explained by the fact that the numerous and diverse problems to which globalization refers have attracted the interest of scholars from a wide range of the traditions and sub-disciplines of the social sciences:

- economists (e.g., Reich 1993; Sachs and Warner 1995)
- students of political economy (e.g., Garrett and Lange 1991; Hall 1995; Scharpf 1996; Berger and Dore 1996)
- political theorists (e.g., Held 1995; Hirst and Thompson 1996)
- sociologists (e.g., Waters 1995; Wiesenthal 1996)

- students of international relations (e.g., Holm and Sorensen 1995; Kohler-Koch 1996)
- students of international political economy (e.g., Strange 1986; Cerny 1993; Jones 1995).

And, in fact, this list is not exhaustive. Academics from subjects beyond the social sciences have concerned themselves with the phenomena of globalization as well. Thus, geographers have analysed the 'global shift' (Dicken 1992) and the relationship between money, power and space (Corbridge et al. 1994), lawyers have investigated the 'globalization of constitutional law and civil rights' (Weissbrodt 1993) and management consultants have analysed the 'borderless world' of the interlinked economy (Ohmae 1990).

Because of the multi-disciplinarity of the writings on globalization and the sheer volume of literature, this chapter cannot attempt to give an exhaustive survey of the theoretical issues related to the discussion of globalization. Hirst and Thompson (1996: 3) are certainly right when they state with respect to the literature on globalization that 'summarizing and criticizing it would be a never-ending enterprise given the scale and the rate of publications on the topic.' Accordingly, this chapter has the character of an excursion into the intellectual territory of globalization, attempting to provide some rough categorizations and hoping to find common threads running through some of the analyses. Necessarily, many questions will have to remain open. But 'unpacking' the debate may already serve somewhat to demystify globalization.

A number of questions will guide my analysis of the globalization literature:

- Is globalization under way?
- If so, in what does it consist?
- How can we explain the dynamics of the process?
- How is this process to be judged?

The underlying question, however, will be what is most interesting in the whole debate on globalization for a political scientist: how far do the developments infringe upon the nation state's ability to act?

In the first part of the chapter I will give a brief description of the precursor theories to globalization, pointing out the relationship to modernization theory; then I will try to give an overview of the field of globalization theories, followed by a discussion of the empirical indicators of globalization used in the literature. In the final section, I will draw some conclusions from the findings of the chapter and present a typology of positions in the globalization debate.

The Intellectual Pedigree: Precursor Theories

The purpose of the following section is to point out connections and relations between the debate on globalization and other debates and theories in the social science literature.[5] No debate is ever completely self-contained; there are always precursor debates which serve as 'inputs' into new discourses. A number of threads can be identified that stand in relation to the debate on globalization. An acknowledgement of the great diversity of these inputs can help to understand the many-sidedness of this debate. Of course, the discussion here cannot claim to be fully comprehensive. My aim is to provide a rough sketch of the intellectual terrain in which the globalization debate takes place. Three strands of precursor theories will be briefly touched upon: sociological theories of differentiation and modernization, discussions in the field of international relations on the role of the state, and the debate in the field of comparative politics on the relationship between foreign and domestic politics.

Theories of differentiation and modernization

Ever since the early stages of industrialization at the beginning of the nineteenth century, there have been theories stating that these developments would inevitably induce commonalities of practice between the disparate cultures of Europe. This was noticed early by Saint-Simon, who, in a spirit of utopian internationalism called for a pan-European government (in a publication presciently entitled *The Globe*) (Waters 1995: 5ff.). His ideas found their way through Comte to Durkheim, who developed them into his theory of the structural differentiation of society. In an elaboration of this tradition, structural-functionalist sociologists in the twentieth century expanded the argument to include the globalizing effects of differentiation. Industrialization, the argument ran, leads to an increase in material wealth. This success gives an incentive for other societies to emulate industrialization, which thereby spreads. The world, in this process, becomes more industrialized. But industrialization has wider societal effects: it induces the pattern of differentiation to other areas of society in a process called 'modernization' which eventually leads to value changes: to individualization, secularity and rationalization. 'As industrialization spreads across the globe, it carries modernization with it, transforming societies in a unitary direction' (Waters 1995: 13).

Most explicitly, this process was forecast by Karl Marx and Friedrich Engels, who in the *Communist Manifesto* predicted the process of globalization of production and consumption and the emergence of a world market out of the logic of the capitalist mode of production: 'The need

of a constantly expanding market for its products, chases the bourgeoisie over the whole surface of the world' (Marx 1977: 224). Its
industries would work up raw materials drawn from all corners of the
earth, and its products 'are consumed not only at home, but in every
quarter of the globe' (ibid.). In this process, the capitalist system, as a
result of superior economic efficiency, would eventually spread over the
whole world: 'The bourgeoisie, by the rapid improvement of all instruments of production, by the immensely facilitated means of communication, draws all, even the most barbarian (sic), nations into
civilization. The cheap prices of its commodities are the heavy artillery
with which it batters down all Chinese walls, with which it forces the
barbarians' intensely obstinate hatred of foreigners to capitulate. It
compels all nations, on pain of extinction, to adopt the bourgeois mode
of production; it compels them to introduce what it calls civilization
into their midst, i.e., to become bourgeois themselves. In one word, it
creates a world after its own image' (ibid.: 225).

The role of the state in international relations

The 'realist' or 'Westphalian' paradigm in international relations theory
has always been state-centred in its analysis, positing *a priori* that states,
and more recently, 'nation-states', are the key actors in international
relations. They have been seen as interacting with each other in a way
not too different from a 'billiard-ball model', whereby the structure of
the international system (i.e., anarchy and the distribution of power)
determine a state's actions. In the last 30 or so years, however, a number
of developments have altered the scene in international relations so that
the discipline is now 'in search for a new paradigm' (Cerny 1996).

On the one hand the power balance between the states has changed,
compared with the situation after World War II when the US clearly
was in a hegemonic position (at least in the West) and the world was
divided into a two-bloc system. Starting in the late 1960s, discussions
began about the way in which growing 'interdependence' could affect
the states comprised in this system (Cooper 1968; Keohane and Nye
1977). In the 1980s, this led to a debate about the situation in the world
'after hegemony', culminating in the discussion on the perceived
'decline' of the United States (cf. Mitchell 1992: 183ff.). International
relations theory had to come to terms with the fact that even a state as
powerful as the US could no longer completely determine its own fate.

A second development was that new actors began to appear in international relations accounts, in a process labelled 'transnationalisa-
tion': states no longer had to deal with their own likes, but with other

non-governmental agencies such as transnational firms or international agencies, rendering narrowly state-centred assumptions that had previously dominated the discipline obsolete. Analysing 'global interdependence', Rosenau (1980: 2) predicted a 'transformation, even a breakdown of the nation-state system as it has existed throughout the last four centuries.' After this sea-change in world politics at the beginning of the 1990s, the once orderly world system seemd to have become completely confusing – its 'turbulence', as Rosenau (1990) now labelled it, characterized by the simultaneous existence of a 'state-centric' world and a 'multi-centric' world. The latter, enduring into the present, is comprised of subgroups of the state system, international organizations, state bureaucracies and transnational actors such as transnational corporations. While the multi-centric world strives for autonomy from the state, the state-centric world seeks the security of political institutions (Waters 1995: 31). In the search for a new paradigm, globalization (or globalism) is a contender: 'The central novelty of globalization as a concept (and therefore as a discourse) lies in the fact that it defies traditional conceptions of levels of analysis in Political Science and International Relations' (Cerny 1996: 3).

The relationship between foreign and domestic politics

The relationship between foreign (or international) and domestic politics has been an issue in both International Relations and Comparative Politics. The old debate about which of the two was dominating the other (*Primat der Innenpolitik* vs. *Primat der Außenpolitik*) was ended in the 1960s in favour of empirical research on the relationship between the two, searching for the 'domestic sources of foreign policy' (Rosenau 1967). One of the main criticisms of the comparativists in IR interdependence theory is that they acknowledge the influence of interdependence on national policy-making, but fail to analyse it (Keohane and Milner 1996: 7). So the comparativists reversed Rosenau's question, seeking the 'international sources of domestic politics'. 'The international system', they argued, 'is not only a consequence of domestic politics and structures but a cause of them. Economic relations and military pressures constrain an entire range of domestic behaviors, from policy decisions to political forms. International relations and domestic politics are therefore so interrelated that they should be analyzed simultaneously, as wholes' (Gourevitch 1978: 911).

The era after the macroeconomic shocks of the 1970s, when the postwar international economic order of Bretton Woods began to disintegrate, provided a particularly interesting time for analysing them. David Cameron's (1978) work on the expansion of the public economy demonstrated that stronger exposure to the forces of the international economy could explain the existence of a large public sector. Moreover, Peter Katzenstein (1985) demonstrated that for the small European countries, political stability and economic flexibility were mutually dependent. Their exposure to international economic forces beyond their control has led them to adapt corporatist political institutions – an 'institutional mechanism for mobilizing the consensus necessary to live with the costs of rapid economic change' (ibid.: 200). Although some of this literature has been criticized for its insufficiently complex modelling of world market forces,[6] the influence of external forces on domestic politics continues to be an issue of growing importance in the comparativist literature.[7]

To sum up this section, we can say that 'inputs' into the globalization debate come from a great variety of different traditions in the social sciences. Sociological theory, International Relations theory and Comparative Politics all have strands of discussion leading to the issue of globalization. It is therefore not surprising that in the ensuing debate(s) very different connotations are associated with the term 'globalization', and that a commonly accepted definition of the term has yet to emerge.

Positions in the Globalization Debate: An Overview

In this section of the chapter, I attempt to categorize positions in the globalization debate. I should, however, add a caveat at the outset: as stated before, this is not and cannot be a fully comprehensive survey of globalization literature. This proposed categorization therefore cannot claim exhaustiveness. Nonetheless, it serves its purpose if it manages to trace some commonalities within the wildly divergent and multi-faceted literature. A number of questions will guide me in this attempt, which can be summarized as follows:

1. what happens?
2. why is it happening?
3. how can what happens be judged?

As will be seen in the course of the following paragraphs, disagreement in the literature rises the further one progresses through this list of questions.

What happens?

With respect to the first question, there is far-reaching agreement in the existing literature. A number of changes are occurring in the economic sphere which have profound consequences, both for the economic and the political sphere: changes in the production sphere lead to production becoming more internationalized, regulations across states become more alike, factors of production like capital, know-how (but also labour, if primarily skilled labour) become more mobile. This causes convergence in a number of policy areas across states, most visibly in the sphere of monetary policy (Andrews 1994; Glyn 1995; Notermans 1993; Strange 1995). After the triumphant progress of the free market economy '[a] global capitalist system is taking shape, drawing almost all regions of the world into arrangements of open trade and harmonized economic institutions' (Sachs and Warner 1995: 61). As far as the political sphere is considered, agreement exists that these developments will reduce the political systems' room for manoeuvre. More recently, however, a number of criticisms have been levelled at these views: that the processes of change are only infrequently specified in detail and, more generally, that many of the assertions concerning convergence in policies and regulations are insufficiently backed by empirical evidence.

Why does it happen?

Concerning the question of what have caused the aforementioned developments, there is also widespread agreement among the contributors to the debate, even if the factors are differently emphasized. In summary, three sets of factors contribute to these changes: they are political, technical and economic-structural (cf. Jungnickel 1995; Scharpf 1996; Reich 1993; Narr and Schubert 1994; Strange 1995).

Among the political factors considered are world-wide liberalizations of markets for goods and capital as well as of conditions for direct investments and privatization programmes both in industrialized and developing countries. Such developments, it is argued, open hitherto protected sectors up to economic activity, inspired by a dominant liberal paradigm in economic policy making. Major technical changes have occurred both in communications and computer technology, allowing new financial transactions, but also more generally lowering distance costs. Such developments and improved transportation systems, allow the precise co-ordination of production over much longer distances than previously. The third factor is a structural change in the situation of corporations: costs for research and development in many new technologies have risen, while at the same time product cycles have become shorter, forcing firms to team up in strategic alliances, thereby increasing the transnationalization of the business sector.

How can this be judged?

While the analysis of what happens and why it happens is fairly similar, positions vary widely as to how these developments are to be judged. While some do not doubt its purely positive effects, others take a more cautious approach, pointing out benefits and costs, while yet again others warn of the dire consequences of globalization. I will distinguish in this section between three positions:

1. *a liberal* position which primarily points out the welfare gains that more efficient international division of labour and increased trade will bring;
2. *a sceptic* position which states that globalization has negative effects both in the economic and political sphere; and
3. *a moderately optimistic* position which agrees with the sceptic position on the potential dangers of globalization but does not subscribe to the view that there is nothing that can be done politically about these.

The liberal position

In this view, the economic sphere is dominant in the process of globalization, and there is nothing wrong with that. After all, it is argued, this assures efficiency, increased welfare and the spread of both around the world. Liberalizing trade has brought welfare gains to all countries in the world which have subscribed to it, and the fact that in the last years most countries have embarked upon that strategy is both proof to its correctness and its promise of a brighter future. Twenty-five years ago, there were still three distinctly different economic systems existing in the world: a capitalist First World, a socialist Second World and the developing Third World. The latter two have failed and have therefore been abandoned: 'In 1995 one dominant global economic system is emerging' (Sachs and Warner 1995: 1). This development is in a way 'natural', because '[. . .] the closed nature of the world trading system at the end of World War II was a historical anomaly' (ibid.: 3). Positive political effects will also be brought about by this development, because institutional harmonization of trade policy, tax systems, ownership structures require more international norms. The treaty setting up the World Trade Organization (WTO) is testimony to that effect. National governments have little impact upon such a system – in fact, little remains to be done for them except to 'buffer' their citizens against the centrifugal forces of the world economy (Reich 1993: 9). The more enthusiastic proponents of this view, however, rejoice in the notion of an 'interlinked economy' which will enhance the well-being of individuals and institutions the world over, creating neither absolute losers nor winners (Ohmae 1990: 216ff.).

As these quotes demonstrate, the liberal position is mainly adopted by economists. It is strongly influenced by considerations of trade and its perceived beneficial effects. In the wider academic debate, few share this unqualified enthusiasm. Such a position, however, seems very influential in the political debate, where both the diagnosis and the policy prescriptions were received especially well in conservative quarters, because 'the prevailing patterns of trade, the global division of labour and the progressive integration of the international financial system, confronted all "national" economies with "realities" that could not sensibly be ignored. The imperative, in this view, was to "liberalise" national economies to the greatest possible level, minimise state interference in industry and encourage the maximum competitiveness, and flexibility, in financial services. Such a policy framework promised its own guarantees of success, while alternative approaches to economic and industrial policy were condemned as inappropriate, misconceived and doomed to failure' (Jones 1995: 80).

The sceptic position

The similarity between the liberal and the sceptic position in the globalization debate is the conviction that the economic sphere dominates the process and that there is no political escape from it. Apart from this, they have little in common. The dominance of the economic sphere is clearly negative to this position. Deregulation and transnationalization have created a monetary system beyond control, decoupled from the real economy (Narr and Schubert 1994). Economic fundamentals have become meaningless in the determination of, e.g., exchange rates, speculation is the dominant force in the 'casino capitalism' (Strange 1986). National economic policies, as already mentioned, have become meaningless, because the symbiosis of the political and the economic sphere, upon which the post-World War II economic strategies were based, has broken down. Capital controls had allowed the state to extract 'rents' from capital owners which were used to fund welfare and other public spending. With the breakdown of the system of fixed exchange rates and the abolition of capital controls national governments lost the ability to determine the rate of interest which is now determined by international financial markets (Scharpf 1996). In addition, the roller-coaster of stock and currency markets also has other negative political implications: 'This cannot help but have grave consequences. For when sheer luck begins to take over and to determine more and more of what happens to people, and skill, effort, initiative, determination and hard work count for less and less, then inevitably faith and confidence in the social and political system quickly fades. Respect for ethical values on which in the end a free democratic society relies suffers a dangerous decline' (Strange 1986: 2). And 'the political choices open to government these days have been so constricted by those forces of structural change often referred to as "globalization" that the differences that used to distinguish government policies from opposition policies are in process of disappearing' (Strange 1995: 291). Additional problems arise in the field of political legitimacy, and international agreements between governments also offer little hope of escape from the dilemmas because they are larded with the traps of strategic interaction (Wiesenthal 1996). Theoretically, this position is inspired by neo-Marxist thought, rational choice analysis, but also by (frustrated or former) adherents of Keynesianism.

The moderately optimistic position

The third and last position that I would like to distinguish I label 'moderately optimistic'. The adherents of this position fall into a number of camps: on the one hand there are those who are convinced that there still is a role for the state to play like the *régulation* school (Boyer and Drache 1996); on the other hand there are those who are discontent with the pessimism of the sceptic position because they want to keep a perspective for political reform (e.g., Glyn 1995; Notermans 1993); and lastly there are those who research the empirical side of globalization and come to the conclusion that things are not as gloomy as is often implied (Jungnickel 1995; Hirst and Thompson 1996).

Boyer and Drache argue that the debate on globalization is centrally concerned with the question of whether markets can be the key mechanism governing modern society (Boyer and Drache 1996: 1). They reject this position, pointing to the importance of the state's role as a regulator: 'markets work best when the state is a strong regulator' (ibid.: 5). And the state also has a strategic role to play in economic development, as the example of Japan demonstrates. Unregulated markets, moreover, could be the source of social upheaval which the state would have to sort out. And the uncertainties that financial markets let loose are detrimental to economic success, which is why their dominance will have to be revised through internationally co-ordinated re-regulation. It is unacceptable that 'they have more control over governments than even democratically elected bodies' (ibid.: 16).

The approach taken by Glyn (1995) is somewhat different: it does not centre so much on theory, but on the causes for the 'disastrous collapse of social-democratic aspirations' for full employment. This pessimism is traced back to two things: the experiences of the Mitterrand government in the early 1980s and the problems of the Swedish model in the early 1990s. Analysing both cases in detail, he concludes that domestic political factors were much more responsible for the problems than international markets and that there still is a reformist political perspective: 'It is a central argument of this paper that the increased international integration, whilst a convenient scapegoat, does not constitute the fundamental block to full employment policies. Openness to trade, and thus the real costs of maintaining external payments balance, has increased only modestly. Openness to international financial flows has added to the speed at which, and the drama with which, financial markets bring retribution to governments whose policies are not "credible"' (Glyn 1995: 54f.). Noterman's (1993) approach and conclusion are similar.

The pessimism inherent in the 'sceptic' position in the globalization debate has, lastly, inspired some detailed research grounded in empirical indicators (e.g., Jungnickel 1995; Hirst and Thompson 1996; Bairoch 1996). All these works agree that recent 'globalizing' developments are not nearly as unprecedented as is often claimed: '[. . .] the level of integration, interdependence, openness, or however one wishes to describe it, of national economies in the present era is not unprecedented. Indeed, the level of autonomy under the Gold Standard up to the First World War was much less for the advanced economies than it is today' (Hirst and Thompson 1996: 49). The conclusion is: 'Global markets are thus by no means beyond regulation and control, even though the current scope and objectives of economic governance are limited by the divergent interests of the great powers and the economic doctrines prevalent among their elites' (ibid.: 3).

The contributors to this third position come from a wide variety of backgrounds: political economists, social theorists and economists. The common thread running through their position is that these are all (and especially the empirical pieces) rather recent writings, inspired probably by the hitherto prevailing pessimism dominant in the academic and political debate, which they aim to counter.

Empirical Indicators of Globalization

The following section of this chapter attempts to give an overview of empirical indicators commonly used in the debate on globalization.

Presenting them in a systematic fashion will enable an assessment of the empirical foundations of the globalization hypotheses and the globalization debate which is often marked by casual empiricism. In this overview, however, I shall mainly present economic indicators. This is because genuinely political indicators which are internationally comparable in a systematic fashion are seldom used in the literature. Nevertheless, this seems to be an important step towards a balanced judgement on the merits of the globalization debate. As will become clear, many of the rather 'alarmist' contributions on globalization are based on the examination of single indicators and/or short time periods, or they abstain completely from any empirical analysis altogether.[8] It does not seem coincidental that those authors who embark upon a systematic examination of the evidence tend to be rather more cautious in their assessments of the extent of globalization.[9] I will present three kinds of indicators:

- macroeconomic indicators;
- indicators of foreign direct investment and corporate profiles;
- financial market indicators.

While in the latter two areas we will find stronger indications for unparalleled changes in recent years, these do not (as yet?) find themselves reflected in the first area: here recent data often only seem to mirror a situation that had already existed before World War I. The developments since the end of World War II in that perspective rather look like a 'return to normality' than like an unprecedented change in the world situation.[10]

Macroeconomic indicators

There is a major problem with macroeconomic indicators in the globalization debate: for many indicators data only exist for very few countries (mostly for the industrialized countries of the OECD). Moreover, where they exist for most or all countries, they only date back for a comparatively short period of time. This is not surprising since most countries in today's world have not been in existence for a very long time. As far as world trade and related things are concerned, however, this seems to be acceptable, since the industrialized countries conduct the major part of it anyway: in the early 1990s, OECD countries conducted what amounted to about 80 per cent of world trade amongst themselves (Hirst and Thompson 1996: 196). The indicators presented here include exports, world trade, growth rates of trade in relation to GDP and the correlation between countries in macroeconomic indicators such as growth, unemployment and inflation.

One of the few contributions to the globalization debate that takes a (nearly) global approach is the paper by Sachs and Warner (1995): they present data for 118 countries, concentrating on economic indicators of trade, data on trade policy and classifying countries according to the openness of their trade policy regime. Viewed from this perspective, rather little has happened between 1960 and 1990. It is only in 1993 that a major change takes place – mainly caused by the introduction of reforms in the transition economies of Eastern Europe. Before that date, only about a quarter of the world population lived in 'open' countries, albeit they accounted for about 50 per cent of world GDP. Now, the respective numbers stand at 50 per cent of the population and 60 per cent of GDP. This is still a relatively modest proportion, indicating that the notion of a 'free world market' is still far from accurate.

World trade, however, is often looked at not from the point of view of policy regimes, but from that of actual trade (e.g., Glyn 1995; Boyer and Drache 1996; Hirst and Thompson 1996). How did this develop? A look at data on openness (defined as the relationship of exports plus imports to GDP) since 1950 demonstrates that openness has grown both in the industrialized and in the developing countries, and that in the 1980s there has been a comparable level of openness in both groups (see Table 1). Closer inspection, however, reveals that the increase in openness is mainly caused by two groups of countries: Western Europe (reflecting the effects of European integration) and East Asia.

But by taking a long-time perspective it becomes obvious that this is by no means as linear a development as it may seem at first sight: as data for 16 OECD countries demonstrate, 1950 was an exception rather than the rule. By the end of the 1980s, on average these countries' openness (here defined as ratio of exports to GDP) was barely higher that in 1913 (see Table 2). When looking at trade, these data suggest, it is best to take the long view to see the complete picture. Moreover, closer inspection of the data shows interesting differences comparing the 16 OECD countries' positions between the start and the end of the twentieth century: while some experience a significant growth in their openness (e.g., Austria, Germany and Sweden) and some stay at roughly the same level (the United States, the UK and Denmark), others experience a drop (Australia, Switzerland and Japan). These differences can be explained through differences of development in the economic structure of the countries and differences in the growth rates of trade and GDP.

Looking at the latter on an aggregated level, it becomes clear that there have been three quite different sub-periods (see Table 3). While

Table 1. Trade Openness since the Second World War (percentage of GDP)*

	1950–59	1960–69	1970–79	1980–89
Industrial countries	23.3	24.6	32	36.8
North America	11.2	11.7	17.8	21.9
Western Europe	37.2	38.9	48.7	56.9
Japan	21.8	19.5	22.9	23.9
Developing countries	–	28	34.4	38.4**
Africa	–	48.2	55.1	54.4
Asia				
East	–	47	69.5	87.2
Other***	–	17.2	19.6	24
Middle East	–	41.5	60.4	46.9
Western Hemisphere	26.3	23.9	24.9	27.9

* Openness defined as nominal merchandise exports + imports as a percentage of nominal output. Aggregates are calculated on the basis of purchasing power parity (PPP) weights.
** 1980–87.
*** Excluding China.
Source: Hirst and Thompson 1996: 28

Table 2. Development of Openness, 1913–87: Ratio of Merchandise Exports to GDP at Current Market Prices

	1913	1950	1973	1987
Australia	18.3	22.0	13.7	13.5
Austria	8.2	12.6	19.0	23.2
Belgium	50.9	20.3	49.9	59.8
Canada	15.1	17.5	20.9	23.9
Demark	26.9	21.3	21.9	25.4
Finland	25.2	16.6	20.5	22.5
France	13.9	10.6	14.4	16.8
Germany	17.5	8.5	19.7	26.4
Italy	12.0	7.0	13.4	15.4
Japan	12.3	4.7	8.9	9.7
Netherlands	38.2	26.9	37.3	43.6
Norway	22.7	18.2	24.4	25.7
Sweden	20.8	17.8	23.5	27.6
Switzerland	31.4	20.0	23.2	26.6
UK	20.9	14.4	16.4	19.3
USA	6.1	3.6	8 .0	5.7
Arithmetic average	21.2	15.1	20.9	24.1

Source: Keohane and Milner 1996: 12

Table 3. Growth Rates of Trade and GDP, 1853–1984: Relationship between growth of Output and Growth of Foreign Trade, 1853–1984 (% per year)

	1853–72	1872–99	1899–1911	1913–50	1950–73	1973–84
Average growth of trade volume	4.3	3.1	3.9	0.5	9.4	3.6
Average growth of output	3.7	3.3	3.6	1.9	5.3	2.1

Average growth of trade volume:
1853–1911: UK, US, France, Germany: 1913–84: UK, US, France, Germany, Netherlands and Japan
Average growth of output:
1853–1911: industrial production only; 1913–84: GDP.

Source: Hirst and Thompson 1996: 22

throughout the nineteenth century both variables grew at about the same rate, the period between the beginning of World War I and the end of World War II displays a dramatic change in the picture: while output slows considerably, world trade on average is nearly stagnant, with a growth rate of only a quarter of that of GDP. After 1950 the situation again changes completely: a significant boost in GDP growth is accompanied by an explosion of world trade which grows at an average rate of more than 9 per cent per year. While after 1973 there is a slowdown in both the growth rate of GDP and the growth rate of trade, the latter is still about 1.5 times the former. The conclusion that might be drawn is that the growth of foreign trade in recent years has been significant but not extraordinary, and that there have been long periods in the past when it grew at a similar or even higher rate.

The last question in this section on macroeconomic indicators of globalization is whether the intensification of trade has in fact led to a convergence in indicators of the real and the monetary economy as a consequence of the increased interconnectedness within the world system. R. J. Barry Jones has looked into this for the G7 countries (USA, Japan, Germany, Canada, France, the UK and Italy) and a number of indicators such as growth of GDP, rates of unemployment and inflation, wage earnings and stock market indices (Jones 1995: 108ff.). The results of his survey are that the correlations are highly variable and far from what could be expected if there really were the massive convergence so often appealed to in the globalization literature. Convergences, if they exist, are on a regional rather than on a global level (e.g., growth rates between France and Germany or Canada and the US), suggesting the influence of regional trading blocs such as ASEAN, NAF-TA and the EU.

Foreign direct investment and corporate profiles

Besides indicators of states' macroeconomic performance mostly based on trade, indicators of foreign direct investment (FDI) and of the behaviour of corporations play an important role in the discussions on globalization (e.g., Narr and Schubert 1994; Glyn 1995; Jungnickel 1995; Hirst and Thompson 1996; Boyer and Drache 1996). It is assumed that developments in these fields lead to corporations' steadily increasing transnationalization with dire consequences both for the labour market and the role of the state (e.g., Narr and Schubert 1994: 139ff.).

Looking at empirical data on FDI flows, it is quite obvious that there has indeed been some change in recent years. While exports and FDI had roughly moved in parallel between 1975 and 1985 (Hirst and Thompson 1996: 55), an enormous expansion in FDI took place in the second half of the 1980s.[11] But suggestions that this provided clear-cut proof of growing globalization may have been a bit premature, since most recent data show them to be on the decrease again after peaking in 1989 and 1990 (see Figure 2). In any case, no too far-reaching conclusions should be drawn from these data without looking at their regional

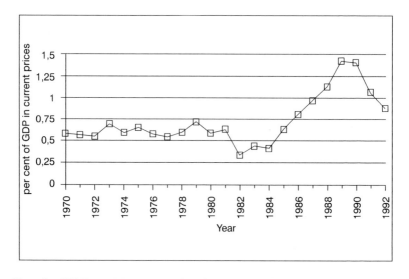

Figure 2. FDI Flows, Western Developed Countries, 1970–92

Table 4. Outward Stocks of Foreign Direct Investments as Percentage of GDP

	Western developed countries	United States	Western Europe	Japan
1950	–	4.2	–	–
1960	7.1	6.2	10.4	1.1
1971	6.6	7.5	6.9	1.9
1980	6.6	8.1	6.4	1.9
1985	7.7	6.2	10.3	3.3
1990	9.8	7.8	12.1	6.9
1993*	11.4	8.2	15.2	6.3

*1993: Preliminary figures.
Source: Boyer and Drache 1996: 182

decomposition. In 1990, 85 per cent of the direct investment flows of the industrialized countries were directed to other countries of the Western world (Bairoch 1996: 183). Much of this could again well be due to European integration.

Looking at the *stocks* of FDI, these also can be seen to have grown in the 1980s, albeit at a much slower rate than FDI *flows* (Jungnickel 1995: 51). But changes are not homogeneous, rather they concentrate in Western Europe and Japan (see Table 4); and in historical perspective, they had by 1990 reached just the level they had stood as a proportion of GDP in 1913 (Bairoch 1996: 188ff.).

Moreover, if one takes a longer-term view, one finds that growth of FDI stocks was just as strong (if not slightly stronger) between 1967–80 as it was between 1980–91 (OECD 1996: 31ff.). Again, there is little new here – what we see is an old phenomenon. There are, however, some interesting changes in regional composition of FDI stocks which demonstrate that the situation is becoming rather less than more 'global': Latin America's share has shrunk from 17.5% to 7%, East Asia's has risen from just below 5% to 13.6%. There are hardly any FDI stocks in Africa and the Middle East.[12]

But have corporate profiles changed as a result of these increased foreign investments? If we look at production abroad (defined as the turnover of corporate subsidiaries that produce abroad), the answer is that since 1980 this has grown faster than world GDP, but by no means as fast as the 'explosion' of FDI flows would lead one to assume. Employment in transnational corporations (TNCs) has not grown very much, in spite of higher FDIs and a wave of mergers and takeovers. FDIs very often only change ownership structures in already existing TNCs (Jungnickel 1995: 50ff.). With respect to international strategic alliances between corporations it can be said that these grow at a rate clearly faster than world GDP. Again here it must be stressed that the basis for these data is rather weak. But all available information points to the fact that the number of strategic alliances in the domestic economy grows just as fast and that therefore internationalization is not specific to that area (Jungnickel 1995: 51).

To sum up the data on investment and corporations it can safely be said that there are indeed changes going on here, but that these are not of a revolutionary nature.

Financial markets

But 'revolutionary' would probably be the right term to describe the developments in the sphere of financial markets. Here, in the last 25 years changes have taken place at breathtaking speed and of a spectacular magnitude. It is not surprising then that financial markets have featured very prominently in descriptions of the turmoils associated with globalization – even at an early stage in the debate (cf. Strange 1986, Hiss 1988). The combination of wide-spread liberalization of financial markets with quantum leaps in the development of computer and

Table 5. Markets for Selected Derivative Instruments: National Principal Amounts Outstanding at year end, 1986–92 ($US billion equivalent)

	1986	1990	1991	1992
Exchange-traded instruments	588	2 291	3 520	4 783
Interest rate futures	370	1 454	2 157	3 048
Interest rate options	146	600	1 073	1 385
Currency futures	10	16	18	25
Currency options	39	56	59	80
Stock market index futures	15	70	77	81
Options on stock market indices	8	95	136	164
Over-the-counter instruments	500 (E)	3 451	4 449	–
Interest rate swaps	400 (E)	2 312	3 065	–
Currency and gross-currency interest rate swaps	100 (E)	578	807	–
Other derivative instruments	–	561	577	–
Memorandum item				
Cross-border plus local foreign currency claims of BIS re posting banks	4 031	7 578	7 497	7 352

Source: Hirst and Thompson 1996: 41
E = estimate

communication technology (and the invention of ever more sophisticated financial instruments made possible by the latter two) has led to
an explosion in the volume of a number of financial instruments. Some
of them are displayed in Table 5.

It can be seen that some of them, like interest rate options or options
on stock market indices, have multiplied their volume ten- to twenty-
fold in the course of only six years. Currency markets are another area
where growth rates have been excessive: as can be seen from Table 6,
daily turnover has skyrocketed in the second half of the 1980s and early
1990s, reaching a volume of nearly $900 bn. in 1992 *per day* and more
than $1 200 bn. in 1995. World trade, in comparison, in 1992 had a vol-
ume of about $7 100 bn. *per year*, or roughly 1/40th (or 2.5 per cent) of
the former. Only five years earlier, in 1987, that proportion had been
twice that size, at 1/20th (or 5 per cent) (Busch 1995: 193).

But not everything in the sphere of financial markets has changed in
such a tremendous way; and not everything is so fiercely internationalized. If one looks for example at the markets for government bonds, one
finds that foreign penetration of these (as a measure of internationalization) is still relatively low at an average of 15 per cent for 11 OECD
countries in 1989 (Hirst and Thompson 1996: 42). But this has grown
from a level of 10 per cent in 1983, and some of these countries already
have quite high proportions of their government bonds held by non-
residents (e.g., Australia, Canada and the Netherlands). So it seems that
the trend in the government bond markets is one towards increased
openness, albeit not at the frantic pace of some other financial markets.

Nevertheless, even in the financial sphere (for all its rapid changes)
taking a long-term perspective reveals interesting similarities again to the

Table 6. Growth of Currency Markets:
Currency Market Turnover per Day

Market	Year	Turnover (US$ bn)
New York	1977	10–12
New York	1980	25
Worldwide	1985	150
Worldwide	1986	200
Worldwide	1989	620
Worldwide	1992	880
Worldwide	1995	1 260

Source: Strange 1986: 11; Busch 1995: 192;
BIS 1996

period at the beginning of the twentieth century. Hirst and Thompson quote from a survey of a wide range of the financial integration literature conducted in 1992 which again points to the highly integrated nature of the international economy before World War I: 'All these measures of transnational securities trading and ownership are substantially greater in the years before the First World War than they are at present. More generally, every available descriptor of financial markets in the late nineteenth and early twentieth centuries suggests that they were more fully integrated than they were before or have been since.' (Hirst and Thompson 1996: 36).

To sum up this section on empirical indicators of globalization, I think one can say that the picture emerging from it is varied. Revolutionary changes in some financial markets contrast with a slow pace of change in many macroeconomic indicators which are being used in the globalization literature. The more systematic, comparative and long term the perspective taken, the more clear it becomes that the notion of a quantitative leap is the wrong one, at least for an overall picture. It is striking to see, however, that the situation in many ways resembles that at the end of the nineteeth century: 'The world economy at the end of the twentieth century looks much like the world economy at the end of the nineteenth century. A global capitalist system is taking shape, drawing almost all regions of the world into arrangements of open trade and harmonized economic institutions' (Sachs and Warner 1995: 61).

Conclusion

This chapter has attempted to shed some light on the current debate on globalization with respect to theoretical considerations and empirical indicators. I have tried to demonstrate that the great diversity of the debate can be attributed to a certain extent to the very different inputs into the debate and the manifold backgrounds of those participating in the debate. In that sense, this is truly an interdisciplinary debate. But at the same time it also bears testimony to the difficulties inherent in such a debate due to the very different conceptual frameworks of the protagonists.

Furthermore, I have tried to identify different positions within this voluminous literature, differentiating between a *liberal*, a *sceptic* and a *moderately optimistic* position. Table 7 summarizes the differences between these approaches.

In the last section of the chapter, empirical indicators on globalization were presented. This demonstrated that there is considerable variation depending on which area one looks at – and hence a need to

Table 7. Positions in the Globalization Debate

	Liberal	Sceptic	Optimistic
Dominant perspective	(liberal) economists	rational choice neo-Marxist Keynesian	*régulation* school
Typical representatives	Sachs Ohmae	Scharpf Strange	Boyer and Drache Glyn
Dominant sphere	economic sphere (which is positive)	economic sphere (which is negative)	(political strategies are still viable)
Economic prospects	positive, because welfare will increase	negative, because instability will rise and incomes decline	uncertain – depends to a considerable extent on political decisions

disaggregate and demystify. While macroeconomic indicators all in all do not display great changes over past performance in the last two decades, the situation looks different with respect to foreign investment or corporate indicators: change here is rather faster than at the macro-economic level. Revolutionary changes have occurred in the sphere of financial markets. But, taking a long-term view, developments in all three areas have been put into perspective: they are not unprecedented, since levels of economic integration both in the real and the financial economy were at the same if not higher level at the beginning of the twentieth century.

Nontheless, there is a significant difference between the situation then and the situation now: in the mass democracies of the late twentieth century the population demands and is used to a high degree of self-determination. Increased interdependence, however, while promising welfare gains, demands the sacrifice of some autonomy – since an ever larger part of a country's or an economy's feasible actions is determined (or at least circumscribed) by the actions of other countries or economies. This dilemma has already been pointed out by Cooper in his book *The Economics of Interdependence* (1968). With the end of the Cold War and the demise of the alternatives to Western democracy and market economy, this dilemma has moved centre-stage in the public conscience and on the political agenda.

For the political system, part of the difficulty of globalization may consist in the fact that, in general terms, it is an extension of the set of options open to most actors, opening up new alternatives that were previously unavailable (Wiesenthal 1996). This will most likely lead to an increase in uncertainty because customary social relations may be subject to change. Indeed, we may not capture the essence of globalization at all if we look at the development of empirical indicators: shifting opportunity costs, to use that economic concept, may be more fundamental than flows in goods or finance themselves. As Keohane and Milner put it with respect to problems of economic policy making (Keohane and Milner 1996: 3): 'the *potential* for international movements of capital, in response to shifts in interest rates or changing expectations about exchange rates, can exert profound effects on national economic conditions and policies even if no capital movements actually take place'.

The challenge for political science in that respect is that a purely domestic analysis is no longer enough: 'It misses central determinants of domestic problems', because 'we can no longer understand politics within countries – what we still conveniently call "domestic" politics – without comprehending the nature of the linkages between national economies and the world economy, and changes in such linkages.', as two participants in the globalization debate from very different backgrounds agree (Narr and Schubert 1994: 159; Keohane and Milner 1996: 3).

Yet this is a very general statement. There is still much work to do on a range of important questions. Is the state's 'capacity to act' (Scharpf 1996) seriously diminished by these developments? Are functional necessities in the process of globalization really forcing states into a process of convergence, with regulatory arbitrage leading to solutions on the lowest common denominator? Or do the different institutional set-ups, legal traditions, etc. and the incentives and restrictions they imply, lead to different reactions to common challenges, and let states maintain nationally distinct and path-dependent configurations? In my view, we will only be able to resolve these questions through the conduct of systematic and detailed comparative studies in as wide a range of policy areas as possible.

Notes

1.	Previous versions of this chapter have profited from discussions at the conference on 'Globalization, Welfare States and Labour Markets' at the Institut für Politische Wissenschaft, Universität Heidelberg, 26–28 September 1996 and the ECPR Workshop 'Globalisation and the Advanced Capitalist State', Berne Joint Sessions, 27 February–4 March 1997. For their comments and suggestions I am especially grateful to Klaus Armingeon, Dietmar Braun, Frank Castles, Hans Keman, Tony McGrew, Chris Pierson and Manfred G. Schmidt.

2. The phenomena discussed in this chapter are sometimes also analysed under the headings of 'internationalization' (e.g., Keohane and Milner 1996) or 'interdependence' (e.g., Garrett and Lange 1991; Hall 1995). Although sometimes different expressions are used for analytical purposes (e.g., Hirst and Thompson 1996, who distinguish between an 'inter-national' and a 'global' economy), more often than not these refer to the same thing. In this chapter, I will therefore (unless otherwise noted) use these terms synonymously.

3. Books which may serve as an introduction to the debate on globalization include Axford 1995, Commission on Global Governance 1995, Held 1995, McGrew and Lewis et al. 1992 and Waters 1995.

4. The figure is based on data from three databases that were queried for publications containing the expressions 'globalization' or 'globalisation' in their title. Databases used are the International Bibliography of Social Sciences (IBSS) and the Library of Congress databases 'WorldCat' (for books) and 'Article1st' (for articles). The survey was conducted in December 1997.

5. For a discussion of these relationships cf. especially McGrew 1992; Waters 1995, chapter 2; and Keohane and Milner 1996: 3–24.

6. See Braun and Keman 1986 for a critical review of Katzenstein 1985.

7. To give just a few recent examples: Armingeon 1993; Garrett and Lange 1991; Garrett and Mitchell 1995; Keohane and Milner 1996.

8. An extreme case of this may be the book by Narr and Schubert, who in a proud example of what Galtung once termed the 'teutonic' style in science state: 'We have, as a rule – a partial exception is part II – , abstained from spreading out empirical facts, presenting illustrations for abstract definitions and and concerning ourselves with other points of view. We wanted to keep our arguments slim.' (Narr and Schubert 1994: 267).

9. E.g., Jones 1995, Jungnickel 1995, Boyer and Drache 1996 and Hirst and Thompson 1996.

10. Cf. Stanley Fischer's comments on Sachs and Warner 1995: 'Many aspects of the global economy are indeed closer now to what they were a century ago than to what they were fifty years ago. At the close of the nineteenth century countries were linked through trade, as well as through massive capital flows corresponding to current account deficits and surpluses on a scale, relative to GDP, that would hardly be acceptable today. The international capital markets were highly integrated in at least two senses: first, that rates of return in the major markets of London, New York, and Paris moved together and, as a result of the invention of the telegraph, very rapidly so; and second, that, as Sachs and Warner tell us, the British colonies and dominions, much of Latin America, and Russia borrowed in those markets to finance development. Then, as now, there were occasional financial panics and debt difficulties in the developing countries, the Argentina-related Barings crisis of 1890 among them' (Sachs and Warner 1995: 100f.).

11. It should, however, be mentioned that FDI data are generally considered to be problematic and not very reliable due to the nature of the basic data that are collected (Bairoch 1996: 181).

12. It should be added that the current fashion of judging the inflows of FDI as a measure of a country s competitiveness should be treated with great caution. As the OECD data reveal, the UK for example has always had a very large share of FDI – it is an outlier in Europe in 1991 just as it was in 1967 (with

about twice as high a share in FDI stocks as Germany). This is mainly due to the strong involvement of the United States in the UK. Japan, on the other hand, surely one of the economically most successful countries in the last thirty years, has always had a negligible share of world FDI stocks: 0.6% in 1967, 0.7% in 1991.

Bibliography

Andrews, D. M. (1994) 'Capital Mobility and Monetary Adjustment in Western Europe, 1973–1991', *Policy Sciences*, 27(4) (special issue, *The World of Money: The Political Economy of International Capital Mobility*, ed. Eric Helleiner), 425–45.

Armingeon, K. (1993) 'Institutionelle Antworten auf Wirtschaftliche Verwundbarkeit. Ein Internationaler Vergleich der Prozeduralen Regulierung der Arbeitsbeziehungen in Kapitalistischen Industriegesellschaften', *Politische Vierteljahresschrift*, 34 (3), 436–54.

Axford, B. (1995) *The Global System Economics, Politics and Culture*, Cambridge: Polity.

Bairoch, P. (1996) 'Globalization Myths and Realities: One Century of External Trade and Foreign Investment', in R. Boyer and D. Drache (eds) *States Against Markets. The Limits of Globalization*, London: Routledge, 173–92.

Bank for International Settlements (1996) Central Bank Survey of Foreign Exchange and Derivatives Markets Activity 1995, Basle, May 1996.

Berger, S. and R. Dore (eds) (1996) *National Diversity and Global Capitalism*, Ithaca, NY: Cornell University Press.

Boyer, R. and D. Drache (eds) (1996) *States Against Markets. The Limits of Globalization*, London, New York: Routledge.

Braun, D. and H. Keman (1986) 'Weltmarkt, Internationale Regime und nationale Politikstrategien', *Journal für Sozialforschung* 26, Heft 3, 357–65.

Brittan, S. (1996) 'Keynes and Globalization', *Financial Times*, 6.6.1996, 12.

Brockhaus-Enzyklopädie (1989) in 24 Bänden, 19. Auflage, Mannheim Brockhaus 1989.

Busch, A. (1995) *Preisstabilitätspolitik. Politik und Inflationsraten im Internationalen Vergleich*, Opladen Leske + Budrich.

Cameron, D. R. (1978) 'The Expansion of the Public Economy: A Comparative Analysis', *American Political Science Review*, 72, 1243–61.

Cerny, P. G. (ed.) (1993) *Finance and World Politics. Markets, Regimes and States in the Post-Hegemonic Era*, Aldershot: Elgar.

Cerny, P. G. (1996) 'Globalization and Other Stories. The Search for a New Paradigm in International Relations', *International Journal*, 51 (4), 617–37.

Commission on Global Governance (1995) *Our Global Neighbourhood*, Oxford: Oxford University Press

Cooper, R. (1968) *The Economics of Interdependence*, New York: McGraw-Hill for the Council on Foreign Relations.

Corbridge, S., R. Martin and N. Thrift (eds) (1994) *Money, Power and Space*, Oxford: Blackwell.

Dicken, P. (1992) *Global Shift. The Internationalization of Economic Activity*, 2nd ed., London: Chapman.

Garrett, G. and P. Lange (1991) 'Political Responses to Interdependence What's "left" for the left?', *International Organization*, 45 (4), 539–64.

Garrett, G. and D. Mitchell (1995) 'Globalization and the Welfare State Income Transfers in the Industrial Democracies, 1965–1990'. [Paper presented to Comparative Research on Welfare State Reform, Pavia, 14–17 September 1995], University of Pennsylvania, Australian National University.

Giddens, A. (1994) *Beyond Left and Right. The Future of Radical Politics*, Stanford, CA: Stanford University Press.

Glyn, A. (1995) 'Social Democracy and Full Employment', *New Left Review*, 211, 33–55.

Gourevitch, P. (1978) 'The Second Image Reversed: The International Sources of Domestic Politics', *International Organization*, 32 (4), 881–912.

Hall, P. A. (1995) 'The Political Economies of Europe in an Era of Interdependence' [Paper prepared for presentation to the Conference on Politics and Political Economy in Advanced Capitalist Democracies, Berlin, 26–7 May 1995], Cambridge, Mass: Center for European Studies.

Held, D. (1995) *Democracy and the Global Order from the Modern State to Cosmopolitan Governance*, Cambridge: Polity.

Held, D. and A. McGrew (1993) 'Globalization and the Liberal Democratic State', *Government and Opposition*, 27, 261–88.

Herr, H. (1996) 'Globalisierung der Ökonomie Entkopplung der Geldsphäre und Ende nationaler Autonomie?', in Kai Eicker-Wolf et al. (Hrsg.), *Wirtschaftspolitik im theoretischen Vakuum? Zur Pathologie der Politischen Ökonomie*, Marburg Metropolis, 251–72.

Hirst, P. and G. Thompson (1996) *Globalization in Question. The International Economy and the Possibilities of Governance*, Cambridge: Polity.

Hiss, D. (1988) 'Geld- und Währungspolitische Implikationen einer Globalisierung der Finanzmärkte', in *Wirtschaftsdienst* 1988, 71–8.

Holm, H.-H. and G. Sorensen (eds) (1995) *Whose World Order? Uneven Globalization and the End of the Cold War*, Boulder: Westview.

Jones, R. J. B. (1995) *Globalization and Interdependence in the International Political Economy: Rhetoric and Reality*, London: Pinter.

Jungnickel, R. (1995) 'Internationalisierung der Wirtschaft – Der Empirische Befund', in W. Schmähl and H. Rische (eds), *Internationalisierung von Wirtschaft und Politik. Handlungsspielräume der nationalen Sozialpolitik*, Baden-Baden: Nomos, 45–77.

Katzenstein, P. J. (1985) *Small States in World Markets. Industrial Policy in Europe*, Ithaca, NY: Cornell University Press.

Keohane, R. O. and H. V. Milner (eds) (1996) *Internationalization and Domestic Politics*, New York, Cambridge: Cambridge University Press.

Keohane, R. O. and J. S. Nye (1977) *Power and Interdependence World Politics in Transition*, Boston Little, Brown.

Kohler-Koch, B. (1996) *Politische Unverträglichkeiten und Globalisierung*, in Ullrich Steger (Hrsg), Globalisierung der Wirtschaft – Konsequenzen für Arbeit, Technik und Umwelt, Berlin, Heidelberg Springer, 89–113.

Marx, K. (1977) *Selected Writings*, edited by David McLellan, Oxford: Oxford University Press.

McGrew, A. G. (1992) 'Conceptualizing Global Politics', in A. G. McGrew, P. G. Lewis et al., *Global Politics. Globalization and the Nation-State*, Cambridge: Polity Press, 1–28.

McGrew, A. G., P. G. Lewis et al. (1992) *Global Politics. Globalization and the Nation-State*, Cambridge: Polity.

Mitchell, J. (1992) 'The Nature and Government of the Global Economy', in A. G. McGrew, P. G. Lewis et al., *Global Politics. Globalization and the Nation-State*, Cambridge: Polity, 174–96.

Narr, W.-D. and A. Schubert (1994) *Weltökonomie. Die Misere der Politik*, Frankfurt am Main: Suhrkamp.

Notermans, T. (1993) 'The Abdication from National Policy Autonomy: Why the Macroeconomic Policy Regime Has Become So Unfavorable to Labor', *Politics & Society*, 21 (2), 133–67.

OECD (1996) *Globalization of Industry. Overview and Sector Reports*, Paris: OECD.

Ohmae, K. (1990) *The Borderless World. Power and Strategy in the Interlinked Economy*, London: HarperCollins Business.

Reich, R. B. (1993) *Die neue Weltwirtschaft. Das Ende der Nationalen Ökonomie*, Frankfurt and Main Büchergilde Gutenberg.

Rosenau, J. N. (1967) *Domestic Sources of Foreign Policy*, New York: Free Press.

Rosenau, J. N. (1980) *The Study of Global Interdependence*, New York: Nichols.

Rosenau, J. N. (1990) *Turbulence in World Politics. A Theory of Change and Continuity*, Princeton, NJ: Princeton University Press.

Sachs, J. D. and A. Warner (1995) 'Economic Reform and the Process of Global Integration', *Brookings Papers on Economic Activity* 1 and 1995 (25th Anniversary Issue), 1–118.

Scharpf, F. W. (1996) 'Föderalismus und Demokratie in der transnationalen Ökonomie', in Klaus von Beyme, Claus Offe (Hrsg.), *Politische Theorien in der Ära der Transformation* [= PVS Sonderheft 26], Opladen Westdeutscher Verlag, 211–235.

Strange, S. (1986) *Casino Capitalism*, Oxford: Blackwell.

Strange, S. (1995) 'The Limits of Politics', *Government and Opposition* 30 (1995), 3, 291–311.

Waters, M. (1995) *Globalization*, London: Routledge.

Wiesenthal, H. (1996) *Globalisierung. Soziologische und Politikwissenschaftliche Koordinaten eines Unbekannten Terrains*, Berlin Max-Planck-Gesellschaft, AG Transformationsprozesse in den neuen Bundesländern (Ms).

Weissbrodt, D. (1993) 'Globalization of Constitutional Law and Civil Rights', *Journal of Legal Education*, 43, 261–71.

3
Izations of the World: Americanization, Modernization and Globalization

Peter J. Taylor

We can all agree with Robert Cox (1996: 21) that it is 'particularly important', with a concept as 'fashionable' as globalization, that we 'place it in historical perspective'. But which history? In the current debate over economic globalization, critics have queried the novelty of the geographical scale of contemporary connections by citing past economic patterns which were seemingly equally world-wide in nature. For instance, Paul Bairoch (1996: 190) has recently shown how analysis of 'one century of external trade and foreign investments' shows international tendencies 'alternating with drawback'. Accordingly he is able to conclude: 'This fact gives a different perspective on the thesis of globalization as an irreversible movement'. Such uses of history are important for the debate but they do not necessarily provide an appropriate historical setting for analysing globalization. Most studies focus on just the last few decades, as in Cox's (1996: 21–2) own brief analysis. This time frame is favoured also by scholars approaching globalization from a more cultural perspective. For instance, Jan Pieterse (1995: 47) refers to globalization theory as 'the 1950s and 1960s revisited under a large global umbrella'. Mike Featherstone (1995: 87) adds a further link interpreting globalization as 'the relentless modernizing force of American cultural imperialism'. In this paper, I take my cue directly from such cultural linkages but develop an analysis much closer to Bairoch's time scale. In short, I take the idea of the twentieth century as the 'American Century' seriously and interpret globalization as its final expression.

I locate globalization within the context of the American hegemonic cycle as theorized in world-systems analysis (Wallerstein 1984; Arrighi 1990 and 1993). This particular historical model defines a periodization of the 'American Century' – a rise phase from *c*. 1900 to *c*. 1945, 'high

49

hegemony' to *c.* 1970, with the demise phase since then. Viewing globalization as a feature of the demise phase obliges us to interpret it as an outcome of processes that have been operating for much longer than the last two or three decades. Using world hegemony as the framing concept of the analysis means that Americanization is brought to the fore, and not only as cultural imperialism, as an evolving pattern of processes that mirror the cyclical periodization. Given this backcloth, modernization and globalization are interpreted as related sets of processes that complement Americanization. All three 'izations' are seen as integral to the unfolding of the US hegemonic cycle. However, our ultimate concern is to throw new light on contemporary globalization with Americanization and modernization as particularly instructive foils because they also stimulated major debates about new trans-state processes.

My play on the common suffixes in the title of this paper is not a trivial semantic point. 'Izations' invite obfuscation. In the English language constructing a noun out of a verb by adding '-ization' creates a peculiar double meaning. The new word provides a name for both the process described by the original verb and the end-state of that process. For example, the noun modernization has been created from the verb 'to modernize' and can mean both the state of being modern as well as the mechanisms for becoming modern (Wallerstein 1979: 134). Thus Göran Therborn (1995: 126) complains '"modernization" is heavily loaded with associations of a single process...a single direction and a given end'. Similarly, the term Americanization can be used to describe both the state of being like American society and the process of imitating America. Globalization is used today both to describe trends towards a more globally-integrated world and to identify the existence of a uniquely global society (Hirst and Thompson 1996: 4). This has important implications for debates over such named phenomena. By conflating becoming with being, alternative future possibilities are discarded: the outcome is literally defined as inevitable. Hence in debates, designating a bundle of processes an 'ization' is a tell-tale sign that we are in a contest between universalizers who are promoting a standardized world and those resisting homogeneity. Just such an 'end of geography' argument is, of course, at the heart of the contemporary globalization debate.

There is an obvious first lesson to draw from this language trap: it is necessary to separate out the two meanings of the izations in any critical analysis. This is quite evident for Americanization and modernization because we know now that the 'pure' end-states never came into being. Hence we are able to decode phrases such as 'this inevitable

"Americanization"' (Brogan 1959: 24) as a 'sign of the times' – a time when Americanization did indeed seem to be 'a kind of global imperative' (Kuisel 1993: 4). But without this historical hindsight, in the case of globalization we must continually remember that we are dealing only with a bundle of processes that define a tendency in contemporary social relations and not, as Cox (1996: 23) terms it, 'a finality' in the sense that there is no alternative (the famous TINA) to a 'globalised world' with attendant claims about the restricted space within which states are able to operate. There is a very good example of this failure of separation in the current literature on world (or global) cities. It is commonplace to refer to a 'world city hierarchy' implying a world-wide connected network of cities ordered by function into distinct levels (e.g. Friedman 1995). No such neat pattern of cities has been shown to exist, rather we have information on current processes that suggest a tendency towards such an ordering of cities. There are, of course, other contemporary tendencies countering such a reordering, so there are no guarantees whatsoever that world city hierarchical tendencies will ever produce a world city hierarchy (Taylor 1997b).

There is a second lesson to be drawn from the nature of izations: separating their two meanings requires that any critical analysis cannot dismiss an ization by exposing the weakness of just one of its two meanings. Although western European countries never became pale reflections of America as many feared in the early post-war years, that does not mean that they did not experience powerful Americanization processes which have in fact contributed in important ways to making Europe what it is today. Similarly, however we interpret the nature of the contemporary 'third world', the fact that it has experienced many decades of powerful processes usually classified under the rubric of modernization cannot be ignored. Again, with globalization we do not have the benefit of such historical insight, but clearly it is inappropriate to test its contemporary salience merely by comparing current social relations with an ideal model of a globalized set of social relations. Unsurprisingly, such a 'straw man' exercise can easily prove that we do not live in a globalized world, but tells us little about the very real globalization tendencies we are experiencing – we will discuss Hirst and Thompson's (1996) strategy along these lines below. If disproving one meaning of globalization causes a neglect of the second, this has dangerous implications for critical research. To return to the world city example, there may be no existing hierarchy but that is no reason not to take very seriously the mechanisms in train that are promoting such a hierarchy.

This preliminary exegesis of izations has provided a provisional illustration of the utility of comparing globalization with Americanization and modernization but the purpose of this paper is to take the argument further as historical interpretation. By treating the American hegemonic cycle as the framework for analysis, the three izations are made part of the same unfolding story. We are not here using the method of historical analogy, their relationships are treated as structurally connected within a changing capitalist world economy. This means that we cannot analyse them separately from their chronological order within the 'American Century': Americanization debates appear in the rise phase, modernization debates in the high hegemony phase, and globalization debates in the decline phase. Each ization is treated in this order in its own section below. But before we come to this triple core of the paper, a brief description of the idea of American hegemony as used in this paper is provided as a necessary backdrop for subsequent argument.

The American Century as Hegemonic Cycle

Most obviously, the 'American Century' is marked by three major US military/political victories – World War I, World War II and the Cold War. These have each had world-wide repercussions. Certainly the USA has been the major political power of the century and during the height of the Cold War it had the largest military arsenal with the longest reach in the history of humanity. But this is not my prime concern here. Although the term hegemony can be used to mean political domination, I will be using it in Gramsci's sense of 'intellectual and moral leadership'. My interpretation of Henry Luce's (1941) original use of the term 'American Century' is that his hopes for America were for much more than mere political superpower status. His notion of the United States as 'the powerhouse of the ideals of Freedom and Justice' is quintessentially Gramscian. This is an hegemony that covers the gamut of social relations, not just the political but also the economic and, importantly, the cultural (Taylor 1996a).

Henry Luce's hopes were, to a very large degree, fulfilled. In the historical model of world hegemonies, the USA comprises the third of three hegemonic cycles as described by Wallerstein (1984), Arrighi (1990; 1993) and Hopkins (1990). As well as being victors in great wars, the Dutch in the seventeenth century, the British in the nineteenth century and the Americans in the twentieth century were the leading economic powers of their eras; the political champions of various forms of liberalism; and accordingly became distinctive civil societies rivals sought to emulate. It is in the latter role that hegemons penetrated the everyday lives of peoples throughout the modern world system. Elsewhere I have interpreted this as the construction of new modernities centred on each hegemon: Dutch-led mercantile modernity, British-led industrial modernity and American-led consumer modernity (Taylor 1996a, 1996b, 1998). In each case hegemons have represented the future for other countries. Contemporaries viewed these hegemonic states as portentous places that you could visit to 'see the future'. By serving to define the future for others, hegemons had a great 'cultural power' to restructure the world in their own image. The world-historical processes of mercantilism, industrialism and consumerism each received their critical stimulus from emulating the Dutch, the British and the Americans respectively. Today we live in a consumers' world largely created in the image of America. It is the latter process that we may term Americanization.

This hegemonic cultural power is in no sense separate from the political and economic components of power – emulation itself is only a reaction to the economic, and to a lesser extent, political successes of the hegemon relative to all rivals. Such a combination of cultural, economic and political power does not arise, or disappear, overnight, hence the concept of hegemonic cycle. In the case of the USA, it was becoming the leading economy in the world by the end of the nineteenth century, by which time it was also flexing its military muscles. As well as US entry into World War I being crucial militarily, this war also marked the transfer of financial pre-eminence from London to New York and the first attempt to impose an American idealism on to international relations. The latter failed with the rise of American political isolationalism but the inter-war years saw the first major international flowering of American popular culture through music (jazz) and film (Hollywood). World War II eliminated isolationalism as a major domestic political force and the US set about constructing the world in its own image. US 'high hegemony' is usually dated from 1945 with the final defeats of Germany (militarily) and Britain (financially): America was the only country to 'have a good war' – production doubled between 1941 and 1945 – creating the success story to be emulated. 1971 is usually chosen to mark the end of high hegemony as this was the year when the dollar was floated thus ending the post-war Bretton Woods financial system anchored on the dollar as the world base currency. Since 1971 the USA has remained the leading economic, political and cultural power but its lead over rivals has been progressively diminished. We will use this rise-to-demise story of the 'American Century' to chart, first, the changing meaning of Americanization.

Americanization: Rise, High Hegemony and Demise

After World War II, Germany was subjected to a propaganda onslaught by the four occupying powers as they sought 'denazification' in their quite distinctive and separate ways (FitzGibbons 1969). In his account of the US occupation, Ralph Willet (1989: 27) makes a curious observation: 'the Occupation (and its Americanization potential) succeeded best when it stopped trying'. It seems that 'Americanization of young Germans was much more successful outside the schools' (Willet 1989: 17). This was because it was not teachers or administrators or soldiers or any other public servants who promoted America best, rather '(i)t was American goods which were to be the revolutionary missionaries for the American Way of Life' (ibid.: 27). What is happening here is the projection of a civil society rather than a state. Even in the strict political conditions of a military occupation and state reconstruction, the dominating force is the 'non-political' appeal of America.

This unusual circumstance is quintessentially hegemonic. There were particular processes unfolding in the American zone of defeated Germany which actualized a much deeper effect than the political domination, however complete the latter. American influence in Germany was beginning to transform the cultural matrix of society by penetrating the everyday lives of the German people. This had nothing to do with the occupation *per se*, but was a much wider process which could be found equally in victor states such as Britain and France. Elsewhere I have interpreted this projection of American civil society – the American Way of Life – as the creation of a new modernity, an integral part of US world hegemony (Taylor 1996a, 1996b, 1998). As such it superseded the 'industrial modernity' that was a product of nineteenth-century British hegemony. This new modernity was based on further revolutionary changes in production enabling a new world of mass consumption to develop: the image of a modern landscape was transformed from cotton mills and industrial housing to corporate skyscrapers and affluent suburbs.

I will define Americanization as this projection of American civil society to create a new general form of modernity. There are three key features we can expect to find in the operation of the process. First, as an aspect of hegemony based upon 'moral and intellectual leadership', the attraction of America should be manifest most in the behaviour of ordinary people and not the local elites with vested interests in 'the old ways'. Second, since this process is not evolutionary but represents an epochal level of social change, we should expect a generational effect with the appeal greatest for young people. Third, given that the process is conceived as a way of becoming modern, we should anticipate America to be widely perceived as the land of the future. In addition, as integral to world hegemony, Americanization should develop in line with the phases of the American hegemonic cycle. We will, therefore, identify three manifestations of Americanization: *incipient* Americanization is part of the rise phase; *capacious* Americanization is the process at high hegemony; and during the demise phase there is a *resonant* Americanization. We will treat the main parameters of each Americanization in turn.

Incipient Americanization

There is a discrepancy between the rise of American political power and the influence of its civil society in the first half of the twentieth century. The US began the century as recent victors in the American-Spanish war and their growing political influence culminated in entry into World War I, victory and the creation of the League of Nations as a US project. Defeat for President Wilson in 1920, however, marked the onset of a political isolationalism by which the US forsook world leadership. In contrast, it was in the 1920s that American cultural influence came to the fore. According to John Lukacs (1993: 273), 'As early as 1925, millions of people in Europe knew the names and faces of American movie stars while they knew not the name of their own prime minister'. Alongside this 'invasion of Hollywood', America was to make its first major foray into dominating popular music through the international spread of jazz. Important as these cultural products were, there was something even more basic to this incipient Americanization.

It seemed as if, in the 1920s, the USA was creating a new type of society. Lukacs (1993: 145) characterizes the changes in terms of the 'shape' of society from pyramid (i.e. with a base consisting of many poor people) to 'onion-shaped' implying a majority of middle-income people. Inevitably this was associated with fundamental changes in the everyday lives of Americans. Higher wages were reflected in more consumption especially in the home. By the middle of the 1920s over 60 per cent of American houses had electricity and their residents consumed over half the electricity generated throughout the world (Rybczynski 1986: 153). This huge market meant lower prices which stimulated more demand with increasing numbers of domestic appliances. Hence the birth of the new suburban life style centred on the home as the locus of consumer durables. These domestic developments came to the notice of the outside world in two main ways. While other countries were developing their propaganda arm of the state with 'official' cultural institutions, Americanization proceeded through essentially private means; the production and marketing of American corporations and visitors' reports and letters home from immigrants (Duigan and Gann 1992: 420–1). In fact, the State Department only set up a cultural relations division in 1938 and Voice of America only began broadcasting in 1942 as part of the war effort. Incipient Americanization was clearly not a public project which was unthinkable in a period of US political isolationism. But the American message got through nevertheless via the two 'unofficial' media.

First, with increased economic protectionism, the fast growing American corporations were forced to set up production behind the tariff barriers. In Europe, Germany became the main US economic base with ITT, General Motors and IG Chemicals leading the way. Coca-Cola opened its factory in Essen in 1929. In Britain, this was the period when a host of companies which were to become famous household brand names built factories, for example: Hoover, Gillette, McLeans, Remington, Firestone and Ford (Marling 1993: 106). The market for consumer goods still lagged far behind America but the beginnings of the new modernity were being put into place.

Second, visitors to America were struck by its unusual civil society and reported back accordingly. Dennis Brogan writes of visiting 'American the Golden' in the 1920s with feelings divided between envy and the desire to emulate. For many, however, there was no such divided feelings. Luigi Barzini, an immigrant from Italy in 1925, was much more insistent on the inherent modernity in the new America:

> What interested me in the United States . . . was the 'modern' concept, in which all things served to be done in a revolutionary 'modern' way. Everything was the product of fresh thinking, from the foundations up. Everything had been 'improved', and was continually being 'improved' from day to day, almost from hour to hour. The restlessness, mobility, the increasing quest for something better impressed me. (Barzini 1959: 73)

As views such as this filtered through to other civil societies, leading intellectuals came to suspect that they were being provided with a glimpse of a new world. Most famously, Antonio Gramsci, writing in 1929, was intrigued by the high wage regime of the USA and asked if this represented 'a new historical epoch' (Hoare and Smith 1971: 277). He was unsure whether the 'new culture' and 'way of life' represented 'a new beacon of civilization' or merely 'a new coating' on European civilization (ibid.: 317–18). Jean-Paul Sartre had no such doubts: 'Skyscrapers were the architecture of the future, just as the cinema was the art and jazz the music of the future' (Duignan and Gann 1992: 410). With the benefit of hindsight, we know today that Americanization was only just beginning.

Capacious Americanization

It was in 1941 that Henry Luce, a prominent Republican, proclaimed 'the American Century'. This has been interpreted, quite properly, as a key step in US abandonment of political isolationalism. Indeed Luce (1941: 260) called for 'a truly *American* internationalism' in order to influence the 'world environment . . . for the growth of American life' (Luce 1941: 23–4). This was part of what Duignan and Gann (1992: 409) identify as a 'sea change' in American society with confidence in the 'American Way' replacing an earlier 'mood of cultural deference' when educated Americans automatically looked to Europe for their cultural lead. This confidence was quite pervasive. At the end of World War II only the USA assumed the good times were coming; Ellwood (1992: 21) reports Keynes' surprise on encountering American optimism at Bretton Woods. As the arsenal and financier of war victory, America was now in a special position to project itself across the spectrum of social relations – political, cultural and economic. This is high hegemony, the period when the rest of the world is offered a comprehensive societal package.

Today, when Americanization is often viewed in narrow cultural terms, it is important to emphasize that the projection of the American Way of Life at mid-century was based upon production processes more than anything else. The technology leadership of US industry – 'American know-how' – meant that American workers were producing two to five times as much per day as European workers (Price 1955: 328). It is not surprising, therefore, that although the Marshall Plan began by emphasizing the need to raise gross production, it soon changed to focus upon raising productivity. In this way, reconstruction soon came to be viewed as the 'modernization of European industry' which in turn brought the 'growth idea' to the centre of decision making. Institutions were set up to take managers and workers on visits to the USA so that they could learn the new and better ways of production at first hand. It was at this time (1950–2) that France sent forty such missions to the United States and, according to Kuisel (1993: 84), discovered 'management' as opposed to traditional French 'direction'. All this created a new politics based upon economic growth leading to higher levels of consumption and thus voter contentment (Ellwood 1992: 94). This

Americanization was to privilege class compromise over class conflict in new political reconstructions in all western European states.

The Marshall Plan as a promise that 'the American Dream could be dreamt without leaving home' (Ellwood 1992: 89) was 'only a qualified success' by the time it finished in 1952 but the events of the next decade resulted in it being hailed as 'one of the great economic success stories of modern time' (Wexler 1983: 254–5). We can see the degree of this American achievement in Franz Joseph's collection of foreign views of America published in 1959. Views from twenty countries constitute a veritable homage to the USA and things American. The elites who are supplying their countries' view of America provide a distinct sense of their societies being undermined by Americanization through its mass attraction with special reference to the lower classes and young people. As the British commentator notes : '(it is) the very aspects of the American way of life that (anti-American elites) despise (which) are those most treasured, envied, and emulated by the mass of the British people' (Brogan 1959: 20). In effect these commentators are reporting on an irresistible new world being created in the USA: from Germany 'an image of the American as being from another world' (Zahn 1959: 97); from Switzerland 'America the symbol of the up-to-date twentieth century, of the brave new world' (Freymond 1959: 83); from Cuba 'America signifies above all else a *new* world . . . being a world *for the new* (with) a *vocation for newness*' (Manach 1959: 340); from France 'in the United States I was above all struck by the originality of American society' (Aron 1959: 58); from Yugoslavia 'I slowly began to realize how vastly the US differs from the industrialized countries of Western Europe' (Yilfan 1959: 119); and finally from Indonesia 'American capitalism is no longer recognizable as the capitalist monster of the nineteenth century', compared with the 'settled' image of Europe when you visit the USA 'you have the feeling that in the United States you are on the threshold of the future, with room and materials to build new values' (Lubis 1959: 200, 204). This illustrates the cultural power of capacious Americanization, immanent in the creation of a new modernity as the future for other countries.

In many ways, the real test case for the power of capacious Americanization was France under President de Gaulle. As an arch opponent of American hegemony, he promoted security and economic policies to lessen US influence in Europe. But the paradox was that it was the decade of the '60s, at the very height of de Gaulle's power, that coincided with rampant Americanization within France itself (Kuisel 1993: chapter 6). It was left to Jean-Jacques Servan-Schreiber in 1967 to produce the massive best-selling book which advocated the opposite to de

Gaulle: accommodation to American power rather than insulation from it. After extolling the prowess of US multinational corporations, he proposed, in Arthur Schlesinger's (1968: x) term, a 'discriminating Americanization', focusing on organisation as an alternative to an 'easy temptation to Americanization' by simple employment of Americans to manage French industry (Servan-Schreiber 1968: 27). The latter was not as outlandish in the 1960s as it now seems. The high point of this type of thinking came with John Ney's book appropriately entitled *The European Surrender* (1970), in which he argued that 'Americans are on top because they are intrinsically different' (Ney 1970: 10), they are 'the only people who can *cope* with technological living at the American level' (ibid.: 6). Nevertheless Europeans will try their best to emulate their superiors (ibid.: 12) because 'the European present can only duplicate the American past' (ibid.: 4). This Americanization argument for 'a predetermined future' (ibid.: 5) represents the essence of an extreme 'ization' position that merges process and end-state to privilege the latter as a universal.

Resonant Americanization

Ironically, Ney's book appeared just as the material conditions that gave it its credibility were beginning to be undermined. After 1970 other countries' corporations began seriously to rival the original US multinationals and the idea of a 'productivity gap' became more likely to refer to American inferiority than superiority. This coincided with a change in the way people began to interpret the new modernity. Raymond Aron (1959: 67–8) had earlier wondered whether the new mass culture should be viewed simply as American culture or more generally as the latest development of material society. Aron proved to be remarkably prescient. In terms of the radical ideas associated with the 1968 revolution in France, for instance, 'America became less the perpetuator of some universal crime and more a fellow victim of a global dynamic' (Kuisel 1993: 186). Kuisel (1993: 6) identifies 1970 as the watershed: 'it has become increasingly disconnected from America . . . it would be better described as the coming of consumer society' (ibid.: 4). But Americanization was too embedded in the everyday lives of Europeans to simply disappear with American high hegemony.

The oddity of Americanization is that it is more visible today than during its high point. Whereas a previous generation experienced Americanization at the cinema or on TV, now it can be encountered directly in any high street as numerous burger, chicken or pizza fast food joints. It is sometimes forgotten how recent this development is:

the first McDonald's did not open in Britain until 1974. Marling (1993: 15) interprets this contemporary Americanization as 'set firmly in a timewarp': 'it's about nostalgia because it is not America *now* that we're in love with, but America as it was when it first swept us off our feet in the 1950s.' Cowboy films may no longer be popular but things American remain fascinating to new generations of Europeans (Marling 1993: 7). This is a resonant Americanization reverberating into our present.

But McDonald's does not represent the universal American society that John Ney envisaged. Rather it is the after shock of a process that never reached its ultimate end-state. The answer to Aron's (1959: 70) question 'Will an industrialized France, concerned with productivity, become a mediocre replica of the United States?' is an emphatic 'no'. The fact the French people buy their Big Macs on the Champs-Elysées does not make them any less French. The outcome of the French engage-ment with Americanization has been neatly summarized as follows:

> Contemporary France is a different society because of changes associ-ated with Americanization ... (but it) neither obliterated French inde-pendence nor smothered French identity. France did change but it remained the same ... The history of Americanization confirms the resi-lience and absorptive capacity of French *civilization* ... Americanization has transformed France – it has made it more like America – without a proportionate loss of identity. France remains France, and the French remain French. (Kuisel 1993: 231, 233, 237)

This is a clear example of universal pretensions that were always tend-encies with no inevitable outcome. Izations are never what they seem. As tendencies they will encounter counter-tendencies, particularities that will challenge their operation. Hence the expected outcome will always be a compromise, a synthesis of the universal and the particular.

Modernization: High Hegemony

Anthony King (1995: 115) has recently drawn an interesting distinction between modernization and the other concepts derived from the idea of being modern, namely modernism and modernity. He argues that whereas the latter are 'Euro-American' with an historical temporality which is spatially restricted, modernization is 'largely American' and has been designed by social scientists to break out of the geographical limits set by the ideas of modernity and modernism. The message of modern-ization was that the modern was open to all. This is quintessentially hegemonic, integral to the United States' promotion of its 'moral and intellectual leadership'. From 1949 when President Truman issued his Point IV plan to promote growth in 'under-developed countries', a massive academic and policy investment was made in the theory and practice of development and this was complemented by a great flourish of theories of modernization in the 1960s, almost totally the product of American social scientists. But its paradigmatic dominance lasted barely a decade and in the 1970s it was under terminal attack: by 1976, Wallerstein (1979: 133) could dismiss modernization in a most patronizing way as 'unquestionably a worthy parable for the times'. In short, this was a theory of American high hegemony and no more.

There is no need to rehearse the well-known debate over modernization of a quarter a century ago, beyond noting that, like Americanization, modernization constituted a comprehensive package of processes – economic, political and cultural (Weiner 1966) – to transform existing societies which were found to be inherently wanting. It was presented as the opportunity to 'catch up'. To show how the theoretical pretensions of modernization theory were entirely compatible with our general explication of izations, we will very briefly outline one, arguably the best, critique presented by John Taylor (1979). Taylor's central point is that the application of Parsonian structural-functionalism to third world countries confounds causation with description. The result is an exercise in 'ex-post-facto generalisation' (Taylor 1979: 29) based upon

> an evolutionary correlation between industrialisation and differentiation (that can) only resolve the problem of future possible directions of change in Third World societies by referring them to a *particular end-state*, namely that attained by the contemporary *most differentiated* social systems. On the basis of its evolutionary postulates, a universal historical path towards greater differentiation emerges, which all social systems *must necessarily follow*. (Taylor 1979: 31)

This is clearly seen in the empirical comparisons made between 'traditional' and 'modern' societal patterns that became ubiquitous to modernization studies. All of this was premised on the ization 'trick' of confusing the process with the end-state so that the latter was accepted as inevitable in the way Taylor shows.

This ization was particularly confusing for third world countries, however, because its 'end-state' of a singular 'modernity' did not fit well with what was happening in the 'first world'. We can illustrate this by reference to the most influential of all writings on development: Walt

Rostow's (1960) model of stages of economic growth. His book is pivotal in this story because it was both the culmination of early development studies in economics and stimulated subsequent modernization studies in sociology. He identified five 'stages' beginning with the 'traditional society' that was to become the sociologists' foil for the modern. But Rostow was an economic historian which led him to identify four other stages beyond the traditional. These consist of two separate processes. First, there are the 'preconditions for take-off' and 'take-off' which is an abstract description of Britain's industrialization, and second, there is the 'drive to maturity' and 'age of high mass consumption' which is a similar abstract treatment of later US economic development. In short, Rostow puts together as a single sequence a pattern that we have described as two distinctive modernities: Britain's industrial modernity and America's consumer modernity. By creating a single scale, all countries are provided with the same path out of tradition and into the modern. But the reality was that the drive to maturity was largely restricted to European countries as Americanization. The 'modernization' on offer to the rest of the world was totally dominated by the process of industrialization. It was about constructing nineteenth-century industrial modernity, a social form superseded by the consumerism of American high hegemony. To the degree that modernization theories were dictated by the necessity to industrialize, Third world countries were being sold an antique model of modernity. Being an ization, nobody seemed to ask the question whether the travails of industrialization could be largely by-passed and the new consumer society instituted through promoting the service sector, a process which we can, perhaps, glimpse in the subsequent success of Singapore.

Of course, theories of modernization and associated ideas on development did not simply succumb to superior intellectual arguments. Rather, it was the absence of the evidence for 'catching up' that spelt the death knoll for such theories. That is to say, it was the failure of the end-state to materialize – a thoroughly modern world of countries moving together towards international economic equality. Crucially, however, this does not mean that the processes modernization theorists were inadequately modelling simply did not take place. On the contrary, they had profound impacts on third world countries and changed their societies irrevocably. This was because, like Americanization in the core of the world economy, modernization beyond the core was fundamentally popular among ordinary people. Modernization was presented as emulating success, and millions of people were seduced by the promise of a better life. The classic example of the power of the modernization process is what came to be known as the 'Baby Powder Milk Scandal' (Chetley 1979). In this case mothers throughout the third world were choosing to spend exorbitant proportions of the family income on powdered milk as an alternative to breast feeding. Increased likelihood of death for the baby (from mixing powder with impure water), and less food for other children in the family, were not strong enough reasons for these women to eschew a product that was marketed as absolutely modern with salespersons dressed up like 'western nurses'. Mother's milk, a better product that was free but fundamentally traditional, just could not compete with being modern. This scandal has repeatedly returned to the news since its first appearance in the 1970s, showing that while modernization theories might be dead, many of the expectations they set in train continue to blight the everyday lives of peoples beyond the 'core'.

Globalization: Hegemonic Demise

Despite a recent reference to 'post-globalization' (Helleiner 1996), I will treat globalization as an important on-going debate about the nature of contemporary social change. Although we can have none of the benefits of hindsight we enjoyed in discussing Americanization and modernization, by focusing on the contemporary process as an ization, we can quickly attune ourselves to its interpretative dangers. Here we are at one with Robert Cox (1996: 23) and his concern that globalization be 'represented as . . . the logical and inevitable culmination of the powerful tendencies of the market at work'. But we must be careful not to use -ization parallels uncritically. As has become common, it might be reasonable to see 'globalization as the corollary of modernity' (Pieterse 1996: 46) but it is definitely not acceptable to elide from modernization to globalization as Mittelman (1996: 1) implies. They are bundles of processes that belong to two different times: modernization was a creature of American high hegemony, globalization is a feature of hegemonic demise. What difference does this make?

Social optimism is an integral part of high hegemony. With the support of a 'can-do' hegemon almost anything can seem possible, even, for instance, the outlandish idea of putting a man on the moon (Taylor 1996a: chapter 3). An important element of Americanization was the transfer of optimism for the future, against all the evidence, across the Atlantic to war-torn Europe. The optimism underlying theories of modernization were an even greater leap in the dark for newly decolonized states. Reading books on development nearly half a century on, one is struck by the implicit naïveté of the thinking behind such claims that 'By the year 2000, we can be living in a world that has overcome poverty – a world without want' (Hoffman 1962: 142). Such optimism was not merely an élite artifice, it was shared by the majority of people and bears a genuine mark of the times. All this changed in the years around 1970 with new economic difficulties associated with political and military disasters, with environmental forebodings appearing, and with cultural assumptions slowly becoming more critical and reflexive. This new despair has been succinctly captured by Charles Cerami (1989: 6) when he says simply that 'the world as a whole is moving in the wrong direction'. This is a new world where the old social optimism could not survive to be replaced by caution, disaffection and indifference. These are the times, the decline phase of the American hegemonic cycle, that have spawned globalization as 'a myth suitable for a world without illusions' (Hirst and Thompson 1996: 6).

Globalization itself, however, is not based upon a pessimistic view of the world. Like the other izations, its universalizing claims are a result of a faith in the beneficial effects of new technology – now with its own name 'high tech' – to create a new world. But unlike the ideologies underpinning consumption and development, high tech is not for all. This is, therefore, a discriminating optimism: not everyone is expected to be plugged in to the new globalized world. Osvaldo Sunkel (1995) describes an 'uneven globalization' and, more specifically, Riccardo Petrella (1996: 77) writes of a 'truncated globalization' or 'triadization' based upon the 'integrated "global" world' of the three core zones of the contemporary world economy. Of course, this relegates the rest of the world to a future as 'increasingly *excluded* fragments outside the Triad' (Petrella 1996: 81). In a related argument, Stephen Gill (1996: 210–11) treats globalization as part of a neo-liberal agenda that legitimates class domination by reifying the market. Hence unlike the optimism of high hegemony, as well as being spatially bounded, globalization's selectivity is also class-based:

> Today we are witnessing a crisis of development of global proportions – a true crisis of global civilization. It involves a counter-revolution of the powerful against the weak. In much of the Third World, the processes of urbanization and economic decline have gone with social chaos, anomie and nihilism. (Gill 1996: 220)

As a professed universalizing process, globalization is much more insidious than either Americanization and modernization were.

Given the above, it is quite reasonable to denote globalization as either a 'necessary myth' (Hirst and Thompson 1996: chapter 1) or 'ideology' (Cox 1996: 23–4). However, we must be careful not to neglect the real material processes that have been the enabling factors in making claims for globalization seem so credible that they threaten to become politically pervasive. This is the old process/end-state conundrum with which we began this paper and which is endemic to izations. Hirst and Thompson (1996: 4) recognize this problem but choose a methodology that seems to me to fall into the ization trap nonetheless. They set up two contrasting economic models, one 'inter-national' and the other of a 'globalized economy', as ideal types against which to compare some crucial information on recent economic trends. Their conclusion is that current patterns can be reasonably interpreted in terms of an international economy that has existed for over a hundred years with no need to resort to postulating a new globalized phase of development. Although this exercise is useful in forcing us to think more precisely about what a genuinely globalized economy would look like, the fact that we have yet to reach that end point is hardly surprising. The key point is in the interpretation of economic changes. But here Hirst and Thompson (1996: 16) make a curious, and I think fateful, initial decision. After stating that their two models 'are not mutually exclusive', they say that

in certain circumstances the globalized economy would *encompass and subsume* the international economy, transforming them as it reinforces them. If this phenomenon occurred there would thus be a complex combination of features of both types of economy present within the present conjuncture.

It is just such a 'complex combination' of tendencies that we would assume to be the outcome of the economic processes Hirst and Thompson investigate. But, perhaps swayed by their own emphasized 'encompass and subsume' – which is not, of course, the only possible relation between the models – they state categorically that 'such a process of hybridisation is not taking place'. There is a brief justification for this by referring to future chapters but no further discussion of a possible hybrid situation – it is not referred to in the final concluding chapter, for example. This really is a pity since much of their evidence for a continuing international economy could be equally interpreted as hybridization. The development of economic blocks, for instance, – and Hirst and Thompson have an excellent discussion of the EU – can be very reasonably depicted as a hybrid situation that marries together national, international and globalizing tendencies. More generally it would seem that focusing on global-local nexus or 'glocalization' (Robertson 1995) is more likely to prove a useful research strategy than simply opposing the global to the non-global.

Although Hirst and Thompson (1996: 3) are avowedly concerned only with *economic* globalization, their eschewing of hybridization is nevertheless remarkable given its new centrality in cultural interpretations of globalization (Pieterse 1995). Post-colonialism has created a new vibrant resistance to universalizing through a conscious mixing of traditions creating innumerable cultural hybrids (Featherstone 1995: 10). Pieterse (1995: 53; 54) describes this as creolization resulting in a 'global mélange'. The argument is that globalization is leading not to cultural uniformity but to 'new levels of diversity' so that 'global culture' should be viewed as 'a field of struggle' rather than 'a common culture' (Featherstone 1995: 13–14). Of course, we should be as wary of the concepts of creolization and hybridization as we have been of the three izations at the centre of this paper, but if we focus on them as tendencies rather than end-states we can see that they represent bundles of processes reacting with extant globalization processes. This reflects the fact that, although both capacious Americanization and third world modernization were contested, in our more self-reflexive times, globalization has suffered particularly acute resistance and critical scrutiny. In terms of politics, two globalizations can be identified. As well as the familiar 'globalization from above' based upon collaboration of leading states and transnational capital, Richard Falk (1992) identifies a second 'globalization from below' which indicts its élite counterpart for global neglect of ecology, liberty and human rights. Using another terminology, this is Gill's (1996) biospheric globalization (versus neoliberal globalization) or what Cox (1996: 22) prefers to call simply 'globalism'.

Concluding Remarks: From Promises to Threat

The kernal of hegemony is an atypical mixture of coercion and consensus with the latter predominating. Hence during American high hegemony the crucial dynamic in the projection of US power consisted of two 'promises' one for the core and one for the periphery: capacious Americanization was for people like us (from the hegemon's point of view) and modernization was for those not like us (the seriously unmodern). Both faltered with the downturn of the world economy and the attendant hegemonic demise. Although these two processes can still be discerned after high hegemony, they are mere shadows of their former selves as globalization comes to centre stage. Here we can see the balance between coercion and consensus becoming what has historically been more typical: globalization's primary role has been as 'threat'. Although it has the most universal name of the three izations, in fact it is the more restrictive in practice, taking the focus away from those who were 'modernizing' and even abandoning some of those who had been comfortably 'Americanized'. Thus, the three 'izations' differ fundamentally in their operation: whereas the power of Americanization and modernization was derived from their promises, it is as threat that globalization has achieved its power.

The world political interpretation of this is quite simple: with the decline and demise of 'real-existing socialism' in the role of alternative world-system, the assurances of modernization could be reneged upon (economic development replaced by economic polarization) and the scope of Americanization could be reduced ('down-sizing' unleashed upon white-collar workers). Nevertheless, although world-wide material changes have been fundamentally enabling for this shift away from building consensus politics, to attain such a gestalt switch requires powerful new mechanisms of legitimation. It is, of course, no surprise that the chief promotors of neo-liberal globalization, Ronald Reagan and Margaret Thatcher, were also primaeval nationalists. However, there was also a curious support for globalization from a most unlikely and equally contradictory source.

Globalism incorporates contested global visions of 'one-world' – all humanity living together – and 'whole-earth' – the world as living planet – deriving from the technological achievements of space travel (Cosgrove 1994). Denis Cosgrove has shown how new global visions are linked to modernist ideals and American projections of power but the connections to contemporary globalization remain to be researched. It seems to me that the global icons which Cosgrove discusses have provided an enabling cultural predisposition for the particular universalism proclaimed as globalization. For instance, the discovery of the 'world population problem' as high hegemony was turning into hegemonic demise (see, for instance, Ehrlich 1968; Club of Rome 1972) was not only providing the excuse for the failure of modernization, it revived a specific geographical scale – the global – as an important part of the world political agenda. And with the development of more ecological concerns, the global came to represent a universal for all of humanity: there is a strong sense in which global warming, ozone depletion, genetic engineering of the food chain and their like are genuinely 'democratic' in their effects. Hence, as well as providing a planetary ethos in which ideas of globalization could flourish, globalism has contributed to the destruction of social optimism so necessary for building consensus. In short, we have moved from the optimistic situation when the 'goods' of modernity were promised to all, to the pessimistic situation with the 'bads' of modernity threatening all. This is the cultural context in which globalization as an idea has been so successful.

Bibliography

Aron, R. (1959) 'From France' in F. M. Joseph (ed.) *As Others See Us: The United States through Foreign Eyes*, Princeton, NJ: Princeton University Press.

Arrighi, G. (1990) 'The Three Hegemonies of Historical Capitalism', *Review*, 13, 365–408.

Arrighi, G. (1993) *The Long Twentieth Century*, London: Verso.

Balroch, P. (1996) 'Globalization Myths and Realities: One Century of External Trade and Foreign Investment' in R. Boyer and D. Drache (eds) *States against Markets: The Limits of Globalization*, London: Routledge.

Barzini, L. (1959) 'From Italy' in F. M. Joseph (ed.) *As Others See Us: The United States through Foreign Eyes*, Princeton, NJ: Princeton University Press.

Brogan, D. W. (1959) 'From England' in F. M. Joseph (ed.) *As Others See Us: The United States through Foreign Eyes*, Princeton, NJ: Princeton University Press.

Broughton, M. (1959) 'From South Africa' in F. M. Joseph (ed.) *As Others See Us: The United States through Foreign Eyes*, Princeton, NJ: Princeton University Press.

Cerami, C. A. (1989) *A Marshall Plan for the 1990s*, New York: Praeger.

Chetley, J. (1979) *The Baby Milk Scandal*, London: War on Want.

Club of Rome (1972) *The Limits to Growth*, New York: Universe.

Cosgrove, D. (1994) 'Contested Global visions: *One-World, Whole-Earth*, and the Apollo space photographs', *Annals of the Association of American Geographers*, 84, 270–94.

Cox, R. W. (1996) 'A Perspective on Globalization' in J. H. Mittelman (ed.) *Globalization: Critical Reflections*, Boulder, CO: Lynne Rienner.

Duigan, P. and Gann, L. H. (1992) *The Rebirth of the West: The Americanization of the Democratic World, 1945–1958*, Oxford: Blackwell.

Ehrich, P. (1968) *The Population Bomb*. London: Pan.

Ellwood, D. W. (1992) *Rebuilding Europe: Western Europe, America and Postwar Reconstruction*, London: Longman.

Falk, R. (1992) 'The Making of Global Citizenship' in J. Brecher et al. (eds) *Global Visions: Beyond the New World Order*, Boston: South End.

Featherstone, M. (1995) *Undoing Culture: Globalization, Postmodernity and Identity*, London: Sage.

FitzGibbons, C. (1969) *Denazification*. London: Michael Joseph.

Freymond, J. (1959) 'From Switzerland' in F. M. Joseph (ed.) *As Others See Us: The United States through Foreign Eyes*, Princeton, NJ: Princeton University Press.

Friedman, J. (1995) 'Global System, Globalization and the Parameters of Modernity' in M. Featherstone, S. Lash and R. Robertson (eds) *Global Modernities*, London: Sage.

Friedmann, J. (1995) 'Where We Stand: A Decade of World City Research' in P. Knox and P. J. Taylor (eds) *World Cities in a World-System*, Cambridge: Cambridge University Press.

Gill, S. (1996) 'Globalization, Democratization and the Politics of Indifference' in J. H. Mittelman (ed.) *Globalization: Critical Reflections*, Boulder, CO: Lynne Rienner.

Helleiner, E. (1996) 'Post-globalization: Is the Financial Liberalization Trend Likely to Be Reversed?' in R. Boyer and D. Drache (eds) *States against Markets. The Limits of Globalization*, London: Routledge.

Hirst, P. and Thompson, G. (1996) *Globalization in Question*, Cambridge: Polity.

Hoare, Q. and Smith, G. N. (eds) (1971) *Selections from the Prison Notebooks of Antonio Gramsci*, London: Lawrence and Wishart.

Hoffman, P. (1962) *World without Want*, London: Chatto and Windus.

Hopkins, T. K. (1990) 'A Note on the Concept of Hegemony', *Review*, 13, 409–12.

King, A. D. (1995) 'The Times and Spaces of Modernity (or Who Needs Postmodernism)' in M. Featherstone, S. Lash and R. Robertson (eds) *Global Modernities*, London: Sage.

Kuisel, R. F. (1993) *Seducing the French: The Dilemma of Americanization*, Berkeley, CA: University of California Press.

Lubis, M. (1959) 'From Indonesia' in F. M. Joseph (ed.) *As Others See Us: The United States through Foreign Eyes*, Princeton, NJ: Princeton University Press.

Luce, H. (1941) *The American Century*, New York: Farrar and Rinehart.

Lukacs, J. (1993) *The End of the Twentieth Century and the End of the Modern Age*, New York: Ticknor and Fields.

Manach, J. (1959) 'From Cuba' in F. M. Joseph (ed.) *As Others See Us: The United States through Foreign Eyes*, Princeton, NJ: Princeton University Press.

Marling, S. (1993) *American Affair. The Americanization of Britain*, London: Boxtree.

Mittelman, J. H. (1996) 'The Dynamics of Globalization' in J. H. Mittelman (ed.) *Globalization: Critical Reflections*, Boulder, CO: Lynne Rienner.

Ney, J. (1970) *The European Surrender: A Descriptive Study of the American Social and Economic Conquest*, Boston: Little, Brown.

Petrella, R. (1996) 'Globalization and internationalization: The Dynamics of the Emerging World Order' in R. Boyer and D. Drache (eds) *States against Markets: The Limits of Globalization*, London: Routledge.

Pieterse, J. N. (1995) 'Globalization as Hybridization' in M. Featherstone, S. Lash and R. Robertson (eds) *Global Modernities*, London: Sage.

Price, H. B. (1955) *The Marshall Plan and Its Meaning*, Ithaca, NY: Cornell University Press.

Robertson, R. (1995) 'Glocalization: Time–Space and Homogeneity–Heterogeneity' in M. Featherstone, S. Lash and R. Robertson (eds) *Global Modernities*, London: Sage.

Rostow, W. W. (1960) *The Stages of Economic Growth*, Cambridge: Cambridge University Press.

Rybczynski, W. (1986) *Home. A Short History of an Idea*, London: Penguin.

Schlesinger, A. (1968) 'Foreword' to J.-J. Servan-Schreiber, *The American Challenge*, London: Hamish Hamilton.

Servan-Schreiber, J-J. (1968) *The American Challenge*, London: Hamish Hamilton.

Sunkel, O. (1995) 'Uneven Globalization, Economic Reform and Democracy: A View from Latin America' in H.-H. Holm and G. Sorensen (eds) *Whose World Order? Uneven Globalization and the End of the Cold War*, Boulder, CO: Westview.

Taylor, J. G. (1979) *From Modernization to Modes of Production*. London: Macmillan.

Taylor, P. J. (1996a) *The Way the Modern World Works: World Hegemony to World Impasse*, Chichester: Wiley.

Taylor, P. J. (1996b) 'What's Modern about the Modern World-System? Introducing Ordinary Modernity through World Hegemony', *Review of International Political Economy*, 3, 260–86.

Taylor, P. J. (1997a) 'Modernities and Movements: Anti-systemic Reactions to World Hegemony', *Review*, 20, 1–18.

Taylor, P. J. (1997b) 'Hierarchical Tendencies amongst World Cities: A Global Research Proposal', *Cities*, 14, 323–32.

Taylor, P. J. (1998) *Modernities. A Geohistorical Interpretation*. Cambridge: Polity.

Therborn, G. (1995) 'Routes through/to Modernity' in M. Featherstone, S. Lash and R. Robertson (eds.) *Global Modernities*, London: Sage.

Wallerstein, I. (1979) *The Capitalist World-Economy*, Cambridge: Cambridge University Press.

Wallerstein, I. (1984) *The Politics of the World-Economy*, Cambridge: Cambridge University Press.

Weiner, M. (1966) *Modernization: The Dynamics of Growth*, New York: Voice of America.

Wexler, I. (1983) *The Marshall Plan Revisited*. Westport, CT: Greenwood.

Willet, R. (1989) *The Americanization of Germany, 1945–1949*, London: Routledge.

Yilfan, M. (1959) 'From Yugoslavia' in F. M. Joseph (ed.) *As Others See Us: The United States through Foreign Eyes*, Princeton, NJ: Princeton University Press.

Zahn, P. von (1959) 'From Germany' in F. M. Joseph (ed.) *As Others See Us: The United States through Foreign Eyes*, Princeton, NJ: Princeton University Press.

4
State Sovereignty, Globalization and the Rise of Soft Capitalism
Nigel Thrift

Introduction

> 14 members of the Ethiopian government recently graduated with MBAs from the UK's Open University, with Meles Zenawi, Ethiopia's President and former Marxist guerrilla, coming fourth among more than 2500 graduates... the government of neighbouring Eritrea, which also has swapped Marxism for liberal democracy and capitalism, was so impressed that 100 politicians, civil servants and other senior people have joined up for the University's two year, part-time MBA course. (*Financial Times*, 18 November 1996: 21)

I believe that something called 'globalization' exists and that, loosely speaking, it is the ability of networks to organize across greater distances in less time than formerly. But I do not believe that this process is a coherent or remorseless one of the kind usually dignified by the single word 'globalization'. Nor do I believe that the impact of globalization on the nation state is as profound as is often pointed. In part, this is because I do not believe that globalization is a coherent process: it is an order of partial connection (Strathern 1991). But, in part, it is also because I do not believe that the nation state is that coherent either. This is because I believe that social life consists of a multiplicity of productive networks with greater or lesser power to align with and translate other networks – sometimes thereby augmenting themselves – which 'supply the necessary basis for the great negative forms of power' (Foucault 1980: 122). Thus the nation state is no longer seen in a reductionist way, but as a multitudinous set of tactics concerned with 'the conduct of conduct', reliant upon many sources of inspiration and systems of expertise, which has achieved some degree of self-referentiality.

Out of the many tactics through which the state is able to produce power – and bring it home – I want to concentrate in this chapter on just one, what I call the state's 'intelligence' capacity, its ability to know others and, in the process, form itself and them. Foucault's account of governmentality stresses that modern nation states were derived from the state getting to know itself through a series of multiple tactics which connect and concentrate knowledge and power. In other words, the state gradually becomes 'intelligent', becoming – all of a piece – the chief source of intelligence, a means of ordering that intelligence, and the vehicle which reflexively monitors and manages that intelligence. The state becomes its own reason for being, constantly creating and steering an inside which defines an outside (Walker 1993). In particular, the state's power of knowledge and knowledge of power comes from the ability of its multifaceted tactics to constitute subjects through which it is able to know and shape the world. Foucault recognized a number of different forms of political power which were concerned with the constitution, maintenance and regulation of subjects. There are basic police apparatuses, referring to the governmental notion of the efficient management of 'men' in their relation to things. A further cluster of apparatuses are based around what he called pastorship and are modelled on the Christian form of confession. These practices, originally extraneous to the state, become more and more prominent techniques of government.

> It is the Christian notion of pastoral power which, during the eighteenth century, is assimilated into governmental apparatuses of security and is to become a fundamental regulatory technique in contemporary society, that is, the confessional. The dissemination of pastoral power into the acts of government involves a corresponding shift in focus from a spiritual to a secular end. It is no longer a question of ensuring the salvation of individuals in the next world, but rather of augmenting their existence in this world. Converging with the governmental concern with efficient management, salvation takes on a new meaning in a series of worldly areas such as health, well-being (in the sense of sufficient wealth and standard of living) security, protection against accidents. (McNay 1994: 121)

Other sources of intelligence on a scale greater than that generated by the nation state were rare. They existed, of course, but many of them, like the circuits of science and education, were rapidly incorporated into the state. However, since the end of the Second World War, things have changed in three ways.

First, the number of sources of intelligence has multiplied. The state can no longer claim to have sovereignty over knowledge. Second, part of the reason for this change has been the extraordinary growth of the mass media. As knowledge has been 'mediatized' through new communications technologies which play a critical role in the disposition of objects, information and persons, becoming a part of a sea of signs, so the rights to knowledge have become crucial since increasingly it is the co-constructive interaction between the knowledge and the media which defines property (Lury 1993). Third, the mode of subjectification has become increasingly reliant on the grip of new forms of pastoral regulation based upon the growth of the 'psy' disciplines (Rose 1996) like psychology, psychiatry, psychotherapy and psychoanalysis, techniques which are 'ways of making visible and intelligible certain features of persons, their conducts, and the relations with one another' (ibid.: 11). In other words, a whole new form of governmentality has been opened up based on new practices of recognition: – 'for it is psy that claims to understand the inner determinants of human conduct, and psy that asserts its ability to provide the appropriate underpinning in knowledge, judgement, and technique for the powers of experts of conduct wherever they are to be exercised' (ibid.: 13).

My argument in the rest of this chapter is that we need to recognize the existence of many comparatively new networks of knowledge operating on a global scale, systems of expertise whose 'function' is to create new cultural systems. These formerly 'underground empires' (Nonini and Ong 1997) are now becoming increasingly visible as self-referential clusters of practices which are generating their own forms of knowledge. Because of the media, this knowledge is more immediately transferable between networks than before and is able routinely to escape the confines of state practices of governmentality.

In the first part of the chapter, I outline the genesis of one of these networks, which I have elsewhere called the 'cultural circuit of capitalism' (Thrift 1997) which has produced new forms of knowledge and new practices of subjectification based on the rise of a body of managerial 'theory' and, in particular, 'softer' management theory.

Then, in the second part of the chapter, I outline the way in which the practices of this network have been adopted by states. One way of looking at this would be to argue that the sovereignty of states has been compromised by the presence of this network and its subsumption into the state. However, I think that this might well be the wrong way to consider the situation. It seems to me to be equally apposite to argue that the hand of certain core nation states has been strengthened, both because the managerial discourse is still predominantly Euro-American in character and because they have adopted practices of intelligence-gathering and subjectification formerly extraneous to them and, in the process, have produced a new 'managerial' state (Clarke and Newman 1993) which is, in its different ways, as potent as what has gone before. In other words, I want to argue that, in certain registers, state sovereignty may even have *increased* in an era of globalization as the result of the increasing adoption of the practices of a global managerialism.

The Cultural Circuit of Capitalism

> These bold new ideas vault business people *beyond* re-engineering, *beyond* total quality management, *beyond* empowerment, and even *beyond* change and toward nothing less than reinvention and revolution. Publisher's blurb for the Tom Peters Seminar: *Crazy Times Call for Crazy Organisations* (1994).

Capitalism has had an intelligence capacity for some considerable period of time. For example,

> The first business school was set up at the University of Pennsylvania in 1881. The University of Chicago and the University of California both established undergraduate schools of commerce in 1899. New York University's Stein School of Business, Dartmouth's Amos Tuck School of Business Administration and Harvard's Graduate School of Business Administration followed in the next decade. The *Management Review* was founded in 1918, the American Management Association in 1925. By the end of the Great War, Arthur D Little, originally an engineering firm, included management advice among its services. James McKinsey set up his consulting firm in 1925. (Micklethwait and Wooldridge 1996: 74)

But, to begin with, this intelligence capacity was primarily based in the United States and founded on notions of efficient, 'scientific' management. In other words, capitalist managerialism was based on producing disciplined workers who produced measurable outputs. But, beginning in the 1950s and '60s a new 'softer' approach based upon the 'human relations' movement started to gain ground. In this guise Foucault's pastoral practices were able to make their way into business and, since this was at a comparatively late date in the history of these practices, they are heavily laced with the influence of the 'psy' disciplines. As Kleiner (1996: 21) shows, in a remarkable history of modern business management:

> what are now standard organisational practices have their roots in a curious mixture of psychology and what we would now call New Age: Kurt Lewin's National Training Laboratories based on T-groups and Douglas McGregor's Theory Y, Eric Trist's experiments with industrial democracy, Elliot Jacques and the Tavistock Institutes psychological experiments, Charles Krone's career at Procter and Gamble and then in California; the work of the philosopher mystic C. I. Gurdjieff who so influenced Krone, the counter-cultural goings on at the Esalen Institute, even the experimentation with LSD to enhance managerial thought.

The result has been an increase in the number and range of discourses of managerialism. Efficient, 'hard' management practices still exist. Indeed, if anything, the tyranny of numbers has probably become greater in modern business with the proliferation of audits, targets, indicators and the like. But, at the same time, the application of pastoral, and especially 'psy' practices, has produced a new softer management discourse. If one had to caricature this new softer managerialist discourse, then it could be described as the result of the application of five principles.

First, the business organization's 'environment' is figured as multiple, complex and fast-moving, and therefore as 'ambiguous', 'fuzzy' or 'plastic'. Of late, most of the inspiration for such a description has come from non-linear systems theory, and especially from the work of authors like Casti, Prigogine, and the like (see *Journal of Management Inquiry* 1994). Second, the business organization is seen as attempting to form an island of superior adaptability in this fast-moving environment. This it achieves in a number of ways, which, taken together, constitute the international business community's 'linguistic turn'. Most particularly, it attempts to generate suitable *metaphors* which allow it to see itself and others in a distinctive (but always partial) fashion (Morgan 1986: 1993). It tries, as well, to *embody* these metaphors in its work-force, a goal which it achieves via a number of means, including experiential learning, learning which involves placing the work force in situations which demand co-operative responses to the uncertain and unknown (Martin 1994). The organization also pays close attention to the resources of *tacit* (familiar but unarticulated) *knowledge* embodied in its work-force and to the generation of trust, both within its work-force and with other organizations. Work on tacit knowledge has been almost entirely generated from the writings of Michael Polanyi (Botwinick 1986) (rather than, for example, Heidegger, Merleau-Ponty or Bourdieu) who, in turn, drew on the ideas of gestalt psychology. Polanyi's (1967: 20) most famous saying 'we can know more than we can tell' has become a vital part of contemporary business discourse, as a way into the problem of mobilizing the full resources of a work-force. In turn, Polanyi's work has underlined the need to generate *trust* or (as Polanyi often called it) confidence, since 'the overwhelming proportion of our factual beliefs continue...to be held at second hand through trusting others' (Polanyi 1958: 208). Third, the business organization must therefore be framed as a flexible entity, always *in action*, 'on the move, if only stumbling or blundering along' (Boden 1994: 192), but stumbling or blundering along in ways which will allow it to survive and prosper, most particularly through mobilizing a culture which will produce traditions of learning (collective memories which will act both to keep the organization constantly alert and as a reservoir of innovation (Lundvall 1992)) and extensive intra- and inter-firm social networks (which will act both as conduits of knowledge and as a means of generating trust). Fourth, the business organization is seen, as has already been made clear, as a cultural entity, which is attempting to generate new traditions, new representations of itself and the world, and increasingly, an ethical stance towards the world because the link between knowledge (as a political economy of information refigured as a culture) and power has been made crystal-clear (Pfeffer and Salancik 1978; Pfeffer 1992). In other words, the business organization is increasingly built on 'a refusal to accept established knowledge' (Kestelhohn 1996: 7).

Fifth, the business organization must be made up of willing and willed subjects. Thus Foucault's pastoral mode of discipline makes its way into the business organization as a set of new definitions of what it is to be a person:

> Breathing strange new life into the old artistic ideal of the 'organic' – of 'the cultivated moral personality' and 'life as a work of art'... – characterises work not as a painful obligation impressed upon individuals, nor as an activity only undertaken by people for instrumental purposes, but as a vital means to self-fulfilment and self-realisation.

As Kanter comments, life in the entrepreneurial corporation has 'a romantic quality'.

> By reorganising work as simply part of that continuum along which 'we' all seek to realise ourselves as particular sets of person-outcomes, self-regulatory, self-fulfilling individual actors – 'enterprise' seeks to 're-enchant' organised work by restoring to it that which bureaucracy is held to have crossly repressed: emotion, personal responsibility, the possibility of pleasure, etc. (du Gay 1996: 25)

As important, in some ways, as this new softer managerialist discourse has been the growth of the agents responsible for its spread across the globe. Together, they form an emergent and increasingly powerful 'cultural circuit of capital' a system of expertise which has only existed in a self-steering form since the 1960s. This circuit is responsible for the production and distribution of managerial knowledge to managers. As it has grown, so have its appetites. It now has a constant and voracious need for new knowledge. Chief amongst the circuit's progress of knowledge are three institutions: business schools, management consultants and management gurus.

Through the 1960s, '70s and '80s formal business education, and especially the MBA course, has produced a large number of academics and students who act both to generate and transmit the new knowledge (Alvarez 1996). In the United States, admittedly the most extreme example, almost one in four students in colleges and universities now majors in business while the number of business schools has grown fivefold since 1957 (Kogut and Bowman 1996: 14) with the result that more than 75 000 students are awarded an MBA every year in the US, fifteen times the total in the 1960s (Micklethwait and Wooldridge 1996). In the top business schools, academics compete with one another to teach students *and* to produce new ideas. Some of these leading schools are now run as *de facto* companies. For example, at Wharton, the Dean, Thomas Gerrity, has tried to put business process re-engineering into operation:

> In companies re-engineering makes a big fuss of tearing down what it calls functional chimneys and reallocating staff to teams. Mr Gerrity has divided both his students and his professors into teams of six: each student team includes at least two non-Americans; each faculty team includes professors from different academic disciplines. Both are evaluated in teams. Mr Gerrity has also torn down

the barriers that divide the school from the University and from the business world. Students now offer consultancy to other parts of the University (on how to bring medical technology to market (for example) and to local businesses. They also study fluffy things like leadership, to the chagrin of many academics but the delight of businesses.

As with other re-engineering exercises, a number of things introduced in its name look like common sense dressed up in fancy language (students are now sent abroad for 'global immersion'). Mr Gerrity has changed the system for granting tenure and awarding annual pay rises in order to shift the emphasis from publishing academic articles (once the only road to success) to teaching and 'leadership'. He has hired a policy firm, Opinion Research, to survey opinion among his constituencies. He has introduced a system of monitoring, so that senior professors can show their juniors how to teach, and quality circles, so that students can tell their teachers what they think of them. (*The Economist*, 13 April 1996: 83)

Another generator and distributor of new knowledge has been management consultancy (Clark 1995). Management consultancy is, without doubt, a growth industry:

Between 1970 and 1980, the revenue of management consultants registered with the Management Consultants Association doubled; from 1980 to 1987 it increased fivefold. In the UK, over the eleven years 1980–1991 the number of consultants registered with the MCA more than quadrupled to 6 963 and their fees increased almost seventeenfold. By the early 1990s there were reported to be 100 000 consultants world-wide. Growth figures in recent years for major players in the global consultancy game confirm the continuing acceleration in business from the late 1980s. Thus the largest company, Andersen Consulting, has been posting 9 per cent growth regularly (and as high as 19 per cent in the recession year of 1992). The second largest player doubled revenue to $1.2 billion between 1987 and 1993. Coopers and Lybrand, third largest (but second in Europe), saw revenue grow 107 per cent over the five years to 1993, and by then had 66 000 staff in 125 countries. (Ramsay 1996: 166)

Using VAT data Keeble et al. (1994) estimated that in 1990 the UK management consultancy industry comprised 11 777 firms with a combined turnover of a little over £2.5 billion. Management consultancies act as a vital part of the cultural circuit of capital. To begin with they provide ideas. For example, Arthur Andersen:

> has three research centres and a massive international database, to which all 40000 consultants are supposed to contribute. The company spent nearly 7% of its budget, or $290 million, on training in 1995, more than any rival. To have a chance of becoming a partner, an Andersenite needs to have put in over 1 000 hours of training – some of it at the company's 150-acre campus outside Chicago. (*The Economist*, 4 May 1996: 90)

Then, they are responsible for much of the packaging of management knowledge, usually producing formulas which can be applied over and over again in different situations. Using Latour's by now familiar vocabulary:

> Each assignment provides consultants with an opportunity to project their special and distinctive competencies to clients by 'bringing home' distant events, places and people. This is achieved by (a) rendering them *mobile* so that they can be brought back; (b), keeping them *stable* so that they can be moved back and forth without additional distortion; and (c) making them *combinable* so that they can be circulated, amalgamated and manipulated. Legge (1994: 3) writes that this is precisely what management consultants do when they make the experience of (distant) firms accessible and combinable through the development of (in Latour's terms) equations or packages – such as McKinsey's decentralisation package, Hay MSL's job evaluation package or even Peters' eight rules of excellence. (Clark 1995: 56)

In turn, to make these packages credible to existing and potential clients requires considerable international work, involving a diverse range of social skills (Clark 1995). And this work is clearly successful. For example, Ramsay (1996) reports that, in an eighteen-month period stretching over 1994 and 1995, 94 of the top 100 British companies had used management consultants.

Then, there is one other major generator and distributor of new knowledge, the management guru (Huczynski 1993; Micklethwait and Wooldridge 1996). Gurus come in many shapes and sizes. Huczyuski (1993) distinguishes between academic gurus like Michael Porter, Rosabeth Moss Kanter, Theodore Levitt, John Kay, Gareth Morgan and Peter

Senge, consultant gurus like James Champy, Peter Drucker, Tom Peters, John Naisbitt, and Kenichi Ohmae, and hero-managers like Mark McCormack, Akio Morita, John Harvey-Jones, Donald Trump and Lee Iacocca. Then, there are other gurus who are less easy to classify, for example Benjamin Zander, conductor of the Boston Philharmonic, who provides inspirational lectures on music as a metaphor for management (Griffith 1996).

These gurus often only run small operations. But, equally, their operations may be substantial. Most impressive of all, perhaps, is the 'leadership centre' run by Stephen Covey in Provo, Utah:

> Having started ten years ago with a staff of two, the Covey leadership centre now employs 700 people and has annual revenues of over $70 million. Mr Covey is building a large campus to house it on the edge of Provo, his home town. But even in its current state, scattered about the town, the centre is a sleek business machine. Its staff are surrounded by enough technology to make a journalist salivate. They have an army of unpaid helpers, thanks to Mr Covey's insistence that the best way to learn his ideas is to teach them.
>
> The centre is divided into three core businesses. The first is management training. Throughout the year high-fliers flock to Provo to spend a week reading "wisdom literature", climbing mountains, discussing personal and business problems and forming into teams. The second is producing personal organisers. These are meant to help people set priorities – so much time for jogging, so much time for your mother-in-law – as well as organise appointments. The third is spinning out new ideas. The centre has a second best seller, "Principle Centred Leadership"; and a third in preparation, the "Seven Habits of Highly Effective Families". (*The Economist*, 24 February 1996: 106)

There is no strong dividing line between business schools, management consultancies and management gurus. For example, Thomas Gerrity, the Dean of Wharton, was formerly a member of CSC Index, the consultancy which produced the idea of 'business process re-engineering' and which is now retailing notions of 'organizational agility'.

Whatever is the case, it is clear that it is these three institutions that are responsible for producing the bulk of management knowledge. That knowledge chiefly comes in the form of a succession of 'business fads' (Lorenz 1989), of which there have now been a remarkable number. Between 1950 and 1988, for example, Pascale (1991) noted 26 major fads.

Certainly the roll call includes quality circles, the paperless office, the factory of the future, entrepreneurship, brands, strategic alliances, globalization, business process re-engineering (including 'core competencies'), employability and more recently, nascent fads and fashions like organizational agility, the accelerating organization (Maira and Scott-Morgan 1996), complexity theory, and even actor-network theory (Latour 1995).

In turn, these ideas have to be distributed. The channels and means of distribution are multiple. First of all, of course, there are the business schools, which teach students the new ideas, the management consultants, constantly presenting clients with new ideas and ways of doing things and the management gurus, taking fees and retainers, to distribute their insights. Then, second, there is a rapidly growing business media industry which packages and distributes this knowledge. Management knowledge sells, most particularly since the establishment of the non-academic management book in the early 1980s. For example, Stephen Covey's 'Seven Habits of Highly Effective People' has sold more than five million copies world wide since its publication in 1989 (*The Economist* 24th February, 1996: 106) and is currently available in 28 languages in 35 countries (it is doing particularly well in China and South Korea). Hammer and Champy's 'Re-engineering the Corporation', published in 1993, had sold two million copies world-wide by September 1996, and had been translated into 17 languages. Of course, management knowledge is not just diffused via books (and, increasingly tapes and videos). Journals like *Fortune, Business Week*, the *Harvard Business Review* and others also dispense such knowledge, as do myriad trade journals. Most broadsheet newspapers also have management knowledge pages (for example, the *Financial Times*, which can claim to be a global business newspaper, started a 'Management Brief' page in 1994 and also produced a major 26-part series on the current state of management knowledge in 1996) (see Crainer 1995). There are also now a number of specific television programmes which communicate management knowledge.

Finally, there is one more means of dissemination which is particularly important in the case of management knowledge. This is the management seminar, which is a mixture of drill and, increasingly, religious revivalism. Such seminars are big business across the world. For example, in 1990 Borks and Swet estimated that corporations in the United States spent $30 billion on business training in general. There are many kinds of seminar, of course. There are, to begin with, the modest seminars which import skills, usually offered by training companies or management consultants.

Their advertising literature about short seminars and courses emphasizes personal and interpersonal techniques. Such offerings include
seminars such as 'Time Management International', 'Liberating
Leadership Team', Leadership Development's, 'Close that Sale', Kar-
rass' 'Effective Negotiating' (named after the management guru Dr
Chester Karass) and the one- day seminars from Career Track with
talks such as 'Management skills for Technical Professionals' and
'How to Set and Achieve Your Goals'. Attendance at these seminars is
substantial if the firm's publicity literature is to be believed. The
'Close that Sale!' seminar claims 59 000 participants from 70 companies. Time Management International claims that 28 000 people
participated in its world-wide series of seminars during 1986. Finally,
Effective Negotiating claims a world-wide participation rate of
150000. Such courses are usually of one day's duration. They are
offered at a low fee and attract a high attendance, often over one
hundred people. They feature a 'high energy' presenter and offer
their audiences 'tested techniques' and 'proven skills'... (Huczynski
1993: 186)

But there are also high-profile series of seminars featuring management
gurus, often stretching over two or three days which communicate
knowledge which is not easily standardised.

Byrne (1986) reported on a type of executive seminar called a 'skunk
camp'. The similarity between his description of it and a religious
retreat is instructive. The 'holy man' leading this event was Tom Peters,
the co-author of one of the world's best selling business books. The cost
to each participant's company was $4000 and at this particular event
the day began with a group jogging session. Following a communal
breakfast, the members gathered in the conference room 'waiting for
enlightenment'. Byrne reported:

In walks our rumpled leader. Head down, hands in the pockets of his
brown shapeless cords, he paces relentlessly. His voice climbs to the
treble clef as he runs through the litany. 'Dehumiliate ... Get rid of
your executive parking spots ... Get everybody on the same
team ... There are two ways to get rich: superior customer satisfaction and constant innovation.'

Byrne's description has similarities with one reported by Oliver (1990)
of a Just-in-Time seminar run by Eli Goldratt (co-author of the book
The Goal):

Goldratt appeared practically at 9.15am, and in contrast to all the delegates who were wearing suits, he wore neither a jacket nor a tie and was wearing a skull-cap and open-toed sandals. He began by saying he had no prepared slides or any notes. The expression 'the cost world' was used to denote the old order and the 'through put world' to denote the new one. Towards the end of the session, Goldratt threw out the question, 'where shall we begin the improvement?'. The audience responded with a chorus of cries of 'Us', 'Ourselves' and other similar expressions.

Often, seminars will include books or videos in the price, so that a seamless web of production and reinforcement of ideas is produced.

Increasingly, seminars are being produced on an extraordinary scale. For example, in September 1996 Stephen Covey, Tom Peters and Peter Senge combined forces in an interactive 'supergroup' presentation on 'How to make your team unstoppable', broadcast by satellite to 30 000 people in 250 cities in 40 countries around the world (in Britain the venue was Birmingham at a cost of £199 per person).

Then, finally, there are management 'audiences'. It is fair to say that we know remarkably little about this aspect of the capitalist circuit of cultural capital: there are only very small amounts of audience research (but see Engwall 1992). Instead, we have to infer the character and motivations of audiences from general trends, and the few studies there are. Thus, first, we know that managers are becoming better educated almost everywhere. For example, 'as more managers complete MBA-type programmes, they become more sophisticated, and are able to under- stand and apply more complicated management ideas' (Huczynski 1993: 48). Second, it is clear that managers do read more books (and listen to tapes and watch videos) than previously. Third, at the same time, through the increased 'packaging' of ideas in seminars and books, management ideas have become more accessible. Fourth, managers clearly want and need new ideas. They need them to make their way in organizations, to solve particular company problems, to act as an internal motivational device, to guard against their competitors' adoption of new ideas, and simply to provide a career enhancer. In the latter case, the new idea demonstrates to others that the manager is creative, up to the minute and actively seeing improvements, thereby increasing that individual's visibility in the organization. Equally, the new idea can act as a defence, can provide a quick-fix solution in a difficult period, or can even simply reduce boredom (Huczynski 1993). Fifth, the management book or seminar can act to raise or boost levels of belief. Thus, attendees at seminars by management gurus may have already read all the ideas in books but this is not the point:

> Managers may attend Tom Peters' seminars to become immersed in his personality. In fact, if he was not to say what they have already read, they would come away disappointed. Lorenz (1986) wrote that "managers may still pay repeated visits in their thousand to sit at [the guru's] feet, or buy his latest book. One executive at a leading multinational talks of needing his 'Drucker fix' every two years".
> (Huczynski 1993: 201)

Again, seminars may retail experiences of such intensity that they change the terms of what it means to be a person, as can happen in experiential seminars. For example, Martin (1994) documents how the initial cynicism of some participants in these kinds of seminar is gradually overtaken by the experience of the seminar. Sixth, and finally, more managers are now women. Some commentators have argued that much of the change in the metaphorical framing of modern capitalism is a result of the feminization of management knowledge which, at least in part, results from the greater presence of women in management and the work-force around the world (Clegg et al., 1996).

To summarize, what seems clear is that managers themselves seek out four main qualities from management knowledge (Huczynski 1993). The first of these is predictability:

> Managers want to find ideas that make a constantly changing environment less confusing and threatening; for however brief a period. In order that they do not appear as part of the problem of constant change, management ideas are packaged so that they can be perceived as something already known but able to be reprioritised. The most popular management ideas seem to be those which successfully integrate a number of ideas into a single bite-size whole. The second quality is *empowerment*. Managers want to be told which ideas will achieve what results and which techniques are to be associated with the actions; managers want 'permission' from accredited sources to act. Third, managers want *esteem*. One way of achieving this is to be seen as the champion of a management idea or ideas.
>
> In a number of companies, the promotion of the latest management fad by managers has been used to help them gain company-wide visibility in the promotion stakes. Management idea championing

can represent a low-risk way of signalling to those with the power to promote that managers are not averse to change, do not mind challenging established views, but that while they are prepared to look critically at the system in which they work, they will not unduly 'rock the organisational boat'.

Further esteem can be gained if the idea is not of the black-box variety, that is it offers (and is seen to offer) the championing managers the scope to make their own contribution to it. Thus it then gives them greater ownership of the idea in the perception of others. It might be thought that this is a high-risk strategy, since the idea may fail to yield the expected benefits. [But] . . . assessments of success and failure tend to be very vague in this area, and all parties concerned have a vested interest in not admitting to failure. (Huczynski 1993: 212–13)

Then, finally, managers want self-belief. In constructing this quality, they are helped by a long history of thinking about the self in management, much of it based on the 'psy' disciplines. For example, Kurt Lewin (1951) invented the so-called T-group, an early form of the encounter group which encouraged colleagues to expose their true feelings about each other, while Maslow's (1954) 'enpsychian' management, McGregor's (1960) 'Theory Y' and Herschberg's (1965) all emphasised 'the need as a human to grow spiritually' (Herzberg 1965: 71). In other words, managers, like many other contemporary individuals, have, for some time, been enjoined:

to live as if running a *project* of themselves: they are to *work* on their emotional world, their domestic and conjugal arrangements, their relations of employment and the techniques of sexual pleasure, to develop a style of being that will maximise the worth of their existence to themselves. Evidence from the United States, Europe and the United Kingdom suggests that the implantation of such 'identity projects', characteristic of advanced democracies, is constitutively linked to the rise of a breed of new spiritual directors, 'engineers of the human soul'. Although our subjectivity might appear our most intimate sphere of experience, its contemporary intensification as a political and ethical value, is intrinsically correlated with the growth of expert languages, which enable us to render our relations with our selves and others into words and into thought, and with expert techniques, which promise to allow us to transform ourselves in the direction of happiness and fulfilment. (Rose 1996: 157)

This emphasis on self belief as a function of personal growth is perhaps best exemplified by the growth of New Age training which attempts to import New Age ideas via techniques like dancing, medicine wheels, and the use of the I Ching in order to engineer the subject (Heelas 1991a, 1991b, 1992, 1996; Huczynski 1993; Rifkin 1996; Roberts 1994; Rupert 1992).

What, then, is the task of the reinvented manager in this newly figured world? The new managerialism depends on the notion that the world is uncertain, complex, paradoxical, even chaotic. The manager must somehow find the means to steer a course in this fundamentally uncertain world, which she or he does by six main means (for a comprehensive review, see Ghoschal and Bartlett, 1995). First of all, there is an emphasis on the competitive advantage, in a business world that is increasingly constituted by information, that is incurred by knowledge. Whereas managers:

> used to think that the most precious resource was capital, and that the prime task of management was to allocate it in the most productive way, now they have become convinced that their most precious resource is knowledge and that the prime task of management is to ensure that their knowledge is generated as widely and used as efficiently as possible. (Wooldridge 1995: 4)

In Drucker's (1982: 16) famous words, 'Knowledge has become the key economic resource and the dominant, if not the only source of comparative advantage'. Second, the task of the manager is increasingly seen as the harnessing of extant organizational knowledge and the generation of new organizational knowledge, most especially by tapping the existing tacit skills and talents of the work-force, and then enhancing these competencies and by stimulating critical thinking skills which can overcome established prejudices; informally by providing greater communication between workers within the organization so that beneficial practices spread, and formally by instituting means of gaining further qualifications and the institution of strategic conversation (Badaracco 1991; Leonard-Barton 1995; Roos and van Krogh 1996). Third, the manager no longer aims to produce an overall corporate strategy which is then mechanistically instituted in and through a corporate bureaucracy. Rather, the aim is to produce an emergent 'evolutionary' or 'learning' strategy which is 'necessarily incremental and adaptive, but that does not in any way imply that its evolution cannot be, or should not be, analysed, managed, and controlled' (Kay

1993: 359). Such a strategy will be based on what are seen as the particular capabilities of a business organization which are then amplified via informal methods of control which rely on a much greater grasp of the issues involved, and which also mean that whole layers of bureaucracy, most of whose time was taken up with oversight, can be shrunk or, in the jargon, 'delayered' (Clarke and Newman 1993). Fourth, in order to achieve evolutionary strategies, and informal control, the manager has to become a kind of charismatic itinerant, a 'cultural diplomat' (Hofstede 1991), constantly imbuing the business organization's values and goals, constantly on a mission to explain and motivate an increasingly multinational and multicultural work-force in an increasingly global firm. Not surprisingly, such a task of producing affective effects is not easy. In earlier studies, Mintzberg (1973), Stewart (1976) and Davis and Luthans (1990) all found that managers spent between a half and three-quarters of their time simply talking to people. Stewart (1976: 92) for example, found that 'Management is a verbal world whose people are usually instructed by personal contact rather than on paper'. More recently, Bruns (1995) found that top managers in multinational corporations spent most of their time talking to people, either via electronic means, or direct face-to-face communication. And much of the rest of the time, they spent travelling, spending as much as three out of every four weeks on business trips as they personally tried to weave the culture of their organization together. In other words, the example of these studies shows that the chief business of business organizations is talk, talk and then more talk in order to achieve some measure of agreement (Boden 1994); 'conversations are the backbone of business' (Roos and van Krogh 1995: 3). Or to put it another way:

> Most of what managers do is discourse: it consists of discussion, ordering, synthesising, presenting, reporting – all activities that take place through the media of various texts and representations of immediate co-presence. Management mostly concerns words that do things, presented in many various arenas, sometimes personally, sometimes impersonally, sometimes in role, sometimes unscripted and unwarranted by the roles that exist already, the narratives already written. Management, above all, is a performative activity: it does what it says and it says what it does: its utterances and its actions are so frequently fused, so politically meshed. (Clegg and Palmer 1996: 2)

Fifth, the manager must not only weave the organization together but must also ensure that, through dedicated networking, she or he can produce and sustain external relationships of trust with other firms, which become vital conduits of information and future business. Through her or his interpersonal skills and cultural sensitivity, the manager not only builds an internal but also an external relational 'architecture' (Kay 1993). Thus, and sixth, management is no longer seen as a science. Rather, it becomes an art form dedicated to 'the proposition that a political economy of information is in fact coextensive with a theory of culture' (Boisot 1995: 7). In other words, the manager sets out to re-enchant the world (du Gay 1996).

What seems clear is that the discourses of the new managerialism being constantly produced and reproduced by the cultural circuit of capitalism have become the hegemonic account of what the business world is like and how best to exercise corporate power within it. This has been achieved this in three ways. First, it has changed the terms of debate. Thus:

> It has contributed to some changes in management practice (however unevenly) and forms of organisational transformation. It has also provided a new and distinctive language of management which has played a significant role in legitimating claims to both organisational and social leadership (Clarke and Newman 1993: 438).

Second, it has spread around the world in quick order. This kind of discourse is now common in many parts of the world outside the United States: it is a rapidly globalizing discourse. It is worth quoting Micklethwait and Wooldridge (1996: 55–7) at length;

> Not so long ago anyone who wanted to understand management went to an American University, studied American gurus, argued about American corporations and probably joined an American consultancy. The great debates in the subject – such as the one about the relative merits of scientific and humanistic management were almost all conducted between Americans. But in the past couple of decades the rest of the world has started to catch up.
>
> From Bradford to Barcelona and Berlin, the cities of Europe are now littered with business schools. A few – Insead just outside Paris, the London Business School (LBS) and Switzerland's Institute for Management Development – deserve a place in America's first division. Britons alone spent around £50m on MBA fees at 100 schools in 1994 – and around half that figure on business books. Continental countries, particularly the French, remain a little suspicious but most of the leading American gurus have broken through. *In Search of*

Excellence sold 100,000 copies in three years in France, and did even better in Germany, Holland, Spain and Sweden ...
And Europe is beginning to produce gurus of its own. There is as yet only one European guru who ranks in the first division by American standards: Britain's Charles Handy. However, a cluster of other names including John Kay and Sumantra Goschal (both at LBS) and Yves Doz (Insead) are knocking on the door. There are also several areas where European gurus look as if they are ahead of their American counterparts. One example is the cultural side of managing multinationals: any big firm in Europe becomes multinational very quickly. Geert Hofstede of the Netherlands Institute of International Culture more or less invented cultural diversity as a management subject, pointing out that attitudes towards pay and hierarchy can vary enormously from country to country. Another Dutchman, Fons Trompenaar, is one of the leading writers on corporate culture.

Indeed in many soft management areas, Europe has a stronger tradition than the more scientifically based Americans. Many gurus, for example, are now re-examining work done in human motivation at Britain's Tavistock Institute back in the 1950s by a team of psychologists led by Elliott Jacques. And at a time when the younger American gurus seem to spend half their lives studying ever more esoteric sub-disciplines, the Europeans' comparative lack of specialisation may be an advantage.

If managerial discourses were limited to the Euro-American sphere of influence only, we might argue them as a global phenomenon. But this is not the case. The discourses have also been making their way into many other parts of the world. In particular, near to Europe management discourses have been introduced to the former Soviet bloc. Most European business schools have Eastern European links or outlets, often funded by the EU. For example, the Stockholm School of Economics has an outlet in Riga which teaches economics and business to 100 students a year from Estonia, Latvia and Lithuania. Even in Moscow, business schools are now starting to appear.

But the most impressive impact of these discourses has probably been in Southeast and East Asia. Of course, for a considerable period of time, the region has exported young people to American business schools. Now Asia is producing business schools of its own.

In China, a country which is desperately short of trained managers, the China Europe International Business School plans to move from its present temporary home on the outskirts of Shanghai into a huge new campus in Pudong, the city's as yet unbuilt financial centre, in 1997; it will also double its annual intake to 120 students (a fair number until you consider that it already gets 4 000 applicants). Despite the fact that most of the big Asian businesses remain family-run the consultancies have already made impressive progress. McKinsey's India Office is the company's fastest growing agency. As the younger business-school-educated generation of Asians take over, the consultancies can expect a bonanza.

Step on to any of Hong Kong's crowded trains and you will find a young Chinese puzzling over the latest offering from Tom Peters or John Naisbitt. In a monumental pan-Asian survey of business people in 1995 roughly half of the respondents had brought a book by a western management writer in the previous two years (although it was noticeable that nearly the same proportion admitted that they had not finished reading it). For many western gurus [at $25 000 a seminar] Asian speaking terms offer much the same enticements that the musical variety do for elderly rock stars. (Micklethwait and Wooldridge 1996: 57)

Third, and perhaps most importantly of all, the new managerialist discourses have empowered their managerial subjects by presenting them with an expanded opportunity to dream 'global dreams' (Barnet and Cavanagh 1995). New forms of managerial subject are being produced through the application of an odd mixture of the 'psy disciplines' (Rose 1996), New Age, and the like. Most particularly, these subjects are being taught to internalize the world as theirs in which to operate with self-esteem and self-confidence (French and Grey 1996) and exercise 'global leadership'. As Strathern (1995a: 179–80, my emphases) puts it, appropriating actor-network theory:

How large, Latour asks, is IBM? An actor of great size, mobilising hundreds of thousands of people, it is always encountered via a small handful . . . We never in this sense leave the local. The local is not just the people you talk to at IBM or BP but the desks, the paperwork, the connections distributed through the system, that is, the instruments that create a global field. From this point of view it makes no sense to go along with the literalism, that 'global' is bigger than 'local'. It is simply where one is at. But if one never leaves the local where is the global? It has to be the infinitely recurring *possibility* of measurement – not the scales but *the capacity to imagine them*.

As part of their ability to act, pressed into operation as design or intention, people's sense of scale produces a reflexive sense of context or locale. That is, it is a capacity which prompts comparisons, whether of commensurate things (along one scale) or of things not reducible to a common scale at all. Either way, we can imagine that it enlarges the world ('deepens it'). If so, we may take such scaling as a technique for knowing oneself to be effective (have relational effects: Law 1994: 102–3) regardless of agency . . . Anthropologists will never understand the power of those who think the world is their market . . . unless they appreciate *the energising effect of such expanded horizons*. The expanded horizon, like the world view, is *how things are made effective locally*.

Back to the state

The new authority will be: member led, officer driven, customer focused: a team environment where the whole is greater than the sum of its parts; a flat management structure where employees and managers are fully empowered and decisions are devalued close to the customer: a culture of learning rather than blame; a clear sense of direction and purpose. A firm commitment to delivering high quality services through a combination of direct provision and effective partnerships. (Recruitment advertisement, Bath and North East Somerset Council. Cited in 'Birtspeak', *Private Eye*, 22 September 1995)

One way in which the advent of these few managerial discourses might be interpreted could be as a part of a more general diminution of state power. These discourses are one of the more visible signs of the triumph of a global capitalism increasingly influenced by the state. But this is, I think, too simplistic a view.

In at least three important ways, the new managerialist discourses are not independent of the state. Indeed, in certain ways the discourses may actually *strengthen* the state's (or, more accurately, some core states') capacities to act.

The first of these ways is cultural. The new managerial discourses are still overwhelmingly American in character. They inscribe American values and they are a part of an American cultural hegemony in this field. Remarkable work by Engwall (1992) and Furusten and Kinch (1992) on the case of Sweden has shown the way in which management training, books, and seminars are all being influenced by thinking from the United States. Swedish managerial thinking is a 'shadow of America'. This situation is replicated in many other countries, giving firms from the United States a signal advantage, and producing variants on American managerial practices in firms of many different nationalities around the world. Of course, each local situation has its own cultural specificities but what we can see, as a class of 'global cosmopolitans' comes into existence, who speak a common managerial discourse (or what Engwall (1992) calls the 'New Latin'), is that new systems of practical rationality, based on an American notion of conduct, are taking hold. Increasingly the world is figured as the American way.

The second of these ways is procedural. Though the state can no longer claim to have sovereignty over knowledge, as multiple means of producing intelligence about the world have come into existence, the key fact that more such sources of intelligence exist is not just a constraint but also an opportunity, since these new sources of intelligence provide both a new set of possible domains to be governed *and* a new set of methods for problematizing what is there to be governed.

And this procedural point relates strongly to the third way in which managerial discourses must be reckoned as complementary to the State, as well as competing with it. Managerial discourses have increasingly reached over into the conduct of the nation state, bringing widespread changes in governmentality.[1] A number of examples of this extension can be cited. In the United States, much of the Democrat and Republican political agenda is now couched in managerialist terms. In Britain, similarly, these discourses have taken hold. Indeed New Labour might be caricatured as a managerialist government. Even in nation states where management theory might be expected to have less hold it is making fast progress.

> In America, on becoming Speaker of the House of Representatives, following the Republicans' triumph in the November 1994 elections, Newt Gingrich supplied his troops with a reading list. As well as the usual suspects the list included, Peter Drucker of Alvin and Heidi Toffler. Not to be outdone, President Clinton spent his holiday holed up in Camp David with two management gurus, Anthony Robbins and Stephen Covey. Al Gore can barely open his mouth without talking about reinventing some part of government. This enthusiasm has been copied around the world, from Sweden to Singapore, and embraced by socialists as well as conservatives. In October 1995, Tony Blair, the leader of Britain's Labour Party, sent his entire shadow cabinet to Templeton College, Oxford, to spend a weekend learning about management theory.

Indeed, it is hard to walk down any corridor of power nowadays without hearing a new and hideous language – 'managing by objectives', 'outsourcing non-care functions', 'negotiating performance measures', and the rest of it. Even generals and admirals are 'downsizing human resources' and 'benchmarking their competitors'. 'Of course benchmarking is only a rough guide' admits one Pentagon bureaucrat. 'The ultimate benchmarking exercise' is war. Given that several thousand Red Army officers have already attended a management course at Minsk, the gurus will have the comfort of knowing that, should the world's two foremost military powers go to war, they will be doing so in their language. (Micklethwait and Wooldridge 1996: 315)

Why have these discourses managed to get a grips on the apparatuses of so many states, infusing their tactics with new practices? There are a number of reasons. The first is that many public servants are now more likely to have been taught business through MBAs and the like: 'increasingly, institutions around the world are being run by people who have been trained in business schools' (Micklethwait and Wooldridge 1996: 315). Second, management theory can give bureaucrats, like managers in business, a competitive advantage by providing a career boost, providing new rationale for action, and so on. Third, management consultancies have been able to move into the public sector via management theory, thus fuelling the process.

In mid 1995 John Major's government admitted in a series of Parliamentary questions that it had spent at least £320m on management consultants – almost certainly a fraction of the real figure. British consultancies are doing so well out of the public sector that they have started hiring former councillors to give them advice: Margaret Hodge, once a head of the notoriously badly managed Islington Council, became a consultant to Price Waterhouse before returning to politics as a Labour MP. In America the public sector has proved such a lucrative client that most big consultancies now have several departments devoted to its needs: one firm, CSC Index, even has a special centre that concentrates on federal customers... (Micklethwait and Wooldridge 1996: 318)

Fourth, management gurus like Michael Porter and Rosabeth Moss Kanter have become interested in the public sector and have started to produce suitable texts. The most successful of the manageralist texts is probably Osborne and Gaebler's *Reinventing Government* which reached the top of the US best seller lists in 1992 (originally it was to be called *In Search of Excellence in Government* in homage to Peters and Waterman). Fifth, there is a purely ideological element: the private sector is regarded as better in some way. Politicians have themselves been able to define a political platform by articulating certain elements of managerialist discourses.

The exact reasons why managerialist discourses have been introduced vary from state to state. In Britain, Australia, New Zealand, Canada and now Scandinavia, the first injections of the discourse tended to be driven from the top. For example, in Britain, Margaret Thatcher set up a succession of powerful bodies, some of them staffed by business people and consultants, to improve public efficiency. In the United States, in contrast, management theory was introduced by lower-level bureaucrats like Bob Stone, deputy assistant secretary for the Department of Defence, who later became something of a management guru himself. Total quality management became something of religion amongst local government officials and was subsequently taken up by Bill Clinton, then governor Arkansas. But:

> Regardless of who first sponsored them, management ideas are now an institutionalised part of government. The Clinton administration has awarded a public-sector equivalent of the Baldridge award for quality. British civil servants can win awards called Charter Marks for things such as successful staff suggestions. Britain has also established the public sector MBA to ensure that civil servants are in tune with the latest in management thinking. There are even special internet sites to which bureaucrats of all nations can log on to discuss subjects such as 'TQM for public servants'. (Micklethwait and Wooldridge 1996: 317)

Of course, one might argue that all the public sector has so far done is to borrow ideas from the private sector (except, perhaps, for the idea of internal markets), and often inappropriately. (Indeed, perhaps the most effective critique has been made by a management guru, Henry Mintzberg (1995)). But, even if this is true, the effects have been clear enough. Efficient management ideas have lead to what has often been massive 'downsizing' or 'delayering'. And, increasingly, softer management techniques based on pastoral modes of regulation are becoming the norm. In the United States, for example:

> Some American government officials carry round small gold business cards which 'empower' them to make decisions without first

going to their supervisors. Some departments are even giving out 'forgiveness coupons', which pre-forgive people their mistakes, in order to encourage them to adopt a less rule-bound approach to government . . .

Thus affection for mixing hard and soft management theory reaches right into the White House. When he is not thinking up ideas for slimming government, Al Gore is coming up with visions or handing out 'heroes of reinvention' awards. No sooner had Bill Clinton been elected President than he organised a bonding weekend, designed to encourage more effective team building, at which two 'facilitators' tried to get everybody to confess to some hidden secret. (Micklethwait and Wooldridge 1996: 326)

What does seem to have occurred is that the injection of global managerialist discourses have given rise to the 'managerial state' (Clarke and Newman 1993). One way to interpret this new form is as weaker than its predecessors, in thrall to business and to business ideas and agendas (the two having become increasingly inseparable). But I am not so sure. Of course, the state (conceived as a multiplicity of regimes of government) has, in certain senses, been 'hollowed out', with some of its rationalities, functions and work-force disappearing. But equally, one might argue that the state has found and been able to draw upon a new set of tactics of government, a new set of political rationalities, which are *more* productive because they enjoin those in the employ of the state and all those touched by the state to break the 'ring of fear' by remaking themselves as subjects who can attain peak performance by achieving a personal 'escape velocity'. The result is that 'the state' may be as or more powerful than before: howsoever defined. This seems to me to be at least a credible alternative hypothesis, especially when one considers the potential (if that is the right word) that might be (and to some extent is being) unleashed by the application of management ideas in totalitarian states like China.

What we might be seeing, then, is the genesis of a leaner, meaner state apparatus, one which though it may be shrinking in size, might, through various new devices and knowing (and constituting) the world – from new regulatory frameworks, though greater subconstracting of state functions, to new more flexible management practices which incorporate postoral modes of subjectification – be able to retain or even increase its power. In other words, a new political rationality may be unfolding in many parts of the world which is based on more positive forms of power.

Acknowledgements

Parts of this chapter are based on Thrift (1997) 'The rise of soft capitalism' *Cultural Values*, 1, and are reproduced by permission of Blackwell Publishers. I would like to thank Colin Hay for his comments on the paper.

Note

1. A number of studies in the United States and Britain have shown the subtle ways in which managerial discourses are inscribed on the state, being changed in the process. The account below is too simplistic in this regard.

Bibliography

Alexander, C. (1995) *Fin-de-Siècle Social Theory: Reduction and the Problem of Reason*, London: Verso

Allen, J. and P. du Gay (1993) 'Industry and the Rest: The Economic Identity of Services,' *Work, Employment and Society*, 3, 18–28.

Allen, T. J. and M. S. S. Morton (1994) *Information Technology and the Corporation of the 1990s*, New York: Oxford University Press.

Alvarez, J. L. (1996) 'The International Popularisation of Entreprenerial Ideas' in Clegg, S. and G. Palmer (eds) *The Politics of Management Knowledge*, London: Sage.

Amin, A. and N. J. Thrift (1995) 'Institutional Issues for the European Regions: From Markets and Plans to Socioeconomics and Powers of Association', *Economy and Society*, 24, 41–66.

Badaracco, J. L. (1991) *The Knowledge Link*, Cambridge, Mass: Harvard Business School Press.

Badaracco, J. and A. Webb (1995) 'Business Ethics: The View from the Trenches', *California Management Review*, 37 (2), 27–36.

Barnet, R. J. and J. Cavanagh (1995) *Global Dreams: Imperial Corporations and the New Order*, New York: Simon and Schuster.

Bauman, Z. (1987) *Legislators and Interpreters*, Cambridge: Polity Press.

Bauman, Z. (1995) 'Searching for a Centre That Holds' in Featherstone, M., S. Lash, and R. Robertson (eds) *Global Modernities*, London: Sage, 140–54.

Beck, U. (1992) *Risk Society: Towards a New Modernity*, London: Sage.

Bhabha, H. (1995) *The Location of Culture*, London: Routledge.

Boden, D. (1994) *The Business of Talk*, Cambridge: Polity Press.

Boisot, M. H. (1995) *Information Space: A Framework of Learning in Organisations, Institutions and Culture*, London: Routledge.

Boje, D. M. and R. P. Gephardt (eds) (1996) *Postmodern Management and Organization Theory*, Thousand Oaks, CA: Sage.

Botwinick, A. (1986) *Participation and Tacit Knowledge in Plato, Machiavelli and Hobbes*, Lanham, MD: University Press of America.

Bowker, G. (1994) 'Information Methodology: The World of/as Information', in Bud-Frierman (1994, 231–47).

Bowker, G. and S. Leigh-Star (1994) 'Knowledge and Infrastructure in International Information Management: Problems of Classification and Coding', in Bud-Frierman (1994, 187–216).

Bruns, S. (1997) *Managers' Lives*, Cambridge, Mass.: Harvard Business School Press.

Bruns, W. (1995) Cambridge, Mass.: Harvard Business School Press.

Bud-Frierman, L. (ed.) (1994) *Information Acumen: The Understanding and Use of Knowledge in Modern Business*, London: Routledge.

Bull, M. (ed.) (1995) *Apocalypse Theory and the Ends of the World*, Oxford: Blackwell.

Callon, M. (1987) 'Society in the Making: The Study of Technology as a Tool for Sociological Analysis', in Bijker, W. E., T. P. Hughes and T. J. Pinch (eds) *The Social Construction of Technical Systems*, Cambridge, Mass.: MIT Press, 83–103.

Chandler, A. (1962) *Strategy and Structure*, Cambridge, Mass.: MIT Press.

Chandler, A. (1977) *The Visible Hand*, Cambridge, Mass.: Belknap Press.

Chanlat, J. (1996) 'From Cultural Imperialism to Independence' in Clegg and Palmer (1996, 121–40).

Clark, J. (1995) *Managing Consultants: Consultancy as the Management of Impressions*, Buckingham: Open University Press.

Clarke, J. and J. Newman (1993) 'The Right to Manage: A Second Managerial Revolution?', *Cultural Studies*, 7, 427–41.

Clegg, S. and G. Palmer (eds) (1996) *The Politics of Management Knowledge*, London: Sage.

Cohen, M. D. and L. S. Sproull (eds) (1995) *Organisational Learning*, London: Sage.

Collins, H. M. (1990) *Artificial Experts: Social Knowledge and Intelligent Machines*, Cambridge, Mass.: MIT Press.

Collins, J. (1995) *Architectures of Excess: Cultural Life in the Information age*, London: Routledge.

Crainer, S. (ed) (1995) *The Financial Times Handbook of Management*, London: Pitman.

Culbert, S. A. (1995) *Mind-Set Management: The Heart of Leadership*, New York: Oxford University Press.

Daly, C. (1993) 'The Discursive Construction of Economic Space', *Economy and Society*, 20, 79–102.

Davis, T. R. V. and F. Luthans (1980) 'Managers in Action: A New Look at Their Behavior and Operating Modes', *Organisational Dynamics*, Summer, 64–80.

Derrida, J. (1994) *Spectres of Marx*, New York: Routledge.

Diamond, C. (1991) *The Realistic Spirit: Wittgenstein, Philosophy and the Mind*, Cambridge, Mass.: MIT Press.

Drucker, P. (1988) 'The Coming of the New Organisation', *Harvard Business Review*, 88, 45–53.

Du Gay, P. (1996) *Consumption and Identity at Work*, London: Sage.

Dymski, G., G. Epstein, and R. Pollin (eds) (1993) *Transforming the US Financial System, Equity and Efficiency for the 21st Century*, Armonk, NY:

Eagleton, T. (1995) 'Review of Derrida's Spectres of Marx', *Radical Philosophy*, 73, 35–7.

Eccles, R. and N. Nohria (1990) *The Post-structuralist Organisation*, Harvard Business School Working Paper 92–103.

Economist (1995) 'Trust in Me', *The Economist*, 16 December, 83.

Economist (1996).

Emery, F. and E. Trist (1965) 'The Causal Texture of Organisational Environments', *Human Relations*, 18, 21–32.

Engwall, L. (1992) *Mercury Meets Minerva*, Oxford: Pergamon.

Foucault, M. (1980) *Power/Knowledge: Selected Interviews and Other Writings*. New York: Pantheon.

French, R. and C. Grey (eds) (1996) *Rethinking Management Education*, London: Sage.

Fukuyama, F. (1992) *The End of History and the Last Man*, London: Hamish Hamilton.

Furusten, S. and N. Kinch (1992) 'Swedish Managerial Thinking: A Shadow of America' in Lunden, R. and E. Asard (eds) *Networks of Americanisation: Aspects of the American Influence in Sweden Acta Umesitatis-Uppsahensies*, 79, 55–79.

Gamble, A. and K. Kelly (1996), 'The New Politics of Ownership' *New Left Review*, 220, 62–97.

Ghoschal, S. and C. A. Bartlett (1995) 'Changing the Role of Top Management: Beyond Structure to Process' *Harvard Business Review*, 73, 86–96.

Gibbons, M., C. Limoges, H. Nowotny, S. Schwartzman, P. Scott and S. Trow (1994) *The New Production of Knowledge: The Dynamics of Science and Research in Contemporary Societies*, London: Sage.

Giddens, A. (1991) *Modernity and Self-Identity*, Cambridge: Polity Press.

Goffee, R. and J. W. Hunt (1996) 'The End of Management? Classroom versus Boardroom', *Financial Times*, 22 March, 3–4.

Gordon, D. (1996) *Fat and Mean: The Corporate Squeeze of Middle Americans and the Myth of Managerial Downsizing*, New York: Free Press.

Griffith, V. (1996) 'Creating Virtuality', *Financial Times*, 22 November, 14.

Gumbrecht, H. U. and K. L. Pfeiffer (eds) (1994) *Maerialities of Communication*, Stanford: Stanford University Press.

Hague, D. (1994) *The Knowledge-Based Economy*, Oxford: Templeton College.

Hammer, M. and J. Champy (1993) *Re-Engineering the Corporation*, A Manifesto for Business Success, London: Michael Brealey.

Handy, C. (1989) *The Age of Unreason*, London: Arrow.

Handy, C. (1991) *The Empty Raincoat*, London: Arrow.

Handy, C. (1996) *Beyond Certainty*, London: Arrow.

Harvey, D. (1989) *The Condition of Postmodernity*, Oxford: Blackwell.

Harvey, D. (1995) 'The Conceptual Politics of Place, Space and Environment in the Work of Raymond Williams', *Social Text*, 42, 69–98.

Heckscher, C. and A. Donnellon (eds) (1994) *The Post-Bureacratic Organisation: New Perspectives on Organisational Change*, Thousand Oaks, CA: Sage.

Heelas, P. (1991a) 'Cutts for Capitalism; Self-religions, Magic and the Empowerment of business' in Gee, P. and J. Fulton (eds) *Religion and Power: Decline and Growth*, London, British Sociological Association, 27–41.

Heelas, P. (1991b) 'Reforming the Self: Enterprise and the Character of Thatcherism' in Keat, R. and N. Abercrombie (eds) *Enterprise Culture*, London: Routledge, 72–90.

Heelas, P. (1992) 'The Sacralisation of the Self and New Age Capitalism' in Abercrombie, N. and A. Warde (eds) *Social Change in Contemporary Britain*, Cambridge: Polity Press, 139–66.

Heelas, P. (1996) *The New Age Movement: The Celebration of the Self and the Sacralisation of Modernity*, Oxford: Blackwell.

Herzberg, F. (1965) *Work and the Nature of Man*, Cleveland, OH: World Publishing Company.

Herzberg, F. (1968) 'One More Time – How Do You Motivate Employees?' *Harvard Press Review*, 46, 53–62.
Hill, S. and Turpin, T. (1995) 'Cultures in Collision: The Emergence of a New Localism in Academic Research', in M. Strathern (ed.) *Shifting Contexts: Transformations of Anthropological Knowledge*, London: Routledge, 131–52.
Hofstede, G. (1991) *Cultures and Organisations*, New York: McGraw Hill.
Huczynski, A. (1993) *Management Gurus: What Makes Them and How to Become One*, London: Routledge.
Ingold, T. (1995) 'Man: The Story So Far', *Times Higher Education Supplement*, 2 June, 16–17.
Jacques, M. (1994) 'Caste Down', *Sunday Times*, Culture Supplement, 12 June, 8–10.
Jernier, J., D. Knights and W. Nord (eds) (1994) *Resistance and Power in Organisations*, London: Routledge.
Journal of Management Inquiry (1994) Special issue on Chaos and Complexity, *Journal of Management Inquiry*, 3, 4.
Jowitt, K. (1992) *New World Disorder: The Leninist Extinction*, Berkeley: University of California Press.
Kanter, R. M. (1991) *When Giants Learn to Dance*, New York: Routledge.
Kay, J. (1993) *Foundations of Corporate Success*, Oxford: Oxford University Press.
Kay, J. (1995) 'The Foundations of National Competitive Advantage', *Fifth ESRC Annual Lecture*, London: ESRC.
Kay, J. (1996) *Why Firms Succeed*, Oxford: Oxford University Press.
Keeble, D., J. Bryson, P. A. Wood (1994) *Pathfinders of Enterprise*, School of Management, Open University, Milton Keynes.
Kestelholn, W. (1996) 'Toolboxes Are Out; Thinking Is In', *Financial Times*, March 22, 7–8.
Kleiner, A. (1996) *The Age of Heretics*, New York: Doubleday.
Knights, D. and F. Murray (1994) *Managers Divided: Organisation, Politics and Information Technology Management*, Chichester: John Wiley.
Kogut, B. and E. H. Bowman (1996) 'Redesigning for the 21st century', *Financial Times*, March 22, 13–14.
Kotter, J. P. (1996) *Leading Change*, New Canaan, CT: Harvard Business School Press.
Lakoff, G. (1987) *Women, Fire and Dangerous Things*, Chicago: Chicago University Press.
Lash, S. and J. Urry (1994) *Economies of Signs and Spaces*, London: Sage.
Latour, B. (1987a) 'The Enlightenment without the Critique: A Word on Michel Serres' Philosophy' in Griffiths, A. P. (ed.) *Contemporary French Philosophy*, Cambridge: Cambridge University Press, 83–97.
Latour, B. (1987b) *Science in Action: How to Follow Scientists and Engineers through Society*, Cambridge, Mass.: Harvard University Press.
Latour, B. (1993) *We Have Never Been Modern*, Brighton: Harvester Wheatsheaf.
Latour, B. (1995) *Organization Studies*.
Law, J. (1994) *Organising Modernity*, Oxford: Blackwell.
Law, J. and A. Mol (1995) 'Notes on Materiality and Sociality' *Sociological Review*, 28, 274–94.
Legge, K. (1994) 'On Knowledge, Business Consultants, and the Selling of TQM', unpublished paper.

Leonard-Barton, D. (1995) *Wellsprings of Knowledge. Building and Sustaining the Sources of Innovation*, New Canaan, CT: Harvard Business School Press.

Lewin, K. (1951) *Field Theory in Social Science*, New York: Harper.

Lorenz, C. (1989) 'The Rise and Fall of Business fads', *Financial Times*, June 24th, 24.

Lundvall, B. A. (ed.) (1992) *National Systems of Innovation: Towards a Theory of Innovation and Interactive Learning*, London: Frances Pinter.

Lury, C. (1993) London: Routledge.

Maira, A. and P. Scott-Morgan (1996) *Accelerating Organisation*, New York: McGraw Hill.

Martin, E. (1992) 'The End of the Body?' *American Ethnologist*, 19, 121–40.

Martin, E. (1994) *Flexible Bodies: The Role of Immunity in American Culture from the Days of Polio to the Age of Aids*, Boston: Beacon Press.

Maslow, A. H. (1954) *Motivation and Personality*, New York: Harper.

McGregor, D. (1960) *The Human Side of Enterprise*, New York: McGraw Hill.

McNay, L. (1994) *Foucault*, Cambridge: Polity Press.

Merriden, T. (1996) 'James Champy', *Management Today*, October: 74–5.

Micklethwait, J. and A. Wooldridge (1996) *The Witch Doctors: Making Sense of the Management Gurus*, London: Times Books.

Mintzberg, H. (1973) *The Nature of Managerial Work*, New York: Harper and Row.

Mintzberg, H. (1975) 'The Manager's Job: Folklore and Fact', *Harvard Business Review*, 53: 49–61.

Miztal, B. (1996) *Trust in Modern Societies*, Cambridge: Polity Press.

Morgan, G. (1986) *Images of Organisation*, London: Sage.

Morgan, G. (1993) *Imaginisation: The Art of Creative Management*, London: Sage.

Morris, M. (1988) 'Banality in Cultural Studies', *Discourse X*, 10, 2–29.

Morton, M. S. S. (1991) *The Corporation of the 1990s: Information Technology and Organisational Transformation*, New York: Oxford University Press.

Naisbitt, J. and P. Aburdene (1990) *Megatrends 2000*, London: Pan.

Nohria, N. and J. D. Berkley (1994) 'The Virtual Organisation: Bureaucracy, Technology and the Implosion of Control', in Hecksher C. and A. Donnellon (eds) *The Post-Bureaucratic Organisation: New Perspectives on Organisational Change*, Thousand Oaks: Sage, 108–28.

Nonaka, I. and N. Takeuchi (1995) *The Knowledge-Creating Company: How Japanese Companies Create the Dynamics of Innovation*, Oxford: Oxford University Press.

Nonini, D. and A. Ong (eds) (1997) *Underground Enemies: The Cultural Politics of Chinese Transnationalism*, London: Routledge.

Norris, C. (1995) 'Versions of Apocalypse: Kant, Derrida, Foucault', in Bull (1995, 227–49).

Pahl, R. (1995) *After Success: Fin de Siècle Identity and Anxiety*, Cambridge: Polity.

Pascale, T. (1991) *Managing on the Edge*, Harmondsworth: Penguin.

Perez, C. (1985) 'Microelectronics, Long Waves, and World Structural Change', *World Development*, 13, 441–63.

Perkin, H. (1996) *The Third World Revolution: Professional Elites in the Modern World*, London: Routledge.

Perniola, M. (1995) *Enigmas: The Egyptian Movement in Society and Art*, London: Verso.

Peters, T. (1989) *Thriving on Chaos*, London: Pan.

Peters, T. and N. Austin (1985) *A Passion for Excellence: The Leadership Difference*, London: Fontana.

Peters, T. and R. H. Waterman (1982) *In Search of Excellence*, New York: Harper and Row.

Pfeffer, J. (1992) *After Power*, New Canaan, CT: Harvard Business School Press.

Pfeffer, J. and G. R. Salancik (1978) *The External Control of Organisations*, New York: Harper and Row.

Pickering, A. (1995) *The Mangle of Practice: Time, Agency and Science*, Chicago: University of Chicago Press.

Plant, S. (1996) 'The Virtual Complexity of Culture', in Robertson, G. M. Mash, L. Tickner, J. Bird, B. Curtis and T. Putman (eds) *Futurenatural: Nature/Science/Culture*, London: Routledge, 203–17.

Polanyi, M. (1958) *Personal Knowledge: Towards a Post Critical Philosophy*, London: Routledge and Kegan Paul.

Polanyi, M. (1967) *The Tacit Dimension*, London: Routledge and Kegan Paul.

Pollin, R. (1995) 'Financial Structures and Egalitarian Economic Policy', *New Left Review*, 214, 26–61.

Porter, M. (1990) *The Competitive Advantage of Nations*, New York: Macmillan.

Porter, T. (1994) 'Information, Power and the View from Nowhere', in Bud-Frierman (1994, 217–30).

Putnam, H. (1981) *Reason, Truth, and History*, Cambridge: Cambridge University Press.

Quinn, J. B. (1992) *Intelligent Enterprise: A Knowledge and Service-Based Paradigm for Industry*, New York: Free Press.

Ramsay, H. (1996) 'Managing Sceptically: A Critique of Organisational Fashion', in Clegg and Palmer (1996, 155–72).

Readings, B. (1996) *The University in Ruins*, Cambridge, MA: Harvard University Press.

Redfield, J. (1994) *The Celestine Prophecy*, London: Bantam.

Rifkin, G. (1996) 'Finding Meaning at Work', *Strategy and Business*, 5.

Roberts, R. (1994) 'Power and Empowerment: New Age Managers and the Dialectics of Modernity/Postmodernity'. *Religion Today*, 9, 3–13.

Roberts, W. and B. Ross (1995) *Make it So: Leadership Lessons from Star Trek. The Next Generation*, New York: Simon and Schuster.

Roos, J. and G. van Krogh (1995) *Organisational Epistemology*, London: Macmillan.

Roos, J. and G. van Krogh (1996) *Managing Knowledge: Perspectives on Cooperation and Competition*, London: Sage.

Rose, N. (1996) *Inventing Our Selves: Pychology, Power and Personhood*, Cambridge: Cambridge University Press.

Rupert, G. (1992) 'Employing the New Age: Training Seminars' in Lewis, J. and J. G. Melton (eds) *Perspectives on the New Age*, Albany: State University Press of New York Press, 127–135.

Sampson, A. (1995) *Company Man: The Rise and Fall of Corporate Life*, London: HarperCollins.

Scase, R. and R. Goffee (1989) *Reluctant Managers*, London: Unwin Hyman.

Schaffer, S. (1996) 'Babbage's Dancer and the Impressions of Mechanism', in Spufford, F. and J. Uglow (eds) *Cultural Bridge: Technology, Time and Invention*, London: Faber and Faber, 53–80.

Schoenberger, E. (1994) 'Corporate Strategy and Corporate Strategists: Power, Identity and Knowledge within the Firm', *Environment and Planning A*, 26, 435–52.

Serres, M. (1982) *Hermes: Literature, Science, Philosophy*, Baltimore, MD: Johns Hopkins University Press.

Serres, M. (1995a) *Genesis*, Ann Arbor, MI: University of Michigan Press.

Serres, M. (1995b) *Angles: A Modern Myth*, Paris: Flammarion.

Shapin, S. (1994) *A Social History of Truth: Civility and Science in Seventeenth Century England*, Chicago: Chicago University Press.

Stehr, N. (1994) *Knowledge Societies*, London: Sage.

Stewart, N. (1976) *Contrasts in Management: A Study of Different Types of Manager*, London: McGraw-Hill.

Stiglitz, J. E. (1994) *Whither Socialism?* Cambridge, MA: MIT Press.

Strathern, M. (1991) *After Nature*, Cambridge: Cambridge University Press.

Strathern, M. (1995a) 'Foreword' in Strathern, M. (ed.) *Shifting Contexts. Transformations in Anthropological Knowledge*, London: Routledge, 1–11.

Strathern, M. (1995b) 'Afterword' in Strathern, M. (ed.) *Shifting Contexts. Transformations in Anthropological Knowledge*, London: Routledge, 177–85.

Stropford, J. (1996) 'Managing in Turbulent Times'. *Financial Times*, 22 March, 5–6.

Taylor, M. J. and N. J. Thrift (1983) 'Business Organisation, Segmentation, and Localisation', *Regional Studies*, 17, 445–65.

Temin, P. (ed.) (1991) *Inside the Business Enterprise: Historical Perspectives on the Use of Information*, Chicago: Chicago University Press.

Thrift, N. J. (1985) 'Flies and Germs: A Geography of Knowledge', in Gregory, D. and J. Urry (eds) *Social Relations and Spatial Structures*, London: Macmillan, 366–403.

Thrift, N. J. (1995) 'A Hyperactive World', in Johnston, R. J. and P. J. Taylor and M. Watts (eds) *Geographies of Global Change*, Oxford: Blackwell, 18–35.

Thrift, N. J. (1996a) *Spatial Formations*, London: Sage.

Thrift, N. J. (1996b) 'Shut Up and Dance, or, Is the World Economy Knowable?', in Daniels, P. W. and W. Lever (eds) *The Global Economy in Transition*, London: Longman, 11–23.

Thrift, N. J. (1997) 'The rise of soft capitalism' *Cultural Values* 1 (1).

Thrift, N. J. and K. Olds (1996) 'Refiguring "the Economic" in Economic Geography'. *Progress in Human Geography*, 20, 311–37.

Van der Pijl, K. (1994) 'The Cadre Class and Public Multilateralism', in Sakamoto, Y. (ed.) *Global Transformation: Challenges in the State System*, Tokyo: United Nations University Press, 200–49.

van de Vliet, A. (1996) 'High Figures Refined', *Management Today*, October, 76–8.

Walker, R. B. (1993) *Inside/Outside*, Cambridge: Cambridge University Press.

Whyte, W. H. (1957) *The Organization Man*, New York: Doubleday Anchor; London: Jonathan Cape.

Wittgenstein, L. (1978) *Remarks on the Philosophy of Mathematics*, Oxford: Oxford University Press.

Wooldridge, A. (1995) 'Big Is Back: A Survey of Multinationals', *The Economist*, June 24–30, 1–22.

Zuboff, S. (1988) *In the Age of the Smart Machine: The Future of Work and Power*, New York: Basic Books.

Part II

Globalization, Regionalization and National Diversity

5
Globalization and Its 'Other(s)': Three 'New Kinds of Orientalism' and the Political Economy of Trans-Border Identity

Ngai-Ling Sum

Introduction

One widely held view of globalization equates it with the Americanization of world society or, at least, with the re-making of the world according to the prescriptions of the neo-liberal 'Washington Consensus'. In this chapter I present a two-pronged critique of this view. It focuses on internal divisions in the American camp over the remaking of geo-economic and geo-political relations; and it also emphasizes the way in which this division is being appropriated across borders to construct new regional identities and interests. One way to tackle this would be to examine the role of regional organizations, such as APEC, in remapping regional identities, such as the 'Asian-Pacific' (see, for example, Higgott 1997). But this chapter considers the dialectic of globalization-regionalization through a study of the evolution of trade-competitiveness-development discourses in the US and Japan since the 1980s. This approach reveals a complex remaking of trans-border identities at the regional and national, as well as firm, levels. A key role here is played by the positing of different types of 'other' in and through three 'new kinds of orientalism'.

Said's account of 'othering' in Orientalism provides a starting point for this case study (1978; 1986). He analyzes Orientalism as an (historically and discursively necessary) 'other' of the West's self-identification; it is a false image through which the West reflects on its own place in the world. Following Said, some scholars in critical international relations have re-examined Western foreign policy discourses about non-Western 'others' through such binaries as 'insider/outsider', 'order/threat', 'North-South', and 'west-rest'. This chapter builds on these latter critical IR analyses but broadens the range of 'others' to be examined, highlights the variety of discourses deployed to construct different types of 'other', and analyzes the political economy of transborder identity and global capitalism. It also examines the structural context(s) in which particular discursive formation(s) are contested and how narrative possibilities are differentially inscribed in specific discursive formations. And it shows how discourses are reinvented or recombined to map a new intersubjective space-time for 'Asian-Pacific'.

Different Types of 'Others' and Three 'New Kinds of Orientalism'

The politics of difference begins with explicit and implicit constructions of boundaries between 'west and rest'/'self and other'. The crucial condition for 'othering' is construction of an inside/outside distinction to establish a division between (a) the nation and communities within and (b) real or potential enemies and, more generally, 'others' without (Walker 1995: 305). These 'others' are often represented as different, a difference couched in terms of inequality, danger, threat, etc. Such discourses are important reference points in examining trade strategy, economic/political development, race, gender, class, religion, etc. For it is through them that 'others' are constructed as 'unfair', 'dangerous', or 'inferior'. To refine such a binary view of inside/outside, this chapter argues that, not only are there different types of 'other' on the outside, but there can also be different types of 'other' on the inside. This blurs some of the spatial boundaries beloved of critics of orientalism and casts doubt on the simple 'othering' of the Orient by those in the Occident. It requires closer attention to the multiplicity of internal/external differentiations and to ways in which global and regional hegemons maintain their influence through the continual rearticulation of such distinctions. Indeed the plurality and heterogeneity of these distinctions is a source of strategic flexibility in a turbulent environment insofar as it widens the repertoire of legitimate actions and alliances. These points can be illustrated from at least three new 'kinds of orientalism' evident in the discursive construction of trade relations between the USA, Japan and the East Asian newly industrializing countries.

Types of 'other'

The two main types of 'other' are outsiders and 'internal others'. They may be adjudged equal or unequal. Equal outsiders are deemed close to the hegemon's time/space and are not differentiated in inferior-superior terms. Few cases exist. One example would be US-EU trade negotiation discourse: this seldom deploys an essentializing evaluative rhetoric even as it criticizes specific trade practices. This case is irrelevant to 'new kinds of orientalism'. More prevalent are discourses about unequal outsiders. They are othered through evaluative 'superior-inferior' and 'fair-unfair' cultural-textual schemata and categories of difference. This subtype occurs in a first 'new kind of orientalism' found in America's post-Cold War 'neo-liberal' trade discourse with Japan.

'Internal others' are defined as 'others' in terms of hegemonic discourses prevailing in the social formation to which these others allegedly 'belong'. Equal 'internal others' are deemed to occupy the same time/space as the hegemon and their difference is seen in relatively non-antagonistic terms. They draw on the same discursive repertoire as the hegemonic centre but offer alternative accounts of similar issues by inverting the otherizing cultural categories/explanations promoted by the latter. Conversely, unequal 'internal others' may be seen (or see themselves) as inferior and/or as located within the (eastern) hegemon's self-defined time/space. Their inequality is constructed through the 'superior-inferior' and 'leader-follower' categories of the latter. In general, where the 'others' (whether internal or external) exist as real subjects (rather than as figments of fevered hegemonic imaginations), social forces have significant incentives to reposition themselves strategically and/or to turn such 'otherings' to their advantage. Such 'internal otherness' is illustrated with studies of the other two 'new kinds of orientalism': respectively, the 'economic nationalism' of America's equal 'internal others' and the rearticulation of the 'flying geese' discourse by Japan's unequal 'internal others'. See Table 1.

Three 'new kinds of orientalism'

After the Cold War, 'discourses of danger' have been redeployed from the geo-political to geo-economic sphere. They are now voiced in international trade, competitiveness, and development relations. In this context, 'neo-liberal' trade discourses about the USA and Japan serve to 'otherize' Japan and define it as deviating from the 1980s' 'universal free trade' model. 'Neo-liberalism' was first championed by Reagan and Thatcher and by US-dominated organizations such as the World Bank

Table 1. Types of 'Other' and 'New Kinds of Orientalism'

	Equal	Unequal
'External Other'	External and close to the western hegemon's self-defined time/space (US-EU trade dialogue)	External but inferior to the western hegemon's time/space (Old orientalism and first 'new kind')
'Internal Other'	Same time/space as the western hegemon Non-antagonistic alternatives by inverting the otherizing cultural categories (second 'new kind of orientalism')	Inferior and within the (eastern) hegemon's self-defined time-space (third 'new kind of orientalism')

and IMF. It eulogizes market-friendly development, minimal state, and free trade and claims these principles are instantiated in the USA. Thus the 'free trade' discourse was deployed by Reagan and Bush to 'otherize' Japan as 'unfair' in its trade practices. They are now entrenched in GATT-WTO discourses. Such discourses illustrate a first 'new kind of orientalism'. This involves a set of 'neo-liberal' narratives centred around the prevailing values/norms, governmentalities, and time/space of the US *qua* hegemon and deployed to otherize powers which are derogated as different and somehow unequal (for instance, because they are culturally inferior, less 'rational', less 'modern', or marginal to American interests and spheres of influence). Thus Japanese economic and political institutions and practices are not only seen as different from those in the USA but are also regarded as 'unfair' and antagonistic to US interests. Geo-economic narratives of 'free trade' thereby serve to impose (new) western standards of economic 'rationality' on (eastern) 'others' to enhance the growth of an open/multilateral global/regional trading system. And, until these 'others' (including Japan) modify their behaviour, they are condemned as 'unfair'.

In the mid-1980s this 'neo-liberal trade' narrative was challenged in the USA by a group of equal 'internal others'. Dubbed 'revisionist' by *Business Week* (1989), they provide a very different account of US–Japan relations. They construct 'the American self/Japanese other' through propositions such as 'Japan is not western' or 'Japan as threat'; and claim that 'American decline can be reinvigorated by economic nationalism' or, more recently, by 'techno-nationalism'. Given the vast literature (both sophisticated and populist) on this topic, my chapter considers those the *Wall Street Journal* (1990) describes in a telling (and 'otherizing') simile as 'the Gang of Four' (Johnson, van Wolferen, Fallows, and Prestowitz).[1] Their work illustrates a second 'new kind orientalism'. This involves discourses centred around the values/norms, procedural and substantive rationalities, and time/space of the West's equal 'internal others'. The latter deploy heterodox economic-cultural discourses (e.g., neo-mercantilism) to interpret Japan as an 'external other' which threatens the values, interests, and superiority of the hegemon on its home ground. Of particular interest here is how these new orientalist discourses have been extended and re-combined in both Japan and the USA to underpin new trade-policy alliances and strategies.

Japan has selectively integrated the heterodox economic discourses of US scholars into its own self-understanding. Thus a body of 'anti-bashing' literature counteracts 'neo-liberalism' and its critique of Japanese trade practices. More recently, Johnson's 'developmental state' narrative has been remapped onto Japanese time and space. A similar selective articulation of heterodox or 'revisionist' themes has occurred in the USA. This is especially clear in the rearticulation of 'trade', 'high-tech Japan' and 'competitiveness' discourses (e.g., Tyson 1992). These are used to redefine the American 'self' (reflected in Reich's debate over 'who is us?') in the face of Japanese threats to American prosperity. Tyson's idea of 'managed trade' signifies a defensive 'self' that is seen from the viewpoint of the hi-tech sectors. This new narrative has resonated in the Clinton Administration and was consolidated as part of his regime of economic truth at least up to 1993.

Around the same time as the USA began constructing 'Japan as threat', the 1985 Plaza Accord between G5 ministers of finance engineered a massive revaluation of the yen and reduced Japanese price competitiveness in export markets. In response Japan sought to reposition itself in East Asia not just by deepening the intra-regional division of labour but also through selective reinterpretation of Akamatsu's idea of 'flying geese'.[2] Japanese research institutes (such as JETRO amd Nomura) now suggest that Japan can lead the flight of other East Asian NICs to industrial success. This illustrates a third 'new kind of orientalism'. This involves a development discourse centred around the prevailing values/norms, governmentalities, and time/space of Japan that assigns a follower identity to the East's unequal 'internal others' (e.g., NICs) – claiming that their interests are best realized by entering the Japan-led framework as junior partners. This discourse creates Eastern unequal 'internal others' and leads to a cultural othering of East Asian economies reminiscent of Western orientalism.

A Strategic-Relational Approach to Three 'New Kinds of Orientalism' in the Post-Cold War Era

Structural and strategic contexts of the post-cold war era and US–Japan trade conflicts

Two broad trends in the global political and economic order help to contextualize the three 'new kinds of orientalism'. First, the end of the Cold War and disintegration of the Soviet Bloc have changed the bipolar geo-political security game into a multipolar one. Japan and China, respectively the current and emerging regional hegemons in East Asia, have joined the sole remaining global hegemon (the USA) in an effort to redefine their respective geo-political identities, interests, and spheres of influence in a multipolar world. Second, in the increasingly dominant geo-economic sphere, growing globalization/regionalization have reinforced tendencies towards global disorder. This chapter concentrates on changes in geo-economic relations between the US, Japan, and East Asian NICs and their links to key textual redefinitions of their identity and interests.

Previously, American pre-occupation with the Cold War (and the resulting need to maintain anti-communist cohesion within the American alliance system) led the federal government to overlook key aspects of its partners' trade and investment practices. Whereas Western Europe was generally expected to comply with free trade principles of the US-led GATT regime, certain exceptions were made for East Asia to promote America's geo-political strategy in the region. Although Japan entered GATT and has developed intense trade and investment relations with the USA, geo-political considerations led the American state to exclude Japan from the demand for reciprocal trading concessions, thereby rejecting calls from domestic business. Indeed, despite the growing imbalance in US–Japanese trade relations, few serious threats to such exemptions arose until the 1980s.

This was when the more general threat to US economic dominance entailed in a changing global economy led to increasing American concern about US–Japanese economic relations – especially as Japan's increasingly favourable insertion in the world economy was combined with America's allegedly declining capacity to adjust to global competition. Thus concerns were raised about Japanese trade barriers (e.g., the domestic and overseas role of *keiretsu*)[3] and about growing trade imbalances (as the 1980 deficit of US$ 7 billion grew to some US$ 55 billion by 1994). See Table 2.

Table 2. USA's Commodity Trade
Deficits with Japan (US$ billion)

1987	52.1
1988	47.6
1989	45.0
1990	38.0
1991	38.5
1992	43.7
1993	50.2
1994	55.0

Source: US Department of Commerce,
Survey of Current Business

The structural and discursive context of these 'new kinds of orientalism' in the USA

These trade imbalances prompted conflicts. Japanese 'otherness' was redefined from the early 1980s onwards and 'reciprocity' was demanded. This discourse goes beyond the 'othering' of Japan under Nixon (Leaver 1989: 430–2). For, uniquely, it links Japan's qualities as an 'other' directly to the economic identity and interests of the USA and its need to reposition itself in the new global economy. This is reflected in various terms of art (e.g., 'multilateralism', 'liberalization', 'developmental state', 'technology policy') that can be flexibly redeployed to construct both the 'Japanese other' and the 'American self'. This section explores these reinterpretations in terms of the first and second 'new kinds of orientalism'.

The 'neo-liberal' construction in the USA: a first 'new kind of orientalism'

The GATT/WTO regime deploys 'neo-liberalism' to define a 'fair' multilateral trading order. In the 1980s, the multilateral regime was disrupted by a relative decline of US domination in world trade. Growing trade deficits with Japan prompted Congressional and wider social disquiet about 'unfairness'. This was articulated in terms of 'restrictive practices' (on agricultural products) and 'structural barriers' maintained by Japanese firms to protect domestic markets (such as the keiretsu system, which restricts entry by foreign firms). Such discourses not only criticize Japan as 'unfair' but do so in an 'otherizing' manner. They contrast Japanese conduct with a (newly constructed) American 'liberal self' and also call for 'national fairness', 'reciprocity' and 'level playing fields' in trade relations with the USA (Kudrle 1995: 168–71).

Of interest during this period is how the USA has strategically connected its new-found 'liberal self' with protectionist tendencies in its
trade relations with Japan. This contradictory 'American liberal-protectionist self' is seen in the promotion, since the 1980s, of 'managed
trade' (i.e., negotiated market shares). This policy includes two sets of
international legal accords: one concerns the management of exports
(e.g., 'voluntary export restraints' (VERs) and 'Anti-dumping Provi-
sions'); and the other covers the expansion of (US) markets abroad (e.g.,
'Voluntary Import Expansions' or VIEs) and 'Super 301' (unfair trade
law) (Sjolander 1994: 46). This contradictory mixture of 'protectionism'
and neo-liberal 'unfairness' creates a symbolic and material space in
which Japan can be 'otherized' as infringing 'liberal' standards; yet it
also permits the USA to justify its own 'protectionist' practices. Examples of practices targetted at different sectors of Japanese industry under
the Bush and Reagan administrations are shown in Table 3.

The 'othering' of Japan as 'unfair' can be seen in the Bush Administration's upgrading of 'Section 301' (i.e., Chapter 1 of Title III of the US
Trade Act of 1974) to become 'Super 301'. Section 301 was intended to
deal with complaints about goods; Super 301 was extended to include a
non-exhaustive list of US-defined 'unfair' practices (e.g., workers' rights
and inadequate anti-competitive policy regimes). In May 1989 President Bush, under serious Congressional pressure, invoked 'Super 301' to
define Japan as 'trading unfairly' in supercomputers, telecommunica-
tion satellites, and wood products.

This US redefinition and broadening of possible areas of 'unfairness'
can be seen as the first 'new kind of orientalism'. It rests on economic
narratives centred around 'fair/unfair' trade policy/practices unilaterally
defined by the USA to serve the interests of the 'American self' against the
'Japanese other'. It provides a discursive framework and sanctions for
the USA to condemn countries which are supposedly departing from
'liberal' standards; and it legitimates the American self-image as 'liberal-
protectionist'. This paradoxical (if not self-contradictory) identity is evident in the view of Senator Max Baucus, Chair of the International Trade
Subcommittee of the Senate Finance Committee, that: '(o)ur trading

Table 3. VERs and VIEs

1982	Automobile VERs
1984	Steel VERs
1985	Machine tool VERs
1986	Semiconductor VIEs
1988	'Super and Special 301s'

partners must realize that the US is firmly committed to opening markets . . . . If we cannot open those market through the GATT, we will use Section 301' (*International Trade Reporter*, January 9, 1990: 60).

The 'neo-mercantilist' construction in the USA: a second 'new kind of orientalism'

This 'American liberal-protectionist self' co-exists with a non-liberal or neo-mercantilist construction of American interests by certain of its equal 'internal others'. This is based on analyses of the non-market foundations of Japanese economic power and the corresponding need for the USA to respond in kind with its own mercantilist or statist policies. The writers considered below are Johnson, Fallows, Prestowitz, and van Wolferen. Despite their 'othering' by critics as the 'Gang of Four', their work is actually quite varied in content and style (with Johnson writing mainly as an academic and Fallows and Prestowitz being more populist). Through their rather different concerns with state, culture, and international strategies, these writers deploy the following constructions in contrasting the 'Japanese other' and 'American self': a) 'Japan as different' (i.e., non-Western); b) 'Japan as threat or danger'; and c) an 'economic nationalist' interest for the US.

First, Chalmers Johnson, a professor of political science at the University of California, San Diego, offers a Eurocentric account of the specificity of post-war Japan. This was first presented in his influential book on the Ministry of International Trade and Industry (MITI), *MITI and the Japanese Miracle* (1982). Without reflecting on its relevance to an East Asian context, Johnson deploys the Enlightenment institutional triplet of 'market economy', 'civil society', and 'sovereign state'. Denying that Japanese development is explicable in terms of simple market forces or a distinctive Japanese culture, he grounds it in a distinctive form of 'state' which dates from the Meiji period. But the Japanese 'developmental state' is analyzed in Eurocentric terms as institutionally autonomous from market forces and as intervening from outside and above the market to pursue a political project. In a manner alien to America's liberal-market traditions, this consensus-building interventionist state has long promoted 'strategic industries'. This is especially clear in MITI's use of special tax incentives, cheap loans, and access to export financing to encourage the dramatic ascent of different high-tech industries (e.g., steel, automobiles, and electronics). This statist reading of Japan's uniqueness has ambivalent implications for America's own identity and interests. It could reinforce the sense of superiority based on a liberal self-identity; or undermine that feeling by suggesting that an allegedly inferior developmental model threatens US interests. Thus it could legitimate demands for liberalization and deregulation in Japan or demands for a similarly effective system of state support for industry in the USA. From the late 1980s onwards, Johnson's work has often been invoked (in admittedly caricatured form) in support of various attempts to redirect US economic policy towards neo-mercantilist and/or interventionist position.

Karel van Wolferen and James Fallows construct (albeit in somewhat different ways) 'Japanese otherness' in terms of specific Japanese cultural traits. Van Wolferen, a Dutch journalist and long-time resident of Japan, argues in *The Enigma of Japanese Power* (1989) that Japan's system is a 'truncated pyramid' with overlapping hierarchies that is 'out of control'. An article in *The National Interest* (1991) reinforces this claim. Van Wolferen notes that there is no final arbitrator among the overlapping hierarchies of the bureaucratic-Liberal Democratic Party-business alliance. He deploys metaphors such as 'a juggernaut with no brakes' and 'kings without power' to portray 'Japan as threat' to the 'international legal framework' (1989: 431).

James Fallows, Washington editor of *Atlantic Monthly*, penned two articles for his journal (1989a; 1989b) and a book, *More Like Us* (1989c). These argue that 'Japan is different'. Rejecting state-centred analyses, he refers Japanese economic success to such essential Japanese qualities as being 'tribe-like' (*sic*), 'lacking universal principles', and adopting a 'situational morality' (1989a: 46–51). Fallows claims that such features provoke US-Japan conflict because Japan lacks real respect for universal free-trade/laissez-faire rules. These threats were proving hard to resist because of the inherent 'individualist beliefs' of America; the 'American self' could never become like the 'Japanese other' and so defend itself in like manner (1989c: x). Not shy of self-contradiction, however, Fallows's second article advocates an 'economic nationalist' identity for the USA, suggesting that it should 'contain Japan' by resorting to 'managed trade' (negotiated market shares) and 'managed competition' (1989b: 63–4).

Clyde Prestowitz, a former trade negotiator, invoked Johnson's arguments to reorient US economic strategy. Johnson had suggested that the Japanese state regards geo-economic goals and industrial performance as akin to national security (1982: 21; 1989: 102). Prestowitz suggested the US state had been so pre-occupied with Cold War geopolitical and laissez-faire goals that its resulting neglect of American industrial and technological leadership had contributed to economic decline. He also claimed that Japanese investment in the USA was a form of colonization and seriously threatened American identity and interests. A research institute established by Prestowitz even concludes that the American auto industry can best be saved from the Japanese threat by offering low-interest loans diverted from military R & D funding.

These 'revisionist' policy recommendations of the 'Gang of Four' (or, in the case of Johnson, based on interpetations of his work) rest on the construction of 'Japanese otherness' based on a curious mix of positive and negative images. Thus we find both positive evaluations of state/ strategic policies/high-tech (future technology); and negative judgments concerning a 'system out of control' or 'lacking universal principles'. These positive and negative features can be condensed into the image of 'Japan as threat' and the concomitant call for a remapping of the 'American self' in terms of 'economic nationalism'. These discourses, popularized by America's equal 'internal others', constitute a second 'new kind of orientalism'. Drawing on a mixture of Enlightenment categories and heterodox economic-cultural discourses, these equal 'internal others' interpret Japanese 'difference' as a threat to the values and interests of the hegemon which requires the latter to adapt or perish.

Strategic and discursive repositionings of Japan and the US

Challenged by these reciprocal constructions of the 'Japanese other' and the 'American self', both Japan and the USA have been seeking to redefine their identities/interests/strategies economically and politically.

Japan's repositionings and the discourses of 'Japanese uniqueness'

Faced with this double othering by the American hegemon and its equal 'internal others', there have been two successive responses in Japan. First, Japanese forces have contested the otherizing discourse by producing 'anti-bashing' literature to counteract 'neo-liberalism' and claims of Japanese 'unfairness'. This is reflected in diplomatic literature warning against 'emotionalism' and 'hysteria' and pleas, on the part of Watanaba Taizo of the Foreign Ministry and Prime Minister Kaifu, for 'calmer attitudes'. This diplomatic approach co-existed with more nationalistic claims that Japan's critics are racists. This can be seen from intellectual magazines (e.g., *Chuo koron*) that were filled with articles on America's conceptions of the 'yellow peril'. Other materials include Shintaro Ishihara and Akio Morita's booklet entitled *The Japan That Can Say 'No'* (1989). This noted Japan's technological superiority over the US and argued that it should further its own interests rather than give in to American threats. Such documents attracted widespread attention in Japan and provoked economic nationalism; but they did not really strengthen Japan's negotiating position – let alone provide an alternative hegemonic discourse (of the kind envisaged in Woo-Cumings 1993: 143). The second phase is more interesting and intellectually more challenging. It involves transforming the debate over the 'Japanese uniqueness' (in terms of, for example, the Japanese model of capitalism and society) into a weapon of empowerment. One form that it takes is to appropriate the positive aspect of the West's heterodox economic discourses on 'Japanese otherness' (e.g., Johnson's earlier idea on 'developmental state') and to assert how these are linked to the unique qualities of Japan. Keizo Nagatani's paper on 'Japanese Economics: The Theory and Practice of Investment Coordination' (1992) is a good example of this approach. By restating the 'Japanese self', it aims to reposition Japan in trade conflicts by refuting negative Western discourses (e.g., from Fallows and van Wolferen) and reworking positive ones (e.g., 'statist' analyses) to provide a restatement of 'Japanese self-identity' rooted in its own historical time and place in the world. In this way it also 'others' the West in a form of 'reinvented orientalism' or a Japanese form of Occidentalism. This two-pronged approach is evident from Nagatani's account of 'Japanese economics' since the Meiji Restoration in terms of the state's 'visible hand' steering economic development (i.e., 'government-guided industrialization', 'modernization through its fiscal authority and financial industry', and 'close government-business partnership') (1992: 192). In particular, he hopes:

> to bring out the essence of 'Japanese Economics' that has shaped Japan's economic policies over the past 120 years. Contrary to the claim by Western critics, it is my belief that Japanese economic policies and strategies are based firmly on principles and quiet consistent with the framework of their doctrines and therefore that knowing Japanese Economics is useful for the Westerners not only to better understand Japan but to cope more effectively with her. . . . Whereas Western Economics is natural – scientific, impersonal, non-historical, static and universal, Japanese Economics is social – scientific, game-theoretic, historical, dynamic and relative. These doctrinal differences naturally lead to different policy formulas and different styles of policy making, the most notable difference having been in the area of investment policy. Whereas Westerners believe that people's free choice over assets in the market place will produce an efficient and socially desirable pattern and pace of capital accumulation and that governmental intervention in this process will necessarily entail distortions and waste, the Japanese believe that economic

growth and development do not come naturally, that different forms of capital have different effects on economic growth and development, and that a proper sequence of investment must be designed and implemented by a "visible hand" in order to succeed. (Nagatani 1992: 178)

Regarding Japan's place in the world, he adds that Japan is a 'latecomer' and a 'follower' that 'must devise its own survival technique . . . in a world already endowed with dominant players and rules written by them' (1992: 188). This creation of the 'latecomer/follower' identity enables Nagatani not only to distinguish Japan's past trajectory from the west; but also creates an alternative discursive space – 'Japanese economics' – that might in future allow Japan to reposition itself in the global economy by engaging in the politics of difference on its own terms. Table 4 summarizes the two discursive formations regarding 'Japanese' and 'Western' economics.

This vignette illustrates a strategic hybrid that links the ambivalent 'statist discourse' of certain equal 'internal others' in America to Japan's own time and space. Besides Nagatani's work, there is a flood of hybridized narratives dealing with Japan's 'unique' form of capitalism (e.g., Gerlach's 'alliance capitalism', Eisuke Sakakibara's 'non-capitalist market economy', and Iwao Nakataini's 'network capitalism'). Such reconstructions of the 'Japanese self' demonstrate a kind of 'reinvented orientalism' that creates intersubjective spaces that are still embedded in discourses of 'uniqueness' but are not too divorced from western

Table 4. Discursive Formations of 'Japanese Economics' and 'Western Economics'

'Japanese Economics'	'Western Economics'
A number of dominant economies	US as the dominant economy
Latecomer and follower mentality	Hegemon mentality
Active rationality in setting goals	Market rationality
Second-best solutions	First-best solutions to constraints
Biological view of the national economy	Physical view of the national economy
State active in economic management	Free trade
The art of organizing people	The efficiency of competitive equilibrium
Co-operation and co-ordination	Competitive individualism
Long-term prosperity	Short-term efficiency

Compiled by the present author on the basis of Nagatani's work understanding. These hybrid identities can be interpreted in many ways: a) by (post)colonial actors as an attempt to build an 'Asian' identity and/or further Japan's economic role in the area; b) by the 'west' as a tendency towards occidentalism in otherizing them in return (Lie 1996: 11); and/or c) as contributing towards a move away from a 'neo-liberal' form of capitalism, which celebrates convergence around a single model (that of Atlantic market capitalism), to an 'Asian-Pacific' kind.

Discourses of 'competitiveness' in the Clinton administration

In the face of Japanese success, the yawning Japan-US trade deficit, and the emerging projection of the 'Japanese self' on the international scene, equal 'others' in the US have sought to redefine American interests in the face of 'Japan as threat'. They sometimes conclude that the USA should not force Japan to become more like itself but should itself seek to become more like Japan. This solution denies Japanese 'uniqueness' (except in so far as Japan pioneered the idea) and paradoxically implies that USA could reduce Japanese imports by importing the Japanese model itself. The most obvious indicators of this strategy are recommendations by research institutes for the USA to evolve strategically and consolidate selectively a 'new' techno-economic approach that emphasizes 'managed trade', 'competitiveness', 'high-technology policies', and 'factory-level Japanization'. These ideas were adumbrated in the writings of Fallows and Prestowitz; but they have since been translated into more sophisticated strategies in various works. Two representative texts have been published by the Berkeley Roundtable on International Economy (BRIE) and the Massachusetts Institute of Technology (MIT).

In one of BRIE's earlier books, edited by Johnson, Tyson and Zysman, *The Politics of Productivity: The Real Story of Why Japan Works* (1989), five key features are said to have contributed to Japanese economic success. They are: a) a pattern of industrial 'catch-up' shaped by import substitution and export promotion policies; b) government agencies such as MITI exerting substantial efforts to build a Japanese position in advanced technologies; c) an industrial and manufacturing organization that builds on flexibility rather than simply mass/volume production; d) the keiretsu trading system; and e) the role of high-technology policies and state policies in promoting competitiveness. This statist/ neo-mecantilist conception of Japan is important because it is bound up not only with American perceptions of Japan; but also with American perceptions of the 'self', especially regarding Japan's 'success' and how it 'threatens' the US.

One particular perception is offered in Laura Tyson's book, *Who's Bashing Whom? Trade Conflict in High-Technology Industries* (1992), which links the 'success of Japan' with 'US high-tech. sectors'. Focusing on sectoral performance, she calls for a 'strategic vision' to develop a 'credible commitment to maintain American strength in high-technology industries' (1992: 288). She then defines the American 'self'/ interests in terms of 'competitiveness' and advances the following microeconomic claims: a) the American government can facilitate 'competitiveness' by raising the quality of public education, increasing the efficiency of infrastructure, making markets, creating high-wage jobs, and promoting 'strategic/high-tech.' industries, etc.; and b) adverse trends in competitiveness are reversible through 'managed trade', which may encompass 'any trade agreement that establishes quantitative targets on trade flows' through a result-oriented trade strategy and 'Framework' talks with Japan (1992: 264, 296).

This remapping constructs a more protectionist, interventionist, and 'techno-nationalist' identity and strategy for the US. This new narrative has found resonance in economic and political circles. Economically, for example, it serves the micro-electronic industry's lobbying for support to high-tech industries. Politically, Clinton was keen to advance a new 'frontier myth' in his election programme. This aimed to expand American 'competitiveness' in a global age and the Tysonian discourse helped to privilege this 'competitor' identity and strategy. This was evident when Tyson was appointed as the Chair of Clinton's Council of Economic Advisors and 'competitiveness', 'managed trade', and 'technological initiatives' became part of his regime of economic truth in 1993. See Table 5.

Discursively, there was a clear remapping of the regimes of economic truth between the Bush and Clinton Administrations through a shift in the image of Japan and its implications for rebuilding the 'American self'. This new 'self' has not gone unchallenged (cf. Krugman's neo-liberal rebuttal, 1994); nor has the intended 'industrial policy' been at all fully or effectively implemented (Froud et al., 1996a). However, what is crucial, in identity terms, is the interpenetration of the Japanese 'other' with the American 'self' in and through the language of 'competitiveness'.

Concurrently, management and business literature attributes Japanese competitive advantage to its production techniques. Thus an influential MIT study, co-authored by James Womack, Daniel Jones and Daniel Roos, *The Machine that Changed the World* (1990), ascribed the success of Japan's automobile industry to a 'lean production system' which is allegedly superior to fordist mass production. It is even hailed as a

Table 5. Clinton's and Bush's Regimes of Economic Truth

Clinton's Regime of Economic Truth	Bush's Regime of Economic Truth
Trade policy is linked to domestic economic policy to strengthen the competitiveness of domestic industry	Links between trade policy and domestic economic policy are not strong
Expansion of exports from US via VIEs (i.e. strategic/managed trade)	Controls of imports to US via VERs
Priority for 'hi-tech.' industries	Priority for consumers
Important role for government	Important role for private sector
Importance of Asian-Pacific and APEC	No general policy on Asia
'Multi-track' (combining global, regional and bilateral approaches)	Unclear 'multi-track approach'

Source: Adapted from T. Sasaki and Y. Shimane, Table 10, 1994: 80

'global symbol of a new era' (1990: 277) and coded in a 'manufacturing infrastructure' language that prioritizes a response through 'factory-level Japanization' (e.g., lean production, just-in-time supply system, and total quality management) in the USA. Synergetic discourses of 'learning from Japan' are also combined with Americanized rhetorics of differences from Japan, and accounts of 'Japanization' as 'a fallen idol' for the US (or elsewhere) (e.g., Froud et al., 1996b). This conjunctural articulation of synergy and differences is prompting another US–Japan discourse – this time on the factory level. This micro-economic narrative of 'synergetic differences', when coupled with Tysonian meso-level discourses on 'competitiveness', allows for further interpenetration of the Japanese 'other' with the American 'self'. Despite their complementary and contradictory aspects, these complex and interpenetrative sets of discourse are (re-)circulated and (re-)constructed by politicians, think-tankers, journalists, business strategists, and social scientists to (re-)create, in a selective manner, a new inter-subjective space-time to be known as the 'Asian Pacific'.

The 'new flying geese' construction in Japan: a third 'new kind of orientalism'
Around the same time as the USA began constructing 'Japan as threat', the 1985 Plaza Accord engineered a massive devaluation of the yen. Saddled with uncompetitive export prices and rising domestic labour costs, and fearing greater protectionism in US and European markets,

Japan has been searching for new production sites in East Asia. These have proved fruitful for the redeployment of the 'flying geese' narrative. As a 'model of development', the 'flying geese' was first proposed by Akamatsu Kaname (1896–1974) as an economic and industrial theory with practical implications for Asian development. As a discursive construction, it was used in a militaristic form to legitimize the 'Japanese Greater East Asian Co-prosperity Sphere' during the Second World War. At the height of the domination of the trans-Atlantic partnership in the 1960s, this theory was further developed by Kojima and Okita to represent Japan and Southeast Asian as laggard 'geese' attempting to 'catch up' with the Euro-American leaders (cf. Korhonen 1994).

In the mid 1980s, the 'catch up' image shifted from Euro-America to the Asian region. In this regard, the 'new flying geese' construction was strategically twisted to remap/redefine the relationship between Japan and other Asian countries. This reinterpretation was promoted by technocrats (e.g., Saburo Okita) as well as Japan-related research institutes such as JETRO and Nomura. A key element in this strategic redefinition was the language of synergy and the image of a flock of 'flying geese'. Japan (as the leader of the flock) spearheads the formation, which is followed by the four NICs, six ASEAN economies, and post-socialist bloc as next to have taken off. This metaphor represents the growth trajectory in a deterministic manner in terms of a movement from traditional to modernized economic orders. It privileges Japan as the industrial leader and advocates a product-cycle approach so that Japan shifts its sunset industries to its EANIC 'flock'. This trajectory envisages the latecomers replicating the development experience of countries ahead of them in the formation. Thus, Japan guides the 'flock of geese' in its techno-economic 'flight to success' but each member of the flock follows under its own independent flight power but following the staging points of Japan (Sum 1996: 225–31).

This strategic reinvention of the 1930s' 'flying geese' metaphor in the 1980s implies: a) a hierarchy promoting the image that US and Japan guides/leads the 'flock'; and b) a realignment of the East's unequal 'internal others', i.e., economies less developed than the Japanese exemplar, to a follower position. As a Japan-centred discursive representation, it has the effect of creating a leader-follower relationship that maps Japan to the former and the other Asian countries to the latter. In this regard, the Asian countries are otherized as 'synergetically inferior'. As such, they become the unequal 'internal others' of Japan. This othering effect is pertinent to the politics of difference in western orientalism. In particular it suggests there is a third 'new kind of orientalism' which is constructed through a development discourse centered on the prevailing values/norms, governmentalities, and time/space of Japan, which assigns a follower identity to the East's unequal 'internal others', and which claims that their interests will best be served by entering as junior partners into a Japan-led framework. As a form of domination in the economic-cultural sphere, this may mean the 'synergetic subordination' of the East Asian NICs to Japanese economic practices that are promoted by its foreign direct investment, oveseas development assistance, and overseas security investment.[4] Thus the transfer of Japanese sunset industries to the East Asian NICs and from the latter to other Asian economies is constructed to be mutually beneficial to a new 'Asian-Pacific'.

Concluding Remarks: Three 'New Kinds of Orientalism' and Cultural Political Economy

Four main sets of remarks can now be proposed about 'new kinds of orientalism' and political economy. The first concerns the plurality of discourses involved in representing the culturally- as well as socially-embedded politics of international trade in the 'Asian-Pacific' region. We can transcend the singular conception of 'first-generation' orientalism by highlighting the unclear boundaries separating western hegemonic forces from the West's equal 'internal others', from its unequal 'external others', and from regional hegemonic forces in the East and their unequal 'internal others'. Accordingly, I have presented a more complex version of the politics of difference and its hybrid discursive forms under the rubric of three 'new kinds of orientalism'. For Western discourses of difference are not always singular and functional: they are multiple, hybridic, and often contradictory. Homi Bhabha's idea of 'decentring history in hybridity and in-betweenness of the postcolonial subject' is a useful guide here to the unclear boundaries of 'inside/outside' in postcolonial analysis. But it can also be criticized on two grounds. First, Bhabha is unclear about how more complex differences and their hybrids are constituted; and, second, he does not adequately pose (let alone answer) questions about the relation between hybrids and power relations, and the repositioning of actors as they rearticulate the discursive and/or material terrains on which they identify themselves, their interests, and strategies.

These two difficulties inform my next two sets of remarks. Thus my second set suggests that the constitution of complex and interpenetrative differences is related to the remixing of time and space. 'Neo-liberal' trade discourses are rooted in a dominant Enlightenment time-space code; the equal 'internal others' in the West also retain this code at the same time as they concede that the Japanese perceive time and space 'differently'. These different time frames have been positively combined in hybridized narratives referring to 'statist'/'Japanese economics' and 'Japanese success'/'US loss of competitiveness'. These narratives enable actors (especially in the East) to reposition themselves in relation to Eurocentric perspectives on time and space, reasserting traditional identities in changed circumstances, and reformulating their interests and strategies in this light. This recoding also has implications for the understanding and construction of space. Thus my case study indicates that Japan can no longer be located in orthodox (Eurocentric) spatial categories such as 'East-West'/'North-South'. In terms of economic space, Japan may be tilting to the North but it is also being 'otherized' as different by the North-North (Europe and North America) in so far as it really belongs to the North-East. Likewise, if Japan belongs to the North-East, the economies/countries 'otherized' by its own 'flying geese' construction may be represented as belonging to the South-East. Such complexities grow if we examine the layers of NICs in the tangled hierarchies of a spatialized geo-economic (dis)order still in the process of a contested becoming. Here the recoding of spatial metaphors and the reterritorialization of economic borders is likely to augment the production of hybridity/synergy/difference.

My third set concerns the production of hybridity/difference/synergy, power relations, and the nature of capitalism. My case study analyzes the political economy of difference in regard to the making of trans-border identity. The construction of synergetic differences helps to understand the complex, still unfolding dialectic of globalization-regionalization. Newly emerging (or revivified) identities, interests, and strategies which combine elements from different sets of discourse (linked variously with western hegemonic forces, the West's equal 'internal others', Eastern regional hegemons, and the East's unequal 'internal others') are (re-)circulated and (re-)constructed by politicians, think-tankers, journalists, business strategists, and social scientists to (re-)create, in a selective manner, a new inter-subjective space-time of the 'Asian-Pacific' at regional, national and firm levels. This new trans-border identity and vision may shape the design of institutions to remap social relations beyond the space-time dominated by 'neo-liberal' paradigm of Anglo-American capitalism. By bringing structure, strategic contexts, strategic capacities, and strategies back into the analysis, one gains a new understanding of the politics of difference, and in this case, of the synergetic difference deployed in the making of new trans-border identities. The discursive and material practices involved herein can be related to the 'commodification of (synergetic) difference'. For, as Dirlik notes, cultures are being broken and remade in response to the operation of capital (1994: 351). One can, indeed, go further and suggest that more than western capitalist powers are involved in the breaking and remaking of cultural traditions. Important roles are also played by counter- or sub-hegemonic forces in the West and, even more significantly, emerging regional hegemons and subaltern forces in the East.

My fourth and final set of remarks concern the need for political economy to take the 'culture turn' more seriously. My case study indicates that micro-economic narratives of the 'synergetic differences' may mediate the re-embedding and reterritorialization of other forms of capitalism that transverse new time and space. This way of reading political economy challenges conventional research boundaries by taking identity, culture, and the process of re-embedding and reterritorialization seriously. Indeed, a 'cultural political economy' approach (Sum, forthcoming) seems called for. This would help to understand such processes, particularly how the dialectic of globalization-regionalization unfolds and how trans-border identities and strategies emerge and react back on that dialectic.

Notes

1. Ó Tuathail (1994) critiques the sophisticated and populist writings on this issue.
2. The metaphor was originally used to legitimize the 'Japanese Greater East Asian Co-Prosperity Sphere' in terms of 'emancipating' East Asia from Atlantic domination. This connotation is absent today.
3. *Keiretsu* are hierarchical networks of interlocking firms organized around Japanese trading companies and banks that operate domestically and internationally.
4. On these economic-political practices, see Arase (1994); Sum (1997).

Bibliography

Arase, D. (1994) 'Public–Private Sector Interest Coordination in Japan's ODA', *Pacific Affairs*, 67 (2), 171–99.
Bhabha, H. K. (1984) 'Of Mimicry and Man: The Ambivalence of Colonial Discourse', *October*, 28, 125–33.
Bhabha, H. K. (1994) *The Location of Culture*, London: Routledge.
Campbell, D. (1994) 'Foreign Policy and Identity: Japanese "Other"/American "Self"' in Rosow, S., N. Inayatullah, and M. Rupert (eds) *The Global Economy as Political Space*, Boulder: Lynne Rienner, 147–70.
Dirlik, A. (1994) '"The Postmodern Aura", Third World Criticism in the Age of Global Capitalism', *Critical Inquiry*, 20, 328–56.

Fallows, J. (1989a) 'Containing Japan', *Altantic Monthly*, May, 40–54.

Fallows, J. (1989b) 'Getting Along with Japan', *Altantic Monthly*, December, 53–64.

Fallows, J. (1989c) *More Like Us*, Boston: Houghton Mifflin.

Fallows, J., C. Johnson, C. Prestowitz and K. van Wolferen (1990) 'The Gang of Four Defend the Revisionist Line', *US News and World Report*, 7 May, 54–5.

Froud, J. et al. (1996a) 'Sinking Ships? Liberal Theorists on the American Economy', *Asia Pacific Business Review*, 3 (1), 54–72.

Froud, J. et al. (1996b) 'A Fallen Idol? Japanese Management in the 1990s', *Asia Pacific Business Review*, 2 (4), 20–43.

Gerlach, M. L. (1992) *Alliance Capitalism*, Berkeley: University of California Press.

Higgott, R. (1997) 'De Facto and De jure Regionalism: The Double Discourse of Region in the Asia Pacific', *Global Society*, 11 (2), 46–65.

Ishihara, S. and A. Morita (1991) *The Japan that Can Say No*, New York: Simon and Schuster.

Johnson, C. (1982) *MITI and the Japanese Miracle*, Stanford: Stanford University Press.

Johnson, C., L. Tyson and J. Zysman (1989) *Politics and Productivity: How Japan's Development Strategy Works?* Berkeley: Ballinger.

Korhonen, P. (1994) 'The Theory of the Flying Geese Pattern of Development and its Interpretations', *Journal of Peace Research*, 31 (1), 93–108.

Krugman, P. (1994) 'Competitiveness: A Dangerous Obsession', *Foreign Affairs*, March/April, 28–44.

Kudrle, R. T. (1995) 'Fairness, Efficiency, and Opportunism in US Trade and Investment Policy' in Rapkin, D. and W. Avery (eds) *National Competitiveness in a Global Economy*, Boulder: Lynne Rienner, 153–78.

Leaver, R. (1989) 'Restructuring in the Global Economy: From Pax Americana to Pax Nipponica?', *Alternatives*, 14 (4), 429–62.

Lie, J. (1996) 'Theorizing Japanese Uniqueness', *Current Sociology*, 44 (1), 5–13.

Nagatani, K. (1992) 'Japanese Economics: The Theory and Practice of Investment Coordination' in Roumasset, J. and S. Burr, *The Economics of Cooperation: East Asian Development and the Case for Pro-Market Intervention*, Boulder: Westview, 175–200.

Ó Tuathail, G. (1994) 'Critical Geopolitics and Development Theory: Intensifying the Dialogue', *Transactions: Institute of British Geographers*, 19, 228–38.

Prestowitz, C. (1989) *Trading Places: How We Are Giving Our Future to Japan and How to Reclaim It*, New York: Basic Books.

Reich, R. (1990) 'Who is Us?', *Harvard Business Review*, 68 (1), 53–64.

Said, E. (1978) *Orientalism*, London: Routledge and Kegan Paul.

Said, E. (1986) 'Orientalism Reconsidered' in *Europe and Its Others*, Volume I, F. Baker, P. Hulme, M. Iversen, D. Loxley, Colchester: University of Essex, 12–29.

Sasaki, T. and Y. Shimane (1994) 'The New Dynamics of the Asian Economy', *Japan Research Quarterly*, 3 (3), 50–88.

Sjolander, C. T. (1994) 'The Discourse of Multilateralism: US Hegemony and the Management of International Trade' in Sjolander, C. and W. Cox (eds) *Beyond Positivism: Critical Reflections on International Relations*, Boulder: Lynne Rienner, 37–58.

Sum, N L. (1996) 'The NICs and Competing Strategies of East Asian Regionalism' in Gamble, A. and A. Payne (eds), *Regionalism and World Order*, London: Macmillan, 207–46.

Sum, N-L. (1997) '"Time-Space Embeddedness" and "Geo-Governance" of Cross-Border Regional Modes of Growth: Their Nature and Dynamics in East Asian Cases', in Amin, A. and J. Hausner (eds) *Beyond Markets and Planning: Third Way Approaches to Transformation*, Cheltenham: Edward Elgar, 159–95.

Sum, N-L. (forthcoming) '"Cultural Political Economy" in the Making: Reconciling with the "Narrative Turn"', *New Political Economy*.

Tyson, L. (1992) *Who's Bashing Whom? Trade Conflict in High-Technology Industries*, Washington: Institute for International Economics.

van Wolferen, K. (1989) *The Enigma of Japanese Power*, New York: Vintage.

van Wolferen, K. (1991) 'No Brakes, No Compass', *The National Interest*, 25, 26–35.

Walker, R. (1995) 'International Relations and the Concept of the Political' in K. Booth and S. Smith (eds), *International Relations Theory Today*, Cambridge: Polity, 306–27.

Womack, J., D. Jones and D. Roos (1990) *The Machine that Changed the World*, New York: Macmillan.

Woo-Cumings, M. (1993) 'East Asia's America Problem' in Woo-Cumings, M. and M. Loriaux, *Past as Prelude: History in the Making of a New World Order*, Boulder: Westview Press.

6
Globalization and Regionalization in Central Europe: Positive and Negative Responses to the Global Challenge

Attila Ágh

The Global Challenge

Globalization has become a magic word in the last decades, first of all after the collapse of the bipolar world order. It has been understood in many ways and in many fields as if the so called 'Global Challenge' had acted as an omnipotent and omnipresent force – inevitably and with the same consequences everywhere (see, Waterman 1996 and Power 1997). When we discuss, however, the transformation of East Central Europe (ECE – Poland, Hungary, the Czech Republic, Slovakia, Slovenia and Croatia) in an inter-regional comparison, we can identify both its ambiguous, dual (positive and negative) effects and indirect consequences or side-effects. It must also be emphasized that globalization has increased the parallel and counterbalancing processes of regionalization. Thus, an inter-regional comparison clearly suggests that all regions have met the global challenge in their own specific way, that is with a particular mixture of positive and negative responses, and with some characteristic side effects.[1]

In the early postwar period, the Western democracies identified their external enemy as the 'evil empire' and this external enemy contributed to their systemic consolidation (Hann 1995: 134–5). When this enemy disappeared, the Western political systems suffered a serious lack of consensus and old problems of secondary rank have come to the fore: 'For the EC itself, the emergence of Eastern Europe from its communist cocoon in 1989 was highly inconvenient, for the EC had partly relied on the Cold War partition of Europe for much of its cohesion, sense of purpose and stability. The new Europe would be much less stable and cohesive and would take time to gain a new sense of direction'

(Bideleux 1996: 248). Frances Millard argues in the same spirit: 'The sudden, dramatic collapse of the common enemy which has done so much to unify Western Europe unleashed a new wave of state particularism and differently perceived national interests' (1996: 221). Indeed, not only the 'East' suffers from the drastic changes in democratic transition and marketisation but the West also suffers from these 'Eastern' changes in its own way. To a great extent, they represent the Global Challenge for each other in the process of European integration. The 'East' – at least East Central Europe – has been faced with a deep structural transformation as adaptation to the EU – and the West has to accomodate to the new partnership with the former 'enemy'.

The Global Reaction: Authoritarian Renewal in the New Democracies

The contradictory, ambiguous or 'dual' effect of global democratization was felt and described first in Latin America as an 'Authoritarian Renewal', then observed also in East Asia and even later extended to Central and Eastern Europe. The statement that 'the East becomes the South' is one of the typical globalist simplifications, presupposing that 'political' globalization would act in the same way – that is homogenizing the countries – on all continents. Of course, Latin America has always oscillated in its cyclical development between democratic and authoritarian rule. However, this time the Authoritarian Renewal has been closely connected not only with domestic and regional issues, but above all with the global transformations associated with the collapse of a bipolar world. New features have also emerged which have influenced similar developments in other continents. As a result, the comparative study of democratizations became a 'boom industry' in the first half of the nineties (see for instance Diamond and Plattner 1993; and Vuylsteke 1995). Within such accounts, the problems of Latin America's 'contagious' effects on other young democracies were discussed, that is the transfer and domestic application of the Latin American authoritarian model on the other continents, above all in Central and Eastern Europe, but also in East Asia.

In the early nineties we witnessed the emergence of a 'global ideology of globalization', that is, the formation of a simplistic-journalistic theory of globalization directly extended to all continents. Globalization, in fact, in its simplistic form became a cheap substitute for a missing Grand Theory of the New World Order. The 'poverty of theory' reappeared in the dual form of 'End of History' and 'War of Civilizations' type of simplifications. The former expressed the tenets of an ascendant, triumphant liberalism; the latter, the extreme local-regional reactions as evidence of emerging fundamentalisms. The obvious contradiction between the two theories can be solved by saying that 'liberalism' wins everywhere except if ethnic-religious fundamentalisms prevent it. It meant, however, the victimization of losers in Western crisis mismanagement, without making the necessary distinctions between extreme fundamentalisms and legitimate national responses, along a continuum of positive to negative reactions. All the contradictions of this simplistic globalism, with its attendant black and white contrast, can be seen in its implementation in Yugoslavia. If the West makes mistakes in the promotion of democracy, the reference to nationalism serves as an excuse for the Western powers, by arguing that 'we tried but because of them we did not succeed – in fact, they did not deserve our assistance' (see Luif 1995: 265–72).

In this spirit, the global connection explaining the emergence of the New Authoritarianism can be described critically as follows:

In the heyday of *Pax Americana*, when American parochialism worked as well as universalism and the reigning social science idea was modernization theory, scholars and policymakers believed in the redemption and ultimate democratization of the heathens. Authoritarianism in East Asia was seen as an aberration, soon to be eclipsed by liberalism. Not so today.... What all this means is that authoritarianism in East Asia is an integral part of development strategy, useful not just for steadying societies in developmental flux, but for creating the class that carried all before the modern world – the entrepreneurial class – and in the shifting of resources to that class. [In Latin America, *mutatis mutandis*, the new authoritarianism has similar functions.] The new authoritarianism presupposes an older version. Latin Americans equate the old authoritarianism with the caudillo or oligarchic politics characteristic of economies that relied on the export of primary commodities, or with the populist regimes that wanted to foster a self-reliant, indigenous industrial base – the Peronistas being the classical example. The new authoritarianism, according to the Argentine political scientist, Guillermo O'Donnell, developed to provide stability in the transition from self-reliance to an export-led system, holding together the rapidly developing, outward-looking, capitalist economy, with transitional actors and technocrats as administrative linchpins. (Woo-Cumings 1994: 413–16)

The New Authoritarianism, mobilizing traditional values and other political devices such as paternalistic hierarchy, has been the development strategy of the modernizing elite in both Latin America and East Asia – as a kind of reform-dictatorship and a particular reaction to the Global Challenge. It is, indeed, some kind of structural accommodation to the global market politically. But at this point the Latin American and East Asian versions differ significantly, since the latter has had stronger continuity with the state-centric tradition, although both models support an export-led accommodation strategy to the global market and to the post-Cold War world system. The state-centric model was also a deeply entrenched tradition in Latin America, its (partial) rejection, however, might have been caused not only by the obvious American pressure of triumphant 'liberalism' (or, rather, neo-conservatism), but also by the failure of this model in the 1980s to deliver its promises and provide a sustainable development following the austerity programmes. These programmes meant a serious deterioration of wages and living standards which led to increasing violence, a breakdown of the social contract and finally, an erosion of democratic institutions and their legitimacy. O'Donnell has described this new variety of the repression as 'bureaucratic authoritarianism', a scheme under which the countries remain 'nominally democratic' whilst allowing for conditions conducive to a certain kind of 'presidential authoritarianism' or delegative democracy.[2]

The New Authoritarianism of the Latin American type performs magically: it solves the contradiction of how to be anti-statist while preserving some features of the state-centred posture, and how to be democratic while resisting democracy, in a form of presidential authoritarianism. We certainly see parallel efforts in Eastern Europe proper, but there are some similarities with the ECE countries as well – all this was discussed several times in the early nineties. First, Adam Przeworski raised the issue of 'The East Becomes the South?', at the American Political Science Association Meeting in September 1990, then subsequently in his book, *Democracy and the Market* (1991). Przeworski states in the conclusion of his book that the reform strategies of 'East European' countries will erode popular support. Accordingly, 'in the face of political reactions, governments are likely to vacillate between the technocratic political style inherent in market-oriented reforms and the participatory style required to maintain consensus. (. . .) Ultimately, the vacillations of financially bankrupt governments become politically destabilizing. Authoritarian temptations are thus inevitable'. Although the roads to democracy and prosperity are not closed, such accomplishments are exceptionally rare. The geographical closeness to Western Europe, Przeworski argues, does not matter much for 'Eastern Europe', since 'The bare facts are that Eastern European countries are embracing capitalism and they are poor. These are conditions East Europeans share with masses of people all over the world who also dream of prosperity and democracy. Hence, all one can expect is that they too will confront the all too normal problems of economics, the politics, and the culture of poor capitalism. The East has become the South' (1991: 189, 191).

In this debate the most valuable contribution in the early nineties was provided by the participants of the symposium entitled 'Is Latin America the Future of Eastern Europe?' These authors accept that there are some parallels between the two regions but do not share either the pessimistic conclusion or the regionally undifferentiated approach of Przeworski, lumping the whole of 'Eastern Europe' together as doomed to failure. As David Ost notes, 'Paradoxically, then, what pushes Eastern Europe away from democracy and toward populist authoritarianism is precisely the neoliberal program that Przeworski and other transition theorists, thinking of Latin America, see as the foundation of democracy. This program fosters authoritarianism because it tells the majority of people, and particularly workers, that post-communism entails decades of hardship ... Such arguments drive workers, particularly those in the still-dominant state sector to authoritarian demagogues' (Ost in Croan 1992: 50).

While Ost sees the main danger which threatens the young East European democracies in elite moves to demobilize the masses politically and marginalize them socially, Lawrence Graham points out that the entire model of comparing Latin America with 'Eastern Europe' is mistaken and that the 'no market – no democracy' model is incorrectly extended to East Central Europe: 'The unifying feature is that before the movement into extended periods of authoritarianism, some societies had a long history of replicating institutional models that grew out of West European experience. It is on this point that you must separate the experience of East Central Europe – Poland, Czechoslovakia, Hungary – from that of Southeastern Europe, just as you must in Latin America differentiate between the Southern Cone countries and the Andean republics. In both regional settings, the first group of states had considerable prior experience with markets before the period of moving into extended state domination of the economic system'. The same contrast has appeared, according to Graham, between the two European and Latin American regions at the political level, but the ECE countries have a much stronger democratic tradition than even the

Southern Cone countries: 'The Southern Cone countries have historically proven to be unable to resolve the question of establishing effective
civilian oversight authority, and this has always made these regimes
tentative... If we move to the Central European context, it is striking
the way in which that issue of civilian oversight authority over military
and security forces was also resolved quickly and definitively' (Graham
in Croan 1992: 52, 53). In this context, it is instructive to note that the
same difference can be observed between the above mentioned four
regions with respect to their political culture. Thus, both continents
have a mixed tradition of democracy and dictatorship but the authoritarian tradition is much deeper and more marked in Latin America (and
Eastern Europe) than the ECE region (see Messner and Meyer-Stamer
1992; Mansilla 1995).

It becomes clear, first, that the 'no market-no democracy' dualistic
model as an undifferentiated view, applied in both Latin America and
'Eastern Europe', is oversimplified for both continents. Second, that
these continents have some very distinct regions and among them in
Europe, the ECE region is particularly close to Southern Europe, with its
legacies in both marketization and democratization. Still, this simplified dualistic model of two simultaneous transitions has become fashionable – as Eric Hershberg has observed. Thus, even Philippe Schmitter
presented it at the International Political Science Association meeting
in Buenos Aires in 1991, as Hershberg quotes him, in the following
terms: 'as the democratic regimes in Eastern Europe try to consolidate,
they will not only have to develop legitimate economic structures as
well. The two transitions are happening at once... in fact, these economic systems will be created together with the political system. And
that puts a much greater burden... on many of East European countries'. This theoretical model reflecting the initial period of democratic
transition, however, is misleading at least in the ECE case, since – as
Hershberg again suggests – the difference between the South European
and ECE countries is not that big in the terms of their domestic developments. The real socio-economic difference in their transitions lies
much more in external factors and in linkage politics. The 'most
favoured nation' situation was quite clear in the case of Spain, since
'when Spain was accepted into the EC, there were substantial transfers
of resources to Spain, both in the form of Community funds sent to
help cushion the cost of adjustment, and in the form of massive
amounts of foreign investment going to Spain' (Hershberg in Croan
1992: 55). In his closing words at the symposium, Melvin Croan himself emphasized that in the ECE countries, actually, despite of all the

dangers, the two processes can not only weaken but also reinforce each other because: 'Those that "make it" in a market society actually help the cause of democratization' (Croan 1992: 56). Consequently, there is a chance that, at least, 'East' as East Central Europe will not become the 'South' (see more recently Weyland 1995).[3]

The Latin American, East Asian and 'East' European comparisons in their simplified ways became unfashionable by the mid-'90s, since it turned out that all the three continents had their distinct and contradictory responses to global democratization, but these dual reactions were region-specific and not the Latin-Americanization of the new democracies. By the mid-'90s, it became evident that 'Eastern' Europe, in any meaningful sense, did not exist. It is but a misnomer based on an early postwar political entity, the Soviet-ruled Europe. But after the collapse of the Soviet empire the internal differentiation immediately re-emerged between the ECE, the Balkan and the East European regions. The ECE region has always been closest to the West, hence, for the ECE countries the inter-regional comparision between Western and Central Europe has always been the most important issue. This is a point of departure for all theoretical debates, even more so currently, when European integration is high on the agenda for the ECE countries.

We can see on all continents the functional equivalents of global reaction, that is the same reactions to the various dimensions of globalization but in different ways. The problem is common for all regions and continents, since masses react angrily to increasing unemployment and other austerity measures, whether they lead to the 'suspension', reduction or breakdown of democracy, that is to elite moves as a 'reform-dictatorship', or democracy can be maintained in an improved way despite all anti-political movements of 'structural losers':

(i) Globalization of economies as loss of jobs, with collapse of some industries producing structural unemployment for a rather high percentage of the population of blue collar workers producing an 'anti-political' movement of the newly emerging parties of the extreme right (see Gerlich 1995).

(ii) Globalization of communication as a cultural shock, leading to attempts at the re-formation and re-assertion of national or ethnic-religious self-identity, even in its extreme forms of fundamentalisms – a clear adverse reaction to the demonstrative effect of Western consumption societies (see Featherstone 1991).

(iii) Globalization of world institutions as their activisation in crisis management reflected in the successes and failures of UN and/or

NATO missions or those of the global monetary institutions, and leading to the demonisation of the IMF and other global actors (Urquhart and Childers 1996).

(iv) Globalization of democratizations as both positive and negative responses, i.e. promotions of democracy or Reverse Waves (in Huntington's term), Authoritarian Renewals or facade democracies.[4]

The European Reaction: Systemic Change in the 'East' and West

At a first glance, the systemic change in East and West due to global transformations has met with the same political dissatisfaction in both East and West. As Peter Gerlich observes, 'Surveys show surprisingly similar dissatisfaction trends both in the old democracies of the West as well as in the new reforming democracies of the East and Central Europe'. It is easily understandable in the East, 'but in the old democracies? Is there a factual basis for the increasing disaffections? Has the Western system not prevailed and clearly won the Cold War?'. He goes on arguing that 'It is my contention that common underlying aspects may be in operation both in Eastern as well as in Western democracies. Therefore similar explanations as well as similar recommendations might be appropriate. The crisis of democratic politics, or to be more specific, of democratic party politics, may be considered part of a general crisis, a consequence of general systemic changes' (Gerlich 1995: 19–20, 23).

The lives of people in both East and West have changed beyond recognition in the New World Order. But the structure of politics, and its chief actors, has remained the same in the West. Accordingly, Western systemic change appears mostly in anti-political feelings. That is what Habermas emphasizes with his notion of *Politikverdrossenheit*. He also refers to the democratic deficit at the EU level which, because of the 'Maastricht Monster', has overdone even the sins of the national political classes (Habermas 1993). The same feeling of impotence in the face of overwhelming external forces has emerged in East Central European countries – 'forced democracies' because of their high transition costs and benign neglect by the EU, that is their fateful dependence on the ambiguous and vague decisions of the EU (see Ágh 1995). EU integration has also reached a critical turning point in the West paralleling the collapse of the bipolar world. The relatively homogeneous European market has drastically changed not only the political but also the policy dimensions of nation-states in the West and markedly underscored their systemic change (see Schmidt 1995). EU enlargement and deepening has merely compounded the problems (Merkel 1995).

We can conclude here, without embarking on a detailed analysis of Western transformations, that systemic change has not happened only to Central and Eastern Europe, it has occurred also in the West, although the depth and forms of the changes are different. The Cold War (or Old World Order) polarized the domestic political systems on both sides at the global level. With the collapse of the bipolar world in the Post-Cold War period (or New World Order), the global transformations have fundamentally concerned both East and West. This Western systemic change is based both on a deepening of the already existing tendencies (crisis of party systems and democratic deficit in the EU) and on the appearance of new features, connected with the 'Eastern' systemic change from the problems of enlargements to the harmful effects of migration and international crime.

The impact of global changes in Central and Eastern Europe, arriving earlier and more drastically, will transform also the West – first of all the EU – slowly and indirectly. The West with its consolidated democracies has to reconsider the problem of democratization for its internal developments. Thus, before beginning an analysis of the ECE region, we can make some general comments on global democratization, including the West European transformations:

1. Democracy is possible and can be consolidated in the long run if it can offer a positive-sum-game in the economy. In the democratic political bargaining process everybody wins through compromises, but the basic principles or values of democracy, competition and participation presuppose an economic foundation and/or solution, in which mass demands, as first articulated through mass participation and then formulated by elite competition, can lead to solid economic results. If the economy is in crisis or submerged in a process of deep transformation, participation and/or competition has to be restricted to some extent even in consolidated democracies. This necessarily unleashes the claim for redemocratization or further democratization. This was the case earlier with the 'new politics', and it is so currently with the democratic deficit in the advanced Western countries.

The precondition of eventual economic consolidation is, however, much more important for the survival of the young democracies. If a given country is not sufficiently sound economically, then mass demands have to be oppressed and elite competition restricted in an 'authoritarian' way. Thus, the authoritarian temptation is there in all democracies, but above all it threatens the life of those young and economically weak, to the extent that they have strong authoritarian traditions. An authoritarian-faced democracy appears also in the form of reform-dictatorship, that is in the authoritarian formation of a globally competitive market economy.

2. The domestic democratic order is more and more a function of the world system and is essentially influenced by regional-continental environmental factors. Democratic maturity is increasingly demonstrated by the fact that a particular country cannot resist but reacts quickly and positively to all favourable changes in its environment, which appear in the ideal case as a conscious promotion of democracy. One can see this in the case of the consolidated democracies, in which the contagious effect of applying the consociational political devices of their partners for their own minorities has increased the level of democracy. Democracy is not a *status quo* situation even in the oldest democracies of the world, but it can only exist in a process of permanent democratization. In this process new and ever newer forms come to the surface as reactions to global changes, for example as an increased control of the executive by the constitutionalism or application of some multicultural-multiethnic devices in a more consensual democracy, all in all, by moves farther away from a ' majoritarian democracy'.

Democratization has also become an international political learning process, with global standards upheld by international organizations and protected by global public opinion. The 'snowball effect' in 1989 in the Central European and Balkan countries showed not only the alien, forced character of the state socialist system for these regions, but also the democratic potential of the ECE region and to a lesser extent, that of the Balkan region. The ECE – and in some ways also the Balkan – countries reacted to the collapse of the bipolar world rather quickly and radically with their domestic transformations, unlike Latin American countries, which have reacted to global – or Latin American regional – changes only slowly and belatedly.

3. Most democratization theories overstress the negative effects of parallel transformations in the economy, society and politics. As seen above, some authors even generalize these into a theory of 'simultaneity' between democracy and market, drawing a fateful conclusion about the necessary failure of this simultaneous exercise. In fact, in those countries having a democratic capacity, as in the ECE countries, these *vicious* circles are only transitory, and the two or three processes

reinforce each other positively in the long run, although the danger of breakdown is there in those countries with less of a democratic capacity, as in Latin America and Eastern Europe. Some positive feedbacks, as experience already shows in ECE, have begun to operate from the very beginning and after some years have turned into a *virtuous* circle, since there is an inherent structural similarity between democratization and marketization, and finally the ongoing processes support each other in both the emerging socio-political institutions and in the quickly changing cognitive structures. For example, the privatization processes create more political freedom and institutional autonomy for social actors, and democratization promotes socio-economic transformations by giving new opportunities for groups and invididuals to act. This historical experience of the mutual reinforcement of the socio-economic and political processes has been very clear in the advanced democracies; in fact, it has always given them the chance to redemocratize, but it has been thought to be only their privilege. Any new theory of democracy definitely has to include this principle of the inherent structural similarity of all domestic transformations and the resulting potential for the consolidation of democracy.[5]

Seemingly, global democratization has taken a big step ahead as a Third Wave. The number of formally democratic states in the world rose from 25 per cent in 1973 to 45 per cent in 1990, while by 1993, 126 (68 per cent) of the 181 states of the world were democratic or were in the process of becoming democratic (see the 'Introduction' by Pridham in Pridham 1995: xii–xiii). It is true that some other generalisations, based on a stronger definition of democracy, produce much lower figures for both the number of democratic states and the size of populations living in these states (see Gaubatz 1996: 140). Although we can discern a large variety of transformations from the real democracies to the fake ones, even if we take the necessary setbacks and reverse waves into account, democracy has still become a global phenomenon. This fact in itself has led to a systemic change in the West, in that it is no longer alone with its democratic systems, but increasingly has similar partners who are becoming actors in global politics. With this, however, differences between procedural and substantive forms of democracy, and regional and continental varieties of democracy, have come to the fore. Competition among these varieties will obviously attract future political thinking but the confrontation between democratic and authoritarian systems still continues to present a more serious problem.

The ECE Reaction: From Vicious to Virtuous Circle

As a result of globalization, in the late '80s the whole of 'Eastern Europe' became a 'disaster area', mostly hit by globalization from among all regions. It was developed enough to get involved in all globalization processes but it was not developed enough to produce a successful and competitive form of structural accommodation to these global changes. In fact, it was globalization in general and its successive stages in particular that brought down the state socialist systems in the 'East'. First, the globalization of economies was fatal for their closed, autarchic economies in the '70s just when they had to open up their economies for further development but they could not make a structural adjustment to the globalization of world economy. Second, the same happened to them in the '80s with the globalization of communications opening up their closed ideological systems and confronting them drastically with the demonstrative effects of a Western way of life. Third, in the '70s and '80s global institutions and international public opinion imposed general criteria of human rights and 'proper' state behaviour upon them which clearly and radically delegitimized their political system before their own populations. It was above all the so-called Helsinki process which put pressure upon the state socialist countries to accept and apply the rules of 'decent' conduct to all European states. Finally, globalization of democratization has come in the '90s as a cumulative result of the former three processes.

These global processes determined not only the collapse of state socialism itself but also those particular forms through which it occured. There were three special factors of this snowball effect in the ECE countries: (1) these countries are small and geographically close both to each other and to Western Europe; (2) they had a similar political system and ideology which was delegitimized in a parallel process and at the same time for all these countries; (3) the West confronted these regimes as a unit, the 'Eastern Bloc', so they all fell together with the fatal weakening of the Soviet Union's external empire. One has to underline that this process of final collapse did not proceed according to a *domino* effect, with countries falling after each other mechanically and in the same way, but according to a cumulative or *snowball* effect through which successive ECE countries fell after each other ever more easily, from Poland to Czechoslovakia, reaching Romania and Albania as well. In fact, by late 1996 a second round of the snowball effect began from Romania which had already reached Serbia, and would involve Albania, Croatia and Bulgaria as well. In general, the demonstrative effect of the transformation in the other countries of the regions concerned still plays a very important role in the democratizations of the ECE and Balkan countries.

The collapse of the former system has exposed the ECE countries even more to the effects of globalization. Consequently, the main theoretical question has been formulated in political science in the following terms: has 'liberalization' (that is the global conditions and institutions) determined the development of these countries or has their historical legacy (that is the local 'inertia' of institutions and cultural patterns – see Crawford and Lijphart 1997). We can state that in the 'confluence' of these two determining factors, globalization takes more and more of an upper hand, but its effect is not 'automatic' as we can see by the simple fact that the reactions in the ECE, Balkan and EE regions are quite different. The ECE region has always had a tradition of following and 'domesticating' the major Western transformations, whilst the Balkan and EE regions have always tended to refuse them as 'alien' factors. In all three regions, however, we observe similar, if differently expressed, developments (see Ágh 1997).

The abrupt changes in the late '80s of course, did not produce 'full' democracies immediately in 'Eastern Europe', but later on a large choice of the regional and sub-regional varieties of immature democracies had taken shape. That is, although the distinction among them is vitally important, still even the most advanced forms in Poland, the Czech Republic, Hungary and Slovenia had some built-in contradictions. In ECE the first period can be characterized as democracy distorted by national-conservatism, as a contrast to the Balkan and EE countries with their national-communism. Both can be treated under the title of Authoritarian Renewal (or Return). Nevertheless, they remain different. In ECE, this was a return to the interwar period to some extent but in the Balkan and EE countries, it was more of a continuity with the 'communist regime' (combined with the traditional nationalism), than a 'return' to some mixed democratic traditions. After some years, the ECE countries have successfully overcome this 'rightist-traditionalist' distortion, but the Balkan and EE countries would need much more time to overturn their rediscovered authoritarian traditions. Consequently, in 'Eastern Europe' we can study the dual effect of global democratization: the global pressure may be favourable towards democratization or may push back to a reverse wave if the domestic preconditions for democratization are not given. Actually, in the ECE case, the countries were ready for democratization much earlier in this century, but the democratization process was interrupted several times because of the unfavourable external preconditions or by direct military interventions (for instance in 1956 in Hungary).

In the advanced democracies, Schmitter and Karl have described four kinds of democracies: the corporative, the consociational, 'elitist' and electoralist democracies (Schmitter and Karl 1992: 67–8). In my understanding, in the next stage of their development, the ECE countries will develop towards a model of corporatist democracy with some consociational features, although it may only be a transitional stage lasting some decades, as in the case of Austria. A careful analysis of all ECE states suggests this assumption (see Ágh and Ilonszki 1996), although even in ECE other types of democracy have appeared as secondary models. Actually, the ECE, Balkan and East European states represent a particular mixture of the four types, with an immature combination of corporative and consociational democracies in ECE, and with an unbalanced combination of elitist and electoralist types in the Balkans and Eastern Europe.

The types of mature democracies may be more or less equally democratic, but the different modes of transition to democracy, for sure, are not. Schmitter and others point out that violent transitions are less likely to produce a stable and genuine democracy than negotiated transitions. Indeed, it is obvious that there has been a marked dividing line between the peaceful ECE transitions and the violent EE ones. Thus the violence itself reflects the immature character of the political actors and their interactions. It shows that the preconditions for democracy are missing because of the lack of strong parliamentary and party traditions in the EE countries.

Actually, there have been four forms of political systems as distorted or immature democracies and as special responses to the pressure of global democratization in the ECE, Balkan and EE regions: (i) *Formalist* democracies (inclusive hegemonies in Dahl's terminology, see 1971: 7) in which there is no actual counter-elite in the form of an organized and institutionalized opposition; (ii) *Elitist* democracies (competitive oligarchies in Dahl's terminology, see 1971: 7) in which there are some competitive elites, but these small groups share the entire power among themselves; (iii) *Partyist* democracies (or *partitocrazia* in Italian) in which parties are the only political actors and they try to exclude all other social and political actors and agencies (organized interests) from political life; (iv) *Tyrannical majorities* as distortions of the majoritarian-type democracy in the young democracies where random (parliamentary) majorities, referring to their electoral legitimation, behave like 'tyrants'.

In my typology of distorted or immature democracies, the formalist and tyrannical types do more harm to the principle of competition, while the elitist and partyist types do more damage to participation. One can indicate with these terms that they are hybrid regimes, somewhat closer to the real democracies. Historically all four types of the typology have existed during the recent emergence of democracy and the general trend has been a political development from the formalist to the partyist democracy through the elitist one. Certainly, the formalist democracies represent, so to say, the zero-level democracy and the tyrannical majorities carry the built-in tendency of the 'majoritarian' systems which become distorted in the absence of systemic checks and balances. This tendency can easily come to the surface in young democracies. Elitist democracies are more characteristic for Latin America. There, one finds presidential systems where parliaments and parties do not play decisive roles. The partyist distortions are more common in the European countries where political life has been organized along the lines of parliaments and parliamentary parties. So we could add to the four-fold schema developed above, their counterparts in parliaments and parties (say, submissive or subdued parliaments; or moderate pluralism, polarized pluralism and hegemonic parties). Nevertheless, let us state here only briefly that in my opinion in ECE and the Balkans, parliamentarism offers a better chance for democratization than presidentialism.

In the Central and East European regions we have to distinguish above all between formalist democracies (that is the facade- or quasi-democracies in EE with their pseudo-participation and pseudo-competition) and the genuine but immature democracies in ECE, usually in the partyist form. It is here that the basic preconditions for real participation and competition have been met, but one or both basic values have been damaged partially. The elements of all four types can be detected (with their combinations restricting participation and competition to a considerable degree) in all ECE countries in different ways, so this typology offers us an opportunity to compare them in the interrelationships of their transitory political systems.

There are no formalist democracies in ECE, but in actual political terms in the Czech Republic until the 1996 elections there were some signs of a bureaucratic-authoritarian system with a paternalistic power concentration and without the real articulation of political alternatives. Poland is a partyist democracy but close to the elitist type, since the political oligarchies are strong and the parties as socio-political organizations are still relatively weak, and the political participation of the

population has been drastically decreased. Hungary – and, to a significant extent, Slovenia – can be described as the classical case of the partyist type, since the (parliamentary) parties emerged early, became strong
politically and successfully monopolized the whole political arena.
They fight against relatively strong organized interests, in a classical
case of overparliamentarization and overparticization. Slovakia and
Croatia have been rather close to the model of (changing) tyrannical
majorities with a national populist overtone. However, in the early '90s
this tendency came to the fore from time to time in the other three
countries as well. Yet the counter-forces and competing-balancing
power centres have been stronger in these latter countries.[6]

Conclusion

1996 was a clear turning-point in regional developments with an
increasing divergence among the ECE, Balkan and EE regions:

1. In the ECE region the recession has come to an end by the mid-'90s
and upward development began, first in the economics then in the
social sphere. In the mid-nineties, the 'U' shaped curve of return had
more or less reached the 'pre-war' (that is, the 1989) level in GDP in the
framework of the market economy and about 70 per cent of the GDP
had already been produced by the private economy. Unemployment
and inflation have decreased, and political systems are now apparently
stable, ready for consolidation. These countries (except for Slovakia) are
eligible for NATO and EU membership.

2. The Balkan countries still have unstable economies, with a stagna-
tion of economic growth, which remains about one-third lower than
the 1989 level, but with high inflation and unemployment. Their
facade democracies started to crumble in 1996 and political stabiliza-
tion is far down the road. Some of them are associate members of
the EU (Romania and Bulgaria), but their full membership can be
expected in the near future. Romania may be eligible for NATO membership.

3. The EE countries, the former Soviet Republics (except for the Baltic
states which must be dealt with separately), began a new downturn in
the mid-'90s, their economic situation has worsened even compared to
the Balkan countries as far as the unemployment, inflation and foreign debt are concerned. They have stabilized to some extent their fake
democracies – or 'delegative democracies'. Their experience is closer to a
reverse wave than to a real democratization process.[7]

The ECE – and the Balkan – countries are, in fact, small states, with even Poland sandwiched between the two powerful neighbours, Germany and Russia. Consequently, one has to consider, finally, the special situation of Central European small states within the globalization process. This time, dependence on external conditions has hinged not so much upon particular great powers, but on the global economic conditions as well as on international integration – above all, on the EU. Paralleling these external changes, some combination of consensual and corporatist constitutional devices has emerged in the domestic structures. These features suggest the following general conclusions:

1. There has been a regional homogenization in ECE as a response to the global challenge. This is parallel to the inter-regional differentiation concerning the Balkan and EE regions.

2. ECE regional co-operation around the mid-'90s has turned from a negative to a positive sum game, first of all in economic and trade co-operation, but slowly followed by the other fields, including political co-operation.

3. Inter-regional differentiation among the ECE, Balkan and EE regions has appeared very markedly in the different forms of 'Europeanization', that is, in various relationships to the process of Euro-Atlantic integration.

Prospects for the future can be indicated in the following tendencies:

1. The West and 'East' must learn how to live together with each other as partners of different kinds (reflecting clear regional differentiations), but within the same framework of the Post-Cold War European Architecture.

2. Painfully and belatedly, the ECE countries have basically accomplished their own global accommodation process and a new period of relative economic and social prosperity can be expected in this region.

3. The young ECE democracies have more or less overcome the difficulties and distortions of the initial period, they have reached an early consolidation. They will soon become more and more similar to the Western democracies within the EU, while preserving their regional character, as the Mediterranean (Spain and Portugal) or Nordic (Finland and Sweden) countries have kept their regional specificities within the EU (see LeDuc et al., 1996).

Notes

1. This paper does not deal with globalization in general, just with its consequences for the ECE region, in an interregional comparison and in a European context. My major statement is that systemic change in a global world cannot be restricted to the 'East', it must be extended to the West as well.
2. O'Donnell describes delegative democracy in the following way: 'With the term "delegative" I point out to a conception and practice of executive authority as having been electorally delegated the right to do whatever seems to fit for the country. I also argue that delegative democracies are inherently hostile to the patterns of representation normal in established democracies (...) Some authors tend to confuse delegative democracy with populism: both, of course share various important features. But, in Latin America at least, the latter entailed a broadening (even if vertically controlled) of popular political participation and organization and coexisted with periods of dynamic expansion of the domestic economy. Instead, delegative democracy typically attempts to depoliticize the population, except for brief moments in which it demands its plebiscitary support and presently coexists with periods of severe economic crisis' (O'Donnell 1993: 167).
3. Socio-economic modernization has the same effect, i.e. it improves both democratization and marketization. Paul Lewis (1995: 393), develops this idea by saying that 'Democratization should, therefore, increase the level of exposure of the East European economies to leading technological processes and facilitate their integration with the mechanisms of the world economy'.
4. The outlines of the 'global policy emerged already in the eighties' (see Soroos 1986). Actually, Samuel Huntington has initiated the new global political paradigm in both ways, that is by both the *Third Wave and Clash of Civilisations* (see Huntington 1991 and 1996a).
5. The simultaneity theories were exposed in the European debates mostly by Claus Offe (see e.g. Offe 1991) and were very fashionable in the early nineties, but the 'no market – no democracy' model has obviously failed in ECE.
6. I have analyzed these forms of global political adjustment in great detail in my book (Ágh 1998).
7. See the theory of delegative democracy in O'Donnell (1994) and its application to Russia in Brie (1996).

Bibliography

Ágh, A. (1995) 'The Paradoxes of Transition: The External and Internal Overload of the Transition Process', in Cox T., and A. Furlong (eds), *Hungary: The Politics of Transition*, London: Frank Cass.

Ágh, A. (1997) 'Small Central European States Facing an Active Future: A Case of Linkage Politics', *Budapest Papers on Democratic Transition*, No. 200.

Ágh, A. (1998) *The Politics of Central Europe*, London: Sage.

Ágh, A. and G. Ilonszki (eds) (1996) *Parliaments and Organised Interests in Central Europe: The Second Steps*, Budapest: Hungarian Centre for Democracy Studies.

Bideleux, R. (1996) 'Bringing the East back in', in Bideleux R., and R. Taylor (eds), *European Integration and Disintegration: East and West*, London and New York: Routledge.

Brie, M. (1996) 'Russland: Das Entstehen einer delegierten Demokratie', in W. Merkel, E. Sandschneider and D. Segret (eds), *Systemwechsel 2*, Opladen: Leske + Budrich.

Crawford, B. and A. Lijphart (eds) (1997) *Liberalization and Leninist Legacies: Comparative Perspectives on Democratic Transition*, Berkeley, CA: University of California Press.

Crawford and Lijphart, (1997).

Croan, M. (organized and introduced) (1992) 'Is Latin America the Future of Eastern Europe? A Symposium', *Problems of Communism*, May-June 1992 (with the participation of Thomas Skidmore, David Ost, Lawrence Graham and Eric Hershberg).

Dahl, R. (1971). *Polyarchy: Participation and Opposition*, New Haven and London: Yale University Press.

Diamond, L. and M. Plattner (eds) (1993) *The Global Resurgence of Democracy*, Baltimore and London: The Johns Hopkins University Press.

Featherstone, M. (ed.) (1991) *Global Culture: Nationalism, globalization and modernity*, London: Sage.

Gaubatz, K. T. (1996) 'Kant, Democracy, and History', *Journal of Democracy*, 7 (4), October 1996.

Gerlich, P. (1995) 'Political dissatisfaction in the new Europe', in P. Gerlich and K. Glass (eds), *Der schwierige Selbstfindungsprozess*, Wien and Torun: Österreichische Gesellschaft für Mitteleuropäische Studien.

Habermas, J. (1993) *Vergangenheit als Zukunft*, Frankfurt: Piper.

Hann, C. (1995) 'Subverting Strong States: The Dialectics of Social Engineering in Hungary and Turkey', *Daedalus*, 124 (2), Spring 1995.

Huntington, S. (1991) *The Third Wave: Democratization in the Late Twentieth Century*, Norman and London: University of Oklahoma Press.

Huntington, S. (1996a) *The Clash of Civilisations and the Remaking of World Order*, New York: Simon and Schuster.

Huntington, S. (1996b) 'Democracy for the Long Haul', *Journal of Democracy*, 7 (2).

LeDuc, L., R. Niemi and P. Noris (eds) (1996) *Comparing Democracies*, London: Sage.

Lewis, P. (1995) 'Democratization in Eastern Europe', in Pridham (1995).

Luif, P. (1995) *On the Road to Brussels: The Political Dimension of Austria's, Findland's and Sweden's Accession to the European Union*, Vienna: Braumüller.

Mansilla, H. C. F. (1995) 'Partielle Modernisierung und politische Kultur des Authoritarismus in der Peripherie', *International Politics and Society*, (FES), No. 1, January 1995.

Merkel, W. (1995) 'Deepening or Widening? The Limits of European Integration', in M. Szabó (ed.), *The Challenge of Europeanization in the Region: East Central Europe*, Budapest: Hungarian Political Science Association.

Messner, D. and J. Meyer-Stamer (1992) 'Latinamerikanische Schwellenländer: Vorbild für Osteuropa?', *FES Vierteljahre Berichte*, September 1992.

Millard, F. (1996) 'Poland's "return to Europe", 1989–94', in Bideleux R. and R. Taylor (eds), *European Integration and Disintegration: East and West*, London and New York: Routledge.

O'Donnell, G. (1993) 'On the State, Democratization and Some Conceptual Problems: A Latin American View with Glances at Some Postcommunist Countries', *World Development*, 21 (8).

O'Donnell, G. (1994) 'Delegative Democracy', *Journal of Democracy*, 5 (1), January 1994.

Offe, C. (1991) 'Capitalism by Democratic Design? Democratic Theory Facing the Triple Transition in East Central Europe', *Social Research*, 58 (4).

Power, G. (1997) 'Globalization and its Discontents', *Development, Globalization: Opening up spaces for civiv engagement*, 40 (2), June 1997.

Pridham, G. (ed.) (1995) *Transitions to Democracy: Comparative Perspectives from Southern Europe, Latin America and Eastern Europe*, Aldershot: Dartmouth.

Przeworski, A. (1991) *Democracy and the Market: Political and Economic Reforms in Eastern Europe and Latin America*, Cambridge: Cambridge University Press.

Schmidt, V. (1995) 'The New World Order, Incorporated: The Rise of Business and the Decline of the Nation-State', *Daedalus*, 124 (2), Spring 1995.

Schmitter, P. and T. Karl (1992) 'The Types of Democracy Emerging in Southern and Eastern Europe and South and Central America', in Volten P. (ed.), *Bound to Change: Consolidating Democracy in East Central Europe*, New York and Prague: Institute for EastWest Studies, distributed by the Westview Press.

Soroos, M. (1986) *Beyond Sovereignty: The Challenge of Global Policy*, Columbia: University of South Carolina Press.

Urquhart, B. and E. Childers (1996) *A World in Need of Leadership: Tomorrow's United Nations*, Uppsala: Dag Hammarskjöld Foundation.

Vuylsteke, R. (1995), 'Third Wave Democracies: Building Democratic Staying Power', *Free China Review*, 45 (11), November 1995.

Waterman, P. (1996) 'Beyond Globalism and Developmentalism: Other Voices in World Politics', *Development and Change*, 27 (1).

Weyland, K. (1995) 'Latin America's Four Political Models', *Journal of Democracy*, 6 (4), October 1995.

Woo-Cumings, M. (1994) 'The 'New Authoritarianism" in East Asia', *Current History*, December 1994.

7
In But Not Of the World? Japan, Globalization and the 'End of History'

John Clammer

Jean Baudrillard has characterized contemporary Japan as 'a satellite of the planet earth' (Baudrillard 1988: 79), as a society and culture both nowhere in relation to the real power centres and points of influence in the modern world system, but yet everywhere in terms of its artifacts and its economic presence. This image of Japan neatly encapsulates the primary tension that has driven Japan forward like the string of a tightly drawn bow from the 1940s until the present. The engine of history for Japan since the Meiji Restoration is not reducible to some internal economic dynamic, but also resides in the problem of the state's and society's relationships with the world. Since the Pacific War, itself seen at the time and justified as a reaction and opposition to Western colonialism in Asia and as a result of Japan's exclusion from the charmed circle of globally significant polities, the 'world' has been a problematic category for Japan. Through defeat (and the American use of the 'A' Bomb), postwar poverty, the 1960s policy of the 'Doubling of National Income', to today's economic dominance, Japan has struggled with its role in the international systems of economic, political and cultural influence which shape global society. Indeed the onset of the processes of globalization has posed this question again in fresh terms, to which answers are being given in distinctively Japanese terms. This fact alone makes the Japanese case of substantial theoretical and comparative interest.

A discussion of Japan's relationship to globalization must pass through the medium of an examination of the ways in which the idea of modernity has been treated. This will be the key motif of this chapter. At the outbreak of the Pacific War, Japan's role in the world (or at least in East Asia) was defined by a group of prominent scholars meeting in

Kyoto to outline an intellectual justification for the escalating conflict as *kindai no chokoku* – 'overcoming the modern' – in which an end to Western hegemony was to be achieved not only by the defeat of the allied powers and their replacement by a Japanese sphere of economic and political influence, but by the radical rejection of the very model on which the West had built its domination of the world – an ideology of universalism, progress and secularism. The new (Japan centred) age to be ushered in by the successful termination of the war was to be based on the rejection of modernity and all that it stood for and its replacement by a world view of fundamentally different form. The break with the West was consequently (or primarily) to be an epistemological one, and not merely a political and economic one. It was to be achieved first by military means, and subsequently by the force of ideas, and the spread of an alternative and hitherto subordinate culture (Matsumoto 1979; Hiromatsu 1989).

The failure, through defeat, to realize the means to achieve this utopian vision, however, did not mean the end of the idea. It did not even really go underground as many postwar events. Among these were the highly succesful attempt to raise the national income and to take on the rest of the world economically through the superior effects of *yamato daishi* - the 'Japanese spirit'; the bitter struggles by the Left, many students and citizen's groups against the renewal of the US–Japan Security Treaty which had allowed Japan to prosper economically under the American nuclear umbrella while removing full autonomy in foreign policy; the current (late 1990s) opposition to the renewal of the leases on land occupied by the US military in Okinawa, to take three prominent examples. These all reflect in various ways the Japanese rejection of the model offered by the West for postwar reconstruction of the world (on postwar Japanese economic and political history see Gordon 1993) while participating in it for what many, within and without Japan, see as selfish economic reasons. This ambiguous relationship to the rest of the world appeared vividly in recent years in Japan's bid for a place on the UN Security Council despite the country's very low profile and level of activity in organization, the serious foot-dragging over agreement to participate in UN peacekeeping activities in Cambodia and the less than active enthusiasm for joining George Bush's crusade against Iraq in the Gulf War.

At the national level, the sense of Japan's separation from the rest of the world when it comes to common international responsibilities is strong. It has even been said that Japan has no foreign policy, not with the immediate postwar meaning that it was 'made by the Americans', but in the more radical form of possessing a political machine that does not understand, and certainly does not like, the outside world. This feeling of isolation is enhanced by two major internal cultural phenomena. One is a discourse of uniqueness and difference (and, by implication, of exclusion) that flourishes in Japan under the collective rubric of *nihonjinron* or 'theories of Japaneseness' and which is devoted to the proposition that Japanese culture, language, psyche and even physical make-up is different from that of foreigners, who thus face serious if not insuperable impediments to understanding Japan (for a thorough if polemical discussion of this position and some of its many manifestations see Dale 1995). Such discourse, occupying much media air time and yards of shelf space in bookstores, is no peripheral phenomenon, but emerges from deep within social strata which might be thought to be amongst the most informed about the outside world – teachers and businessmen as well as intellectuals (Yoshino 1992). The other is a rather interesting form of struggle for self-determination amongst many Japanese in which freedom is seen as the right to be different, not from each other, but from the restraints imposed by outside models. The result is a society in which generational differences are muted, in which to a great extent consumption has replaced political involvement and in which debates about human rights are muted or transposed into a discourse of the expectation of 'benevolence' from those 'superior' in the social hierarchy and in which geographical knowledge and concern tends to evaporate very rapidly with geographical distance from Japan. It is still cheaper to call the US than it is China, and cheaper to fly to Hawaii than to Hong Kong. Much of Asia, most of Latin America and almost all of Africa are *terra incognita* for most Japanese, including university students.

All this has had interesting results on internal cultural debates. It has fueled the deep political conservatism of the last forty years, deflecting the felt need for change from indigenous political institutions to the unwelcome (and opposed) pressures from the outside world to open markets, and even to eat more foreign rice (Ohnuki-Tierney 1991), to allow in more foreign workers and to moderate the negative impact of aid (Japan is now the world's biggest donor) and economic activities, especially on local ecologies, in areas such as Southeast Asia where the Japanese presence is large (Clammer 1993). It has largely trivialized what looked in the 1980s to be one of the most promising social trends towards kokusaika or 'internationalization' and turned it into little more than a fad for learning a little English, sprinkling advertisements with foreign words, consuming a small amount of foreign foods or other goods and enjoying travel abroad. Its effect on fundamental attitudes towards the world has been minimal (Mouer and Sugimoto 1986). Recent debates about the 'end of history' fueled by Francis Fukuyama (interestingly a Japanese American) and his triumphalist book signalling the victory of capitalism and the end of ideology (again!) have been closely followed in Japan (Fukuyama's book was rapidly translated into Japanese and was a best seller in the months after its publication). This was reinforced as Fukuyama subsequently praised Japanese capitalism for its 'civility' (Fukuyama 1992). However, if Fukuyama sees the 'end of history' in the perhaps somewhat prematurely announced victory of capitalism, the Japanese see it slightly diferently: as the victory of *Japanese* capitalism, not primarily over communism, but over the competing alternative forms, especially the American one.

To understand these postwar developments and their contemporary incarnations, it is necessary not so much to poll the Japanese on what they mean by 'globalization', but rather to explore in a little more detail Japanese responses to modernity and to postmodernity and the nature of counter-Orientalist voices which are proposing a somewhat different reading of history from that proposed by the West. Japan's positioning of itself in relation to globalization is refracted through these debates. It takes place within an environment in which the assertion of a peculiarly Asian form of identity is once again possible, especially given Japan's much asserted pacifism and its self image as a source of cultural flows and economic influence through investment, trade and aid (but most certainly not of political domination). To pose these questions at all raises, as indeed they do in Japan, the question of the universality of Western social theory and conceptions of history. This provokes in a rather uncomfortable way the issue of whether such theory, especially as it now expresses itself in a sudden interest in globalization, might not actually be an attempt to establish intellectual hegemony in a form that reproduces classical Western concerns for universalism while actually suppressing the possibility of alternative visions of the world and forms of social knowledge from arising not only on the periphery, but even in the new centres of real global power.

Discourses of Modernity and Postmodernity

A surge of interest in postmodernity amongst Japanese intellectuals in the 1980s (e.g., Imada 1987) reopened in a very public fashion the problems of modernity, its preceeding and succeeding stages and of Japan's relationship to these concepts. They had, after all, arisen in the West and not out of native soil, however eagerly they were fallen upon by sociologists, media and advertising people and the horde of cultural commentators who fill magazines, newspapers and journals with daily updates on trends or *boomu* ('booms'). Books on the subject which one would hardly expect to have mass appeal became best-sellers, the most conspicuous example being Asada Akira's treatise on structuralism and post-structuralist thought *Kozo to Chikara* (Asada 1983) which sold in vast quantities. These debates reopened in fresh form the inevitable motif of modern Japanese history: how and by what routes did Japan become the only non-Western nation to achieve industrialization without, apparently, passing through the same trajectory as the Western industrialized nations and their particular form of state formation? This is an enigma that has exercised both historians of and within Japan, and has been a particularly acute problem for the large community of intellectual Marxists in the country. Indeed their varying positions on the issue of the periodization of history has been one of the key elements in determining the geography of their inevitable sects and factions both prewar, when debates about the nature of modernity and its universality began to be raised (Hoston 1986) and today. Engagement with the question of postmodernity began rapidly to suggest to many fertile Japanese imaginations the possibility that not only was Japan a postmodern society, but that it was also the only one yet to emerge.

This exciting hypothesis was suggested by two things: firstly the apparent existence in Japanese culture of all those elements which appear in the lists that postmodernists make when attempting to characterize their subject – elements such as the absence of metanarratives, the appearance of eclecticism and pastiche in contemporary popular culture and the decentred nature of the self and society; and secondly the fact that Japan had evidently made the transition from an agrarian, semi-feudal society to a highly urbanized industrial one with extraordinary speed and with remarkably little obvious social disruption, and certainly no riots, revolutions or major disturbances. Although this view was firmly opposed by some, including the most significant of postwar Japanese social theorists, Maruyama Masao (1985), who argued that Japan could not have achieved postmodernity since it had not in his view yet achieved modernity, in his view defined by the emergence of autonomous and responsible individuals, it became immensely popular not least because it suggested that Japan was in some sense *beyond* history, rather than merely in one of its universal stages. Postmodernity, in this argument, was seen not indeed as a *stage* (i.e., post something else, presumably modernity), but as an ontological condition, a state of being (Miyoshi and Harootunian 1989; Arnason and Sugimoto 1995; Fu and Heine 1995).

If the chief advantage for Japanese theoreticians of embracing postmodernism is that it places Japan outside of history, it has other effects too. If 'Modernity is a risk culture' as Anthony Giddens suggests (Giddens 1991: 3) then by transcending or 'overcoming' modernity, the risk of risk might be averted. And since much of what happens in Japanese foreign policy (e.g., reluctance to become involved in the Gulf War), in internal social arrangements (e.g., the pursuit of *Wa* or harmony and the corresponding minimalization of conflict) and even in psychic organization (the celebrated theory of *amae* or 'dependency' as the fundamental structure of Japanese psychological make-up) can be reasonably interpreted as the avoidance of risk, it makes sense that modernity, as the source of many of these risks, should indeed be actively avoided. Globalization, it hardly needs to be pointed out, is a risky business: chains of causality lengthen, formerly inviolate borders become porous, imponderables multiply. Furthermore as Giddens, and his mentor in these matters Ulrich Beck agree, a key ingredient of modernity is that it forces individuals to reflexively construct their own biographies. But yet, as Maruyama had argued a decade or more ago, Japan is actually characterized by low levels of individualization, indicated by low levels of divorce, relatively little social mobility, a rigid labour market and low income differentials. For Beck, the labour market is the engine of individualization, but in Japan that market is closely structured by cultural norms and the society as a whole correspondingly is one in which while 'liberty' is low, stability is high. Japan is consequently still far from Beck's understanding of Western individualization: 'Individualization in this sense means that each person's biography is removed from given determinations and placed in his or her own hands, open and dependent on decisions' (Beck 1994: 135). The 'democratization of techno-economic development' which Beck assumes defines the structural transition to modernity has certainly not yet taken place in Japan, partly because of the power of the corporate and national bureaucracies, but also because the conditions of selfhood antecedent to such a transition have not yet come about, or are simply culturally absent. Transition to an active sense of globalization is restricted not only by conservative political forces, but also by the mode of selfhood which itself rejects the demands of modernity. Whether such selves can be characterized as 'postmodern' is open to debate, but this point certainly does throw into relief the often subtle connections between the internal organization of a society and its relationship to the wider world system, which are by no means only mediated through economic and political structures.

The refusal to see postmodernity as an evolutionary stage, but rather as a state of being beyond that yet achieved by the West, however, has yet a further twist to it. It could of course turn out that the West, or some bits of it, *do* eventually achieve true postmodernity (rather than the fragmented bits of it, mainly expressed in culture, that are all that it has so far shown). While this creates the problem that after all postmodernity *was* a stage, it nevertheless provides Japan with the satisfaction of having got there first, and with that one step overcoming the historical humiliation of having been for a very long time an importer and adaptor of Western science, medicine and technology. It has not escaped the attention of some Japanese commentators that the enthusiasm of some foreign scholars to fit Japan into the category of the postmodern places the country in the danger of being assimilated after all into an alien category, by which the intellectual hegemony of the West and the extension of its Enlightenment project and its implicit universalism absorb Japan once again back into a common world history. This can only be avoided by being there first, by constructing a culturalist and (paradoxically for a society set against metanarratives) essentialist (ahistorical) view of Japan which argues for its permanent and ancient 'postmodernity', or by dropping the use of the term altogether as soon as foreigners begin to use it about Japan, something that has widely happened since the early 1990s.

This leaves certain strategic objectives and problems to be managed. Japan's own economic success in dominating the markets of Asia and penetrating deeply through trade, aid and investment into the heart of the global economy has brought with it some fairly obviously expected problems. These include demands that Japan's market be similarly opened to foreign competition, that its positively Byzantine distribution system be clarified and simplified to allow foreign goods to circulate, an increasing flow of foreign students, workers (legal and illegal) and tourists. Moreover, as ever larger numbers of Japanese travel and work abroad they discover alternative models of social organization and also how incredibly expensive goods are on the domestic market in Japan compared with those almost everywhere else abroad. Globalization is perceived as the integration of Japan, as a society increasingly dominated by consumption, into the world economy.

These trends are potentially extremely disruptive of the carefully orchestrated theme of difference and consequently require managing through a number of channels. The first of these is the very selective introduction of foreign foods, products and services, all of which are, if possible, assimilated to distinctively Japanese patterns of usage and meaning: the global is localized in other words (Clammer 1997). The second is the maintainance of a public rhetoric of 'internationalization' while ensuring that society does not reward the actual practice. For example attendance at a foreign rather than a Japanese university is often a barrier to employment rather than a positive factor; many company employees resist being posted abroad because they will be out of the inner political circles of their corporations while on distant stations; many UN agencies have less than their full quotas of Japanese, who refuse to seek such work (and those that they do have are significantly often women, already semi-marginalized in mainstream Japanese life). Furthermore children who have lived abroad and know a foreign language often will conceal the fact from school-mates to avoid teasing and even bullying. The third is the transposition of the *nihonjinron* into ever new keys. While the production of nativist literature continues, much of the insinuation of a unique Japanese identity has shifted to advertising and the popular media, where it is reproduced through images and symbolism as much as through text (see for instance Moeran 1995). The fourth is the invention of fresh variations on the theme of cultural nationalism orchestrated around developing world events as well as local ones: the aforementioned importation of foreign rice being one, and responses to the great Hanshin earthquake of 1995 being another when foreign advice and specialist rescue teams were refused until it was too late to actually help many of the victims. Cultural nationalism indeed in Japan is not something really separate from other forms of nationalism since Japanese nationalism *is*, as I have elsewhere argued (Clammer 1995) deeply cultural and is likely to continue to be so in many subtle ways.

The Decentring of Power and the Forms of Modernity

Debate about the nature of globalization from the perspective of Japan then is based on a small number of fundamental assumptions. The first is that the world itself is not unitary, but is given an illusory appearance of being so by the very coining of the term 'globalization' itself. In other words the term, as used by Western theorists such as Robertson (1992) is not descriptive, but both prescriptive and ideological. It often represents a moral vision (of how the world should be) and a universalist image of how it is structured. The second is that while there may be many modernities (Taiwan or Singapore for example might claim, and to some extent do through a rather different discourse of 'Asian values' and the refurbishment of Confucianism) to be found in the world, each one may achieve the *fruits* of the Western model in material and technological terms, while eschewing the *means* by which that model reached its goals.

Indeed a fundamental Japanese (and more generally East Asian) critique of the Western model and of the globalization implicit in it, is that while it has delivered the technological goods, it has conspicuously failed to deliver the social harmony to accompany it. Rising crime, family disorganization and a disintegration of values have been the bedfellows of economic progress in the Western capitalist societies. The Japanese model however is supposed to deliver development without alienation by retaining the social nexus as the primary value, a value reinforced rather than undermined by practices within work, education and mechanisms of justice and social control.

The third relates to the nature of power. If the world itself is decentred and with multiple locations of power, so is Japanese society, and those analysts who have sought for the centre of Japan in one place or institution while discounting the significance of culture (e.g., Van Wolferen 1989) are mistaken. While state and capital do very definitely work hand-in-glove in Japan, even they are bound by cultural rules and a dense network of other and sometimes competing and contradictory organizations. And it is precisely this constellation of historical antecedents, cultural forces and social practices that give Japan both its inherent uniqueness and its special-case status as outside universal history (e.g., Hamaguchi 1982). The fourth relates to the terms in which the globalization debate has been phrased. Running through the discussions has been the recurrent motif of 'the global and the local', which of course acknowledges the continuing existence of the local, even if it is as the reception point of global forces. Japan however is assumed to be the 'local' on a huge scale, not as the recipient of global forces, but as a transmitter of such forces. The Japanese social project is a fundamentally utopian one: to create within a 'pure' society, one untramelled by the pollutions of the wider world; and to create without a world, if not exactly in Japan's image, at least one that shares Japan's postwar discovery of pacifism and universal harmony. Universalism then reappears in an interesting guise – as a Japan-centred view of the world with Japan reappearing not as a source of particular institutional arrangements (those are peculiar to individual societies), but of values. Significantly, it has been the *Shinshukyo* or 'New Religions' which have been the main agents of this new vision of Japan as the promised land, the one with material plenty and social harmony. This vision, not very thoroughly theorized in relation to the role of Japanese capital and popular culture, both being exported rather vigorously too, nevertheless should not be mistaken for simple racism or neo-colonialism. Despite its continuities with Japan's pre-war past, it does contain some very new elements, and ones which define in a new way Japan's relationship to the rest of the globe. It does, however, have its roots in a genuine perception of sociological distinctiveness (the interpretation of that distinctiveness from a *nihonjinron* perspective – as uniqueness and superiority – is another matter). When Long for example attempts to define, globally, social changes that are allegedly transforming the whole world in terms of transformation of the nature of work, of the state and of knowledge and technology (Long 1996: 38–9) he gets it quite wrong when his typology is applied to Japan: in fact Japan fails to meet almost all of his criteria. For instance there has been little or no decline in 'corporatist modes of regulation and organization', there has been no transformation of social or political identities or the diversifying of social commitments through commitment to transnational or cosmopolitan notions of citizenship (Long 1996: 38).

It is unfortunate that Long's essay is devoted to the proposition that globalization means diversity, not uniformity, yet by typologizing in this way he contradicts his own premiss that previous attempts to theorize globalization have failed precisely because of the attempt at 'formulating a general (or universal) theory that seeks to identify certain '"driving forces" ... "prime movers" ... or "cultural facilitators"' of change' (Long 1996: 37). Japan has long had a 'post-Fordist' mode of industrial organization, and has proved highly talented at creating an industrial and corporate structure based both on vertical integration *and* on horizontal linkages and flexible accumulation without creating a fragmentation of economic life. Indeed Japan's economic expansion has been based largely on the ability to combine what other societies separate – the vertical and the horizontal, hierarchy and egalitarianism, capitalism and classlessness, and by ensuring that, as economies become increasingly informationalized, it controls the technology that makes this possible and ensures access to global communication networks while retricting access to its own networks of communication and information, largely through the expedient of using a language which is still not widely known.

Japan and Its Others

Japanese identity then, as identity to some extent always is, is defined as against 'others'. But while the struggle for intellectual autonomy is largely against Europe, whence came the ideas of modernity and of universal history and its periodization, the struggle for political and economic autonomy is against the United States. The historic 'Other' – China – against which earlier struggles for cultural autonomy took place, especially as encapsulated in language, religion and social organization (Pollack 1986) is still there, but now more as a potential political rival than as a source from which Japan must differentiate itself. This redefining of the globe in terms of significant others – the US first, immediate (East) Asia next, Europe third, and the rest of the world a very poor fourth (reflected in a host of surveys of Japanese geographical knowledge and perceptions of the world) – has had an interesting effect on the *nihonjinron*. This has in the last decade shifted increasingly from a purely internal debate about the unique properties of the Japanese language, thought patterns, brain, silent methods of communication, art and so on, to a debate about Japan's role in the world phrased as Japan in *opposition* to that world, especially the modern world as represented by the United States (e.g., Morita and Ishihara 1989; Kato 1988). Such polemics have even gone to the extent of enrolling other parts of Asia in its crusade under the banner of a pan-Asian opposition to Westernization in general and Americanization in particular, as with the book by the somewhat xenophobic Prime Minister of Malaysia and one of Japan's leading isolationists (Mahatir and Ishihara 1994).

This isolationism is of a peculiar kind, since under the new conditions of the production of cultural knowledge, Japan is 'everywhere': people in London eat Japanese foods, teenagers in Bangkok read Japanese comics, children in Malaysia watch Japanese TV programmes, adults in New York drive Japanese cars, women in Singapore, Paris and Rio wear Japanese fashions and people just about everywhere listen to their music, take their photographs or watch images on their televisions by way of Japanese technology. It is actually Japan as much as or more than anywhere else in the world that is promoting cultural flows, especially of images, technologies and people. Isolationism is then clearly ideological rather than a reflection of any empirical reality, and is fueled by the fact that Japan is no longer trying, in material terms at least, to catch up with the West, but has in many ways surpassed it, without however desiring or being able to enter the international political arena in any significant sense. Yet, because presumably of the 'postmodern' conditions of Japanese society, Japanese intellectuals find it very difficult to produce a sustained critique of the West, or of modernity Western style. What is rather easier is to both applaud and attack the 'decline' of the West while maintaining, meanwhile, ever new variations of the theme of Japanese identity (e.g., Sakaiya 1991). We are left with a paradox: that examination of the Japanese case effectively undermines the universalist claims of modernity/capitalism/globalization in a way that goes well beyond the analytical weight of such alternative critical approaches as subaltern theory in ways similar to that which the exploration of the Chinese case suggests (Ong 1996: 64), but also that the resulting Japanese position turns out to be a highly conservative and utopian one.

Some Japanese intellectuals are aware of this paradox: that Japan, held up as a model by many other developing countries such as Singapore (Stanley 1988), is actually fundamentally resistant to emulation. And, significantly, the only model to which the Japanese refer to is that of themselves: wider discussions, especially in Southeast Asia, about pan-Asian values and the power of Confucianism tend to be passed over in silence. This, for the Japanese is a peculiarly Chinese, and especially 'overseas-Chinese' phenomenon. The global networks of language and ethnicity to which the Chinese can appeal do not apply to the Japanese, the greatest tourists perhaps, but hardly the greatest sojourners or settlers. Moreover the colonial experiments of the 1930s and '40s partly failed for this reason: Japan was still the self-proclaimed centre in a way that Britain never was (except nostalgically) to colonists in South Africa or Australia. Japan's love affair with its great cultural other – China – had by the beginning of the twentieth century turned into a despising attitude as China declined both politically and economically and fell further and further under the influence of the Western colonial powers. Earlier pride that it was through Japan that much Western science and learning had reached China was replaced by war and then with the escaping of China altogether from the Japanese (and Western) sphere of influence with the transition to communism in that country even as Japan chose the capitalist path.

What has happened, as a consequence of this choice, has been the attempt to theorize Japanese capitalism in a way that radically distinguishes itself from other models in terms of work practices, organizational structures, linkages with the wider society and its cultural 'fit' with the rest of Japanese society and the postwar economy of consumption (Matsumoto 1991). This is an interesting approach as it not only asserts the existence of many capitalisms (again in opposition to universalizing tendencies), but it sees the relationship between capitalism and society as not only benign, but as positively healthy – an attitude which has led some Japanese commentators to actually equate contemporary Japanese civilization with (Japanese) capitalism (Sakakibara 1993) – an interesting idea both for its recycling of the uniqueness model and for its congruence at a certain level with one of the most radical ideas of Western social theory: that modern society is basically just capitalism writ large. But whereas the Western version tends to lead on to critique of the commodity form, in Japan it tends to lead to its celebration. Giddens, who is so often wrong in these matters once he is off his familiar territory of middle-class England and California, again stumbles rather badly when he suggests that the necessary accompaniment of modernity must be the dismantling of the forces of nature and of human culture (Giddens 1991). Japanese modernity, if that is still the right word for that which has been 'overcome', affirms both of these and sees them indeed as essential parts of the constitution of its distinctive society, as things destroyed in the Western version, but retained at the heart of the social vision in Japan (Clammer 1995). Economy, culture and nature are related to one another in Japan in unexpected ways, and the contestation with Western visions takes place as much on this plane as it does on the level of universalization and periodization. It is not only a 'geopolitical unconsciousness', to use Frederic Jameson's phrase (Jameson 1992: 3) which underlies imagination and the construction of narratives, but also a 'geopolitical consciousness', an articulated image of identity based on the production of difference, East/West distinctions and understandings of social order (Amino 1994).

Japanese particularism, in challenging the claims of any individual form of capitalism to either universality or to a monopoly on colonizing the future, stands in an interesting relationship to another notable discourse of difference and otherness – Orientalism (Said 1978). If it is difficult for small-scale localities to stand against the global power of capital, there are two sources of encouragement: that global capitalism is in many ways divided against itself, and that Japan, as the exponent of one of these competing varieties, is hardly small scale in its own global reach. If the (Western) Orientalism of the past, the one described by Said in terms of its construction of representations, is mostly over (it lives on, at least residually, in advertising and the exoticization of the Other in the media) with the disappearance of its colonial basis, new forms may come into being, forms paradoxically generated from within the Orient itself. The *nihonjinron* in presenting itself as a discourse of uniqueness represents the assertion of the principle of difference certainly, but from *within* the culture that is generating it. The self, as it were, defines itself as 'other', before it can be so named. At one level it subverts the Orientalist project by indigenously constructing itself; the West is consequently deprived of the power to define. The vigorous polemics against the *nihonjinron* on the part of Western scholars suggests that it is indeed a deeply threatening thing to those both committed to universalism on their terms, the terms, that is, of implicit superiority.

But if the threat of definition by the West is a paramount concern in Japanese intellectual circles in an attempt to avoid being the signified, in relation to much of the rest of East and Southeast Asia, Japan is the signifier, especially in relation to the traditional and troubling otherness of China and Korea. Together with Thailand, (another predominantly Buddhist country and at present the biggest recipient of Japanese aid), Japan was one of the only two societies in East Asia never to have been colonized. It does in this sense stand outside of the history of most of Asia. The appearance of Edward Said's famous book (Said 1978) in Japanese translation triggered lively debate, as it seemed to describe exactly what Japan had been doing to large tracts of Asia while hiding behind mystifications of its own making in order to avoid the same representational fate at Western hands. By the late nineteenth century, prominent Japanese intellectuals, and most notably Okakura Tenshin, were arguing for a concept of the unity of Asia, but with two rather special characteristics: that this new Asia was Japan-centred and that 'Asia', defined as against the 'West', was assumed to be superior to that West. Asia, a macro-civilization organized along the two great axes of Chinese and Indian cultures (with Japan as the pivot having perfected the best attributes of both through its native genius) is defined as possessing continental stability, and as being characterized by its roots in agriculture, its emphasis on harmony understood as self-sacrifice and tolerance, its universality, willingness to investigate the world phenomenologically and its commitment to seeking for the true meaning of life as exemplified by its great religious teachers, Confucius and the Buddha being paradigmatic of this quest. The West, on the other hand, is characterized by oceanic restlessness, a civilization based on hunting and war, a psychology of individualism, freedom and equality, an enthusiasm for analytical methods and a seeking for the means, rather than the meaning or object, of life (Irokawa 1984).

This kind of argumentation, which has most recently resurfaced in the latter-day pan-Asianism of Lee Kuan Yew of Singapore and Mahatir Mohammad of Malaysia, is interesting not only for its reproduction of the very binary mode on which classical Orientalism is based, but equally for its self-Orientalizing characteristics in which the most astonishingly essentialistic 'characteristics' of the 'East' (a large place!) are made reducible to a set of categories mainly defined by their absolute contrast with those of the 'West' (also a fairly large place). The self

Japanizing of Japan has gone to great lengths and the very low foreign content of programmes on television and the general management of the influx of exotic culture seems to suggest that the Japanese have long since learnt Turner's principle that the main threat to indigenous cultures and especially religions – the sources of secularization that is to say – come not from intellectual dispute and argumentation with them, but from the spread of global popular culture. Japan has more to fear from Madonna than it does from all the regiments of anti-*nihonjinron* scholars entrenched in their Western universities (Turner 1994: 10). The avoidance of cultural domination has been a major plank in Japan's dealing with the threat of globalization to itself, while of course simultaneously exploiting that same global system for purposes of trade and the exporting of its own culture. As Turner suggests in responding to the idea that globalization is simply westernization by another name: 'there are profound social movements coming out of Japan and the other strong economies in the Asian region which are shaping the globe to such an extent that one could easily talk about the orientalization of modern culture' (Turner 1994: 9). This is true both in the sense of cultural flows and in the sense of the self-orientalizing of Japan and other parts of Asia, since being different creates moral leverage against the West (with its bad record as the former dominator), allows internal developments to occur without exposing them to universalist standards (the suppression of democracy and human rights in Singapore, say) and of course it attracts the tourists.

Japan then allegedly is the one society which has passed directly from premodernity to postmodernity without passing through modernity at all. It is already dwelling in post-history, a point Kojeve made a generation ago when he spoke of Japan as having experienced life at the 'end of history' for the last three centuries, as having no religion, politics or ethics in the European sense of those words and as being now engaged in the process not of assimilating the globe, but of Japanizing the West (Miyoshi and Harootunian 1989: xii–xiii). Japan has industrialized but not modernized according to the thesis of Maruyama Masao, and has done so by its unique ability to adapt the foreign, be it technology, institutions, or ideas to Japanese patterns (the remarkable indigenizations of Marxism, Christianity and Psychoanalysis, surely three of the great metanarratives of the modernist West, are all excellent examples of the latter). The attraction of this to the comparative theorist is all too apparent. It might be remembered as well that the prewar version of counter-Orientalism, of which Okakura's was probably the most worked out example, was closely connected with ultra-nationalism and through this to the path that led to war. Maruyama elsewhere argues (Maruyama 1963) that it was precisely the lack of modernity that led Japan to that disaster. The absence of the attributes of the Enlightenment project – personal autonomy, respect for rights, a conception of universal justice – were the reasons why Japan marched to the abyss. And since everything is now supposed to be postmodern, those attributes are still not present and so the road to future disaster is still open.

Japan Beyond History?

As Japan approaches the century's end many of the problems that have occurred elsewhere are beginning to appear at home. Some of these are the effects of over-development (urban crowding, high prices, slowly rising indicators of social disorder such as divorce and crime); some are the results of the pressures which the ultra-conservative and almost entirely one-party government political system is facing as it outlives its perceived utility, but still fails to respond to economic and social demands, and is becoming increasingly marginalized as its credibility drops; others are due to international pressures for more open markets and more participation, befitting such a rich nation, in the needs and concerns of the rest of the world. Internationalization, as a bureaucratically led policy designed effectively to keep the world sweet in order to keep it open to Japanese products (Harrison 1995: 229–30) has 'worked' so far. But some Japanese observers have begun to note that in an increasingly multipolar international environment the benign nature of the world trading environment can to be taken for granted less and less. In these circumstances, rather than an open world, absolutely necessary for peaceful Japanese domination, one comprised of many little (or big – think of China) Japans might emerge, fatal indeed to Japanese economic hegemony. Not without reason do the Japanese keep a wary eye not only on China and the EU (the fear of 'fortress Europe', but on its own ex-colonies South Korea and Taiwan, both of which have learnt the lessons their erstwhile mentor had to teach only too well.

Back to the Future?

A double essentialism then pervades Japan's relationship with the world: the common depictions of Japan from abroad as tribal, inward looking, exclusivist; and the self-images of the uniqueness, inpenetrability and homogeneity of Japanese culture. The two are mediated by the notion of Japan the great assimilator, as Marilyn Ivy suggests: 'The

image of Japan as the great assimilator arises to explain away any epistemological snags or historical confusions: Japan assimilates, if not
immigrants and American automobiles, then everything else, retaining
the traditional, immutable core of culture, while incorporating the
shiny trappings of (post)modernity in a dizzying round of production,
accumulation, and consumption' (Ivy 1995: 1). The Japan which is
everywhere, but which yet constantly reinvents the absolute gulf
between itself and the 'West', which internationalizes by domesticating
the foreign, is actually, to use a popular contemporary term, a'hybrid'.
The empirical convergences between Japan and the West are subsumed
within a discourse of cultural difference which has the double effect of
both absorbing the cutting edge of postmodern cultural criticism
(Yoshimoto 1996: 136) and stopping the thrust of anti-Orientalism and
the demand for historical specificity short of a 'truely critical anthropology (or history, or literary analysis')' (Ivy 1995: 8).

The question becomes one of how to move beyond the self imposed
limits of cultural particularism to this genuinely critical anthropology.
Several suggestions have been made in this direction which avoid the
reabsorption of Japan back into a homogeneous world history or concept of globalism. The first is that contemporary Japan be examined as
primarily a society of consumption in which both the realities of local
cultural production and Japan's relationship with the wider world be
read from the perspective of the domination of culture by capital (with
Japanese characteristics) and in which the transnational and 'nomadic'
aspects of Japan's presence in the world be seen as the congruence of
the 'Japanese model' with the development strategies of the West and
of many other hitherto 'developing' societies. Having started at different points, and proceeded by different strategies, Japan and the world
have now met in the moment of consumption (Clammer 1997). The
second is that it be recognized that Japan in fact has passed through, or
is still in, the phase of modernity, and that many of its current cultural
strategies (the orchestration of nostalgia, the recent appearance of new
museums devoted to history and to folklore, forms of religiosity) are to
be seen as attempts to manage precisely that modernity and the damage
that it inflicts on tradition, and to manage it, not through a policy of
opening to the world, but through the utopian option of reinscribing at
every turn the 'national-cultural phantasm' of Japan, precisely through
the invoking of the vanishing, those things which are passing away
because of modernity (Ivy 1995). The third, which has as yet hardly
been begun, is to explore the ethnography of postmodernity and its
connection with actual everyday life. To talk about, say, space-time

compression at the macrolevel is one thing. Its meaning in the life-world is another. The idea of the global system is an abstraction that it is difficult to grasp; its selective practice in consumption or entertainment activities however is another. If globalization has in fact contributed to the diversity rather than the homogenization of cultures, then it does make sense to explore it in its manifestations rather than from the level of the totality. The sociology of modern Japan has suffered from being largely pursued from within a set of pre-existing abstractions; a return to the study of actual cultural practices would both clarify what contemporary Japanese culture is, and how, if at all, it relates to tradition. The social organization of memory in fact becomes a key to the understanding of the construction of cultural self-images, and much of the *nihonjinron* turns out to be little more on close examination than nostalgia writ large.

The transition of the idea of modernity from the *universal* to the *global* which 'means merely that everyone everywhere may feed on McDonald's burgers and watch the latest made-for-TV docudrama' (Bauman 1995: 24), does suggest that it may be something in its contemporary manifestation worth avoiding. Lying behind Bauman's perhaps slightly cynical formulation is, of course, the idea that this new globalization is a largely *cultural* phenomenon, whatever its economic basis. The new cultural nationalism of Japan *is* new precisely because it takes place within a global context, and that context is its constant referent, opponent and market, all at the same time. Nowhere is this better seen than in Japan's confused policy about the presence of foreign workers in the country, many of them illegal, and many of them from poor countries which were either former Japanese colonies or which are recipients of Japanese aid. They are known to exist, are discussed in the press, are needed economically, are considered a cultural problem, yet no official policy exists on managing, legalizing or even stopping the 'problem'. This is not because there is any shortage of bureaucrats in Japan capable of formulating such a policy: it is because to *have* a policy would be to public-acknowledge Japan's historical and economic debts and to link itself morally with the fate and future of those nations from which migrants (and a tiny number of refugees) come.

The Japanese case is a fascinating one for the comparative social theorist, and the problems it raises are not easily resolvable. Its very existence does strike at the foundations of Eurocentric theorizing, at the universalizing and unity-of-capitalism assumptions of precursors to globalization theory such as Wallerstein's world systems approach and at the mainstream definitions, contested although they already are, of modernity and postmodernity. Japan is even an awkward case for post-colonial theory, since its analysis necessitates the dialogue of political-economy and culture, something which it has not so far proved to be very good at, and because it is a non-colonized ex-colonial state which has produced one of the most radical varieties of social and cultural particularism, something which is supposed to be the property of the formerly colonized.

The enigma is not unresolvable, but involves the *critical* examination of Japanese society through the very categories that it has used to explain itself. The conceptual challenges to social theory are real, and so are the questions facing the Japanese as they are integrated further into a multipolar world of porous boundaries in which the old certainties of the nation-states system is collapsing, and a world from which, moreover, they benefit enormously as the source of the raw materials which sustain their economy and as the market for their finished goods. Much can be understood if it is realized that Japan, for all its economic reach, is still a society of anxiety, and has been at least since its first opening to the West: a society convinced of the workability of its own social arrangements, but deeply concerned that the rest of the world will not recognize it as a real 'civilization'. Much of its history at least for the last century can be read as the attempt to create a front for the world behind which the true sense of uncontaminated being can flourish: to allow innerness (a constant theme of Japanese literature) to grow not in the sense of subjectivity and individualism, but in that of absorption into the totality. The lack of *gaibu* – exteriority – is the cultural strategy which allows, and has done so for centuries, the society of feeling to flourish in a world of facts. The real question to be addressed to Japan in order to grasp its relationship to globality is consequently a very simple one, rarely asked by those whose model is founded on either 'culture' in a narrow sense (art, film, architecture), or 'economy': how, in fact, does postmodernity work at the level of everyday life, and how is that life, in today's world, both encapsulated and globalized at the same time?

Bibliography

Amino, Yoshihiko (1994) *Nihon Shakai saiko* [Reconsidering Japanese Society], Tokyo: Shogakkan.

Arnason, J. P. and Y. Sugimoto (eds) (1995) *Japanese Encounters With Postmodernity*, London: Kegan Paul.

Asada, A. (1983) *Kozo to Chikara*, Tokyo: Keioshobo.

Baudrillard, J. (1988) *America*, London:Verso.

Bauman, Z. (1995) *Life in Fragments*, Oxford: Blackwell.

166   *Demystifying Globalization*

Beck, U. (1994) *Risk Society*, London: Sage.

Clammer, J. (1993) 'Nihon to tonan Ajia' [Japan and Southeast Asia], *Sophia*, 42, 5.

Clammer, J. (1995) *Difference and Modernity: Social Theory and Contemporary Japanese Society*, London: Kegan Paul International.

Clammer, J. (1997) *Contemporary Urban Japan: A Sociology of Consumption*, Oxford: Blackwell.

Dale, P. (1995) *The Myth of Japanese Uniqueness*. London: Routledge.

Fu, C. W-H. and S. Heine (eds) (1995) *Japan in Traditional and Postmodern Perspectives*, Albany: State University of New York Press.

Fukuyama, F. (1992) *The End of History and the Last Man*. New York: Free Press.

Giddens, A. (1990) *The Consequences of Modernity*, Stanford: Stanford University Press.

Giddens, A. (1991) *Modernity and Self-Identity: Self and Society in the Late Modern Age*, Stanford: Stanford University Press.

Gordon, A. (ed.) (1993) *Postwar Japan as History*, Berkeley: University of California Press.

Hamaguchi, E. (1982) *Kanjinshugi no shakai: Nihon* [Japan: The Contextual Society], Tokyo: Toyo Keizai Shinposha.

Hamaguchi, E. (ed.) (1993) *Nihongata moderu to wa nanika: Kokusai jidai ni okeru meritto to demeritto* [What is the Japanese model? The merits and demerits of the Japanese approach in the age of internationalization], Tokyo: Shinyosha.

Harrison, P. (1995) 'The Japanese postmodern political condition' in Arnason and Sugimoto (1995, 213–3).

Hiromatsu, W. (1989) *'Kindai no chokoku' ron* [On transcending the modern], Tokyo: Kodansha.

Hoston, G. (1986) *Marxism and the Crisis of Development in Pre-War Japan*, Princeton: Princeton University Press.

Imada, T. (1987) *Modan no datsukochiku* [Deconstruction of the Modern], Tokyo: Chuo Koronsha.

Irokawa, D. (1984) *Okakura Tenshin*, Tokyo: Chuo Bakkusu.

Ivy, M. (1995) *Discourses of the Vanishing: Modernity, Phantasm, Japan*. Chicago: University of Chicago Press.

Jameson, F. (1992) *The Geopolitical Aesthetic: Cinema and Space in the World System*. Bloomington: Indiana University Press.

Kato, T. (1988) *Japamerika no jidai ni* [In the age of Japamerica], Tokyo: Kadensha.

Long, N. (1996) 'Globalization and localization: new challenges to rural research', in H. L. Moore, (ed.) *The Future of Anthropological Knowledge*, London: Routledge.

Mahatir, M. and S. Ishihara (1994) *'No' to ieru Ajia* [The Asia that can say 'No'], Tokyo: Kobunsha.

Maruyama, M. (1963) *Thought and Behaviour in Modern Japanese Politics*, London: Oxford University Press.

Maruyama, M. (1985) 'Patterns of individuation and the case of Japan: a conceptual scheme', in M. B. Jansen (ed.) *Changing Japanese Attitudes Towards Modernization*, Tokyo: Charles E. Tuttle.

Matsumoto, K. (ed.) (1979) *Kindai no chokoku* [Overcoming the Modern], Tokyo: 1979.

Matsumoto, K. (1991) *The Rise of the Japanese Corporate System*, London: Kegan Paul International.

Miyoshi, M. and H. D. Harootunian (eds) (1989) *Postmodernism and Japan*, Durham: Duke University Press.

Moeran, B. (1995) 'Reading Japanese' in *Katei Gaho*: The art of being an upper class woman", in Skov, L. and B. Moeran (eds) *Women, Media and Consumption in Japan*, London: Curzon Press.

Morita, A. and S. Ishihara (1989) *'No' to ieru Nihon* [The Japan that can say 'No'], Tokyo: Kobunsha.

Mouer, R. and Y. Sugimoto (eds) (1986) *Images of Japanese Society*, London: Kegan Paul International.

Ohnuki-Tierney, E. (1991) *Rice as Self*, Princeton: Princeton University Press.

Ong, A. (1996) 'Anthropology, China and modernities: the geopolitics of cultural knowledge', in H. L. Moore (ed.) *The Future of Anthropological Knowledge*, London: Routledge.

Pollack, D. (1986) *The Fracture of Meaning: Japan's Synthesis of China from the Eight through the Eighteenth Centuries*, Princeton: Princeton University Press.

Robertson, R. (1992) *Globalization: Social Theory and Global Culture*, London: Sage.

Said, E. (1978) *Orientalism*, Harmondsworth: Penguin Books.

Sakaiya, T. (1991) *Nihon to wa nanika*, [What is Japan?] Tokyo: Kodansha.

Sakakibara, E. (1993) *Bunmei toshite no Nihon-gata shihonsugi* [Japanese capitalism as a civilization], Tokyo: Toyo Keizai Shinposha.

Stanley, T. A. (1988) 'Japan as a model for economic development: the example of Singapore', in G. L. Bernstein and H. Fukui (eds) *Japan and the World*, London: Macmillan Press.

Turner, B. S. (1994) *Orientalism, Postmodernism and Globalism*, London: Routledge.

Van Wolferen, K. (1989) *The Enigma of Japanese Power*, London: Macmillan Press.

Yoshimoto, M. (1996) 'Image, information and commodity: a few speculations on Japanese televisual culture', in Xiaobing Tang and S. Snyder (eds) *In Pursuit of Contemporary East Asian Culture*, Boulder: Westview Press.

Yoshino, K. (1992) *Cultural Nationalism in Contemporary Japan*, London: Routledge.

8
Globalization and European Integration
Daniel Wincott

Introduction

The relationship between European integration and globalization has been conceptualized in a number of different ways. European integration might be 'caused' by globalization. It could represent the unfolding of globalization in Europe and facilitate further globalization. Alternatively, globalization might have provoked a defensive reaction in Europe, blocking (however inefficiently) further globalization and perhaps leading to the creation of a 'fortress Europe'. In the first case, globalization could be viewed as 'causing' integration fairly directly. Even when it is portrayed as operating through various European actors, this view tends to be structurally deterministic. The space for the 'selection' of strategic alternatives is limited. The second view gives a larger role to political actors who construct barriers to globalization. It is worth pointing out, however, that neoliberal/globalist critics of integration depict this reaction as an inevitable consequence of 'politics', but one which is ultimately doomed to failure. Some social democrats develop a variant of this argument according to which the autonomy lost at the national level can be partially regained by action at a European level, 'rolling back' the frontiers of globalization (for an example of this view see Hutton 1996: 315–16).

In examining political and economic developments in Europe over the past two decades, we are then apparently faced with a stark choice between competing and mutually exclusive interpretations and theories. Paradoxically, these positions take as their starting point a widespread agreement that social democracy and the welfare state (topics with which I am particularly concerned) have been placed under enormous strain in the recent past by pressures not unrelated to 'globalization'. From here, in effect, we are asked to choose between two different interpretations of these changes: (i) as a characteristic or consequence of globalization which may, but need not, act through the European Community (the 'globalization' interpretation); or (ii) as a repudiation of globalization due to the resistance of the European Community to pressures which might otherwise undermine social democracy and the welfare state (the 'European resistance' position). While finding some suggestive ideas in these literatures, I reject both as general positions. In contrast to much of the existing literature, I develop an interpretation which emphasizes the role of European integration in undercutting welfare regimes and restricting the space for social democracy. The politics of constructing the European Community after about 1980 is understood here as a process of institutionalizing the outcomes of struggles between and choices made by a variety of actors. This process was open or contingent to some extent, but it reshaped the terrain or space for subsequent developments.

My argument in this chapter is that the debate around globalization obscures more than it clarifies. I argue that globalization theorists and their opponents share more than either side seems prepared to acknowledge. Moreover, what they share is usually more interesting than what divides them. I make these arguments in the context of an analysis of the relationship between European integration and (the trends and tendencies often labelled as) 'globalization', in which I suggest that Europe is a particularly important site for the assessment of 'globalization': its extent, intensity and consequences. After considering the significance of Europe for globalization, I develop critical analyses, respectively, of the concept(s) of globalization deployed within this literature and the role of European integration in the critique of globalization. I then turn to the way in which globalization and the state have featured in analyses of integration. The most interesting of these accounts either explicitly deploy an analysis of European integration as a difficult process of political construction, or suggest that such an approach would be most fruitful. I present a brief analysis of this sort myself, before concluding with a call for a rapprochement between the two sides of this debate. This is based, it should be noted, on a more selective and cautious use of the concept of globalization that appears typical at present, together with the development of more detailed work on the episodes which both sides agree to be crucial turning points.

Globalization and Europe

There are two reasons why Europe is particularly significant for 'globalization' theory. First, within the 'Triad' of North America, Europe and

Japan, it is in Europe that social democratic and welfare statist projects have been most successful. Secondly, globalization is connect to 'regionalization' and the European Union is the most complex or 'best developed' regional organization in the world. The EU plays a particularly important role for critics of the concept of globalization, who emphasize 'European resistance' to it, although some globalization theorists see it as a local form of the general phenomena.

On the first of these issues, globalization is thought to have decisively restricted, if not wholly eliminated, the space for left of centre political projects, particularly those associated with a positive role for the welfare state. Among the (Triad) states with which globalization theorists primarily concern themselves, it is primarily states in Europe which approximate welfare state regimes. For the most part North American and Asian states do not come close to, never mind meet the criteria of social citizenship classically used to define the welfare state. States must have had the capacity to be social democracies at some stage in order meaningfully to have lost it. 'Within' the Triad only European states have had this capacity recently, so only they can have lost it.

This argument has to be made carefully, for a number of reasons. I will focus on two in particular. First, a powerful argument can be made that few, if any states have ever approximated to the status of welfare state, rigorously defined (see Esping-Andersen 1990; Orloff 1993; Hay 1996). Moreover, the social policy effort of many states, including European states, may never have been motivated by social democracy or social citizenship (Esping-Andersen 1990; Baldwin 1990). In other words, even where the state and social policy are 'interventionist' they need not be social democratic or 'welfare statist' – other patterns of state 'organization' of capitalism (have) also exist(ed). In this case, the distinctiveness of the European experience, particularly from that of North America, where the retrenching of social policy has been attempted, at least partly under the banner of globalization, is reduced. Nevertheless, I would to argue that whatever differences there are among European states, when compared with North America, European social and welfare policies are substantially more important to the political economy and society. Moreover, social democratic parties play an important role in most (western) European states, so it is important to consider the impact of 'globalization' on the strategic context faced by these parties. Finally, whether or not it stands up to critical scrutiny (and I suspect that it doesn't), a powerful discourse has developed around the notion of a 'European Social Model'.

Secondly, it would be wrong to overlook the cases of states which fall outside the Triad, at least as it is usually defined. Outside of Europe, in two relatively affluent countries – Australia and New Zealand – the left has had the power (particularly through control of central government) to institutionalize a significant displacement of the market. There is some disagreement in the literature about the significance of the welfare effort of these two states. In some classifications they appear as cases of stingy and marginal welfare (Esping-Andersen 1990) while others classify them as a distinctive, and in its own terms relatively successful 'wage earner' welfare state (Castles 1985; Castles and Mitchell 1993; Castles and Pierson 1996). From a European perspective these two states can appear as strong confirmation of some versions of the globalization thesis. Indeed, they may seem to represent the defining cases of market oriented, welfare policy restricting reforms, introduced by governments of the left.

Research (at least within the extra-Antipodean academy) has not yet focused critically on the question of the *causes* of these reforms, beyond the invocation of globalization. It seems to be widely accepted that by the end of the 1970s, the previous policy regime was exhausted, and the economies of these states were exposed by economic factors beyond national control (Castles and Pierson 1996: 242) although these factors do not necessarily amount to 'globalization'. However, recent research has shown significant differences in the policy paths followed by these two states. Although the New Zealand case might seem to support an argument of globalizing convergence, the Australian one does not. While the historic commitment to targeting (means testing) benefits (a characteristic which helps to explain its poor standing in some comparative typologies) has been intensified in Australia there was also 'a conscious move towards greater generosity for certain categories of beneficiary and major new welfare state departures in the area of health and [old] age pensions' (Castles and Pierson 1996: 243).

On the question of the relationship between globalization and European integration, the central argument of this paper is that although there has been a restriction of the scope for social democracy and welfare statist policies in Europe, this restriction is bound up with the process of European integration 'rather than' being a consequence of globalization. Broadly, from the late 1970s, the series of developments or events which constitute European integration has served to strengthen the role of the market, constraining that of the state and authoritative political decision more generally. This general trajectory has tended to reduce the space and/or resources for left of centre political projects and

to bolster the right. Of course, a number of European Community/
Union initiatives and proposals have seemed or attempted to counter
this general tendency. Most notable among these are the Social Charter
of 1989 and the Social Agreement of the Maastricht Treaty. However,
the contention that the EC's Social Dimension amounts to a manifesto
for socialism or social democracy is fatuous.

The assertion that European integration has reduced the space for
social democracy might seem odd, given recent experience in the UK.
Here, the European issue has fractured arguably the most successful
right wing party of the twentieth century. It still seems set to split the
party (see Ludlam 1996 and Wincott, Buller and Hay 1998), while contributing significantly to the recent revival of the (nominal) 'left'. However, the looking glass world of British politics may provide an ironic
confirmation of the general hypothesis. In Britain public debate on Europe has produced bizzare, mutually strengthing discourses. The European Community is constructed as a set of regulative constraints on a
mythical wholly self-sustaining free market, rather than viewed as an
attempt at the difficult task of overcoming collective action problems
among capitalists and states in the creation of a big market (see Wincott, Buller and Hay 1998 on the relational construction of images of
the EU in 'Westminster in wonderland'; Mount 1992 for an unusal right
wing perspective on 'weights and measures stuff' of market construction; and Grahl and Teague 1989 on the 'Big Market'). The symbolic use
of Europe's social dimension has helped partially to disguise or render
more palatable a dramatic shift to the right within the Labour Party on
integration and many other issues. It seems unlikely that this use of the
social dimension would have been possible had the Conservatives not
'demonized' the social dimension as socialism 'by the back door'.

The analysis of European integration developed here (building on
some existing work in the field of EU studies) is an effective counter to
what I will define as 'simple' – economically or technologically deterministic – versions of globalization theory. Yet, it does not in itself constitute a counter to, far less a total rejection of, the recent profusion of
more 'complex' ones. Indeed, some complex globalization theorists
might want to incorporate an account of this sort 'within' their analyses.
While I do not find such an account convincing, its flaws can only be
exposed if they are engaged on theoretical or conceptual terms. Although
certain complex globalization theorists display some sensitivity to
questions of structure and agency, such approaches still tend to exhibit
a certain tendency to reify globalization – by treating it as a process beyond (and sometimes wholly without) agents. This can only result in a

structuralist bias. Equally important, if accurate, the integration analysis presented here undermines important critiques of 'globalization' insofar as they are rooted in the image of the European Union resisting the forces of globalization. If globalization theory is characterized by a tendential structuralism, then the 'European resistance' approach is flawed by voluntarism – the attribution of too much autonomy to the agent.

What Is Globalization?

While there is a good deal which is of value in the discussion of globalization, there is a risk that a fruitless, polarizing and even obfuscatory 'debate' (perhaps labelled 'globalization or internationalization') may develop around the concept, its associations and perceived consequences. Otherwise fruitful analyses have been flawed by the use of arguments about globalization for other, not always fully explicit, purposes. Moreover, while interesting arguments have been developed by both 'globalizationists' and their opponents, each 'side' resorts to caricatures, vulgarities and simplifying distortions. Internal flaws in each version have arisen from the argumentative and rhetorical strategies adopted on both sides.

Some theorists who welcome globalization do so for reasons which seem to owe a great deal to skirmishes within the academy. If a dominant intellectual 'paradigm' can be constructed around 'globalization' it would sound the death knell of neo-realism (Cerny 1996). Whatever the attractions of such a development, to my mind, they are insufficient to make the concept worth embracing. They are certainly no reason for failing to speak to the silences, or of the elisions, of the 'globalization' concept. On the other hand, while critics of globalization may be correct to argue that even sophisticated uses of the term validate an extreme neo-liberalism (Hirst and Thompson 1996), sometimes these critics concentrate their fire on a straw doll. In other words, rather than engaging with the strongest versions of 'opposing' arguments, each has constructed what almost amounts to a parody of the other. Positions which have a good deal in common are thus divided from one another. This can only divert attention from a series of crucial theoretical and political issues which are therefore considered inadequately, if at all.

Globalization theorists draw attention to extremely important changes which *have* occurred, for example, in the organization of financial markets. These changes reinforce the position of state actors following neo-liberal economic strategies and constrain social democrats, consequentially undercutting existing welfare regimes (although this argument can be exaggerated – see Hay and Watson 1998). However, the concept of globalization seems to me to be of little *analytic* use in the investigation of these developments – it would be better to focus on the precise causal mechanisms and relationships between, say, developments in financial markets and slow squeeze of welfare retrenchment. The notion of globalization is thus – at best – unnecessary to carry out the conceptual work attributed to it; at worst it spawns confusion. Not only is the field of 'globalization studies' already vast and growing at a seemingly exponential rate, it is confused by multiple and competing interpretative frameworks.

Even leaving aside sociological and cultural analysis (as I do here) the political economy of globalization falls into two broad camps, which I identified briefly earlier. One is deterministic, explicitly arguing that globalization produces a powerful economic convergence. This 'simple' globalization is simply the latest – triumphalist – version of neo-liberalism. It can be dismissed relatively easily *as an analysis*, although doing so remains an important task given the political uses to which it is put (see Watson 1998 for a discussion of this issue in the British context). This is the version of globalization on which many critics concentrate – treating the entire literature as one-dimensional. This critical reaction is thoroughly inadequate; it neglects the second variant of globalization analysis which self-consciously celebrates its 'complexity'. In particular 'complex globalization' theorists take pains to repudiate the notion that we ought to expect globalization to take the form of, or cause, a general (political, social or cultural) convergence or homogenization (see Cerny 1996). Despite their loud protestations to the contrary, however, I believe that the concept of globalization at best suggests some sort of unity (of a 'complex' kind, if you like) behind the continuing morphology of (political, social or culture) difference. Moreover, for present purposes it *is* worth pointing out that on one crucial point even influential proponents of the complex globalization perspective agree with the neo-liberals: they associate globalization with the removal – or at least severe limitation – of the space for the left and the restriction of the state to a residual form (see especially Cerny 1995: 611–12 and 618–21; also Cerny 1996).

Be that as it may, it seems to me that 'complex globalization' theory needs to be met on its own terms, rather than assuming that the critique of more crudely neo-liberal variants of globalization will do for it as well. Although I do not have the space here to set out the argument in detail, I believe that complex globalization theory generally falls into the trap of reification – it treats the concept of globalization as if it were a (real) 'thing' which could have causes and (still more problematically) consequences. For analytical purposes it seems to me that the most helpful use of the term 'globalization' is to describe a process, within which various trends and counter-trends, tendencies and counter-tendencies need to be specified. It is to these latter notions, rather than the notion of globalization itself, that we should look for causes and consequences. In my view 'globalization' is best reserved for the description of the process as a whole (in so far as one can be identified). Even here 'globalization' should only be used if the process is leading to a condition which could be labelled as 'global' (although the meaning of this concept would be open to contestation as well). As a result, my preference would be for the use of 'globalization' as a hypothesis about something which may, but may not, be occurring.

Before closing the discussion of the meaning of globalization, there is one final issue I have avoided so far, but which needs to be addressed. There is a sense in which globalization is a 'cause' and does have 'effects' – as a discourse or social construction (MacNamara 1997; Hay and Watson 1998). Too often the critique of globalization depends on a rather crude separation of the 'ideational' from the 'real'. First, real changes in, say, the economy are 'shown' to be insufficient to justify the claims of globalization theorists. Secondly, globalization is labelled as a 'fashionable idea'. Finally, the 'real effects' of globalization are attributed to, and explained away as a consequence of, ideational fashion. Taken more seriously, the notion that the discourse (or 'paradigm' – see Cerny 1996) of globalization constructs actors, or contributes powerfully to their construction, is more difficult to dismiss. Of course, one discursive strategy with which to counteract it is ('while the opportunity remains open') to point to the gap between the rhetoric and reality of globalization. However, while this strategy *might* have an appeal for those increasingly marginalized by 'globalization' it is unlikely to cut much ice with those at the core of the construction. Here playing on the internal contradictions and perverse consequences of the globalization discourse might have more impact.

Although critical of the ways in which the term 'globalization' has been used by academics and 'business gurus', nevertheless, I believe that the debates around the notion are of crucial importance. Moreover, if defined more precisely and used more carefully a concept of 'globalization' may be helpful within those debates. In a similar vein, I believe while the existing critique of globalization has some flaws, there is a good deal that is useful within it. It is to the critique of globalization that I now turn, and particularly to the role attributed to the European Union within it.

Social Democratic Delusions

This section centres on a discussion and critique of Hirst and Thompson's analysis of *Globalization in Question* (1996). While there is a great deal with which I have sympathy in this text, particularly if it is viewed as a political or ideological intervention, it is nevertheless ultimately flawed. I should make it clear that these flaws are not necessarily characteristic of all its authors' work. Its flaws are revealed particularly clearly in its analysis of, and recommendations for, European integration, which are characterized by a striking voluntarism.[1] This flaw is particularly damaging, as in their analysis the EC/EU is held to play a crucial role in resistance to what amount to potentially globalizing tendencies. As the most fully developed regional grouping of states the character of governance within the Union is portentous and its contribution to wider (global/international) patterns of regulation is key.

The European Community is not merely the (potential) saviour of Europe (and EC member states), it also points the way forward for (states in) other regions and is called on to play a lead role in inter-regional co-ordination to regulate the global/international economy. Their account requires that Europe should at least have the potential to 'succeed' as a site of regulated ('social') capitalism. Even in the text on globalization they are not utterly starry-eyed about European integration (and elsewhere a bleaker image of the future is shown, see Hirst 1995).[2] Nevertheless, the logic of their argument requires that the barriers to European 'success' cannot be too great. As a consequence, while not wholly one-sided, their argument has a bias. In my view, this strongly influences the overall tenor of their discussion – giving it a voluntaristic quality. This quality can be discerned most clearly in their discussion of questions of accountability in the Community/Union. It also spills over into their view of the major issues of contemporary European political economy.

The question of accountability looms large in debates about the future of Europe (as do the closely associated issues of legitimacy and democracy). It quickly becomes clear that major substantive issues connected to the elitist character of the European project and the detachment of popular forces from it are begged in any analysis of accountability. Hirst and Thompson's solution to the problem is quite simple: Europe's politicians should change their attitudes. Then 'without large structural changes' a crucial change in the accountability of the Union would result (1996: 156). This recommendation embodies a strikingly voluntaristic conception of political action. It suggests that political agents freely select their attitudes and are capable of changing them at will. No analysis of the sources or genesis of existing attitudes of politicians is presented. The ways in which the attitudes of Europe's politicians are created in, and constrained by, national and European structural contexts are not adequately considered here, never mind the manner in which these structures developed around and institutionalized the attitudes of past and present politicians. Indeed, as we shall see, the undemocratic character of the Community/Union may be its 'efficient secret', a characteristic essential to its success.

Hirst and Thompson's account of the orientation of European economic policy also has a somewhat voluntaristic tone. They develop a critique of the terms of monetary union and subsequently canvass the possibility of a continental Keynesianism. There is much to agree with in their critique of the deflationary character of the monetary union and the abstracted model of central bank independence on which the European Central Bank is based. However, there are reasons why such arrangements take this form. The most important concern the perceived acceptability of the EMU to financial markets and the effective veto of the German government over the project, particularly at its formative stage. Within the German state, the position of the Bundesbank on monetary union has been and remains crucial, with both direct and indirect means of restricting the government's options, as well as external influence via its sway on financial markets. There *is* an important sense in which the politics of monetary union has been open. Thus, at the time of writing the countries likely to join the union appear to have some leeway as regards the strategies and goals which Europe's central bankers will adopt. Indeed, even the overall 'success' or 'failure' of the project remains in question. However, if it is open, it is certainly not unconstrained. Hirst and Thompson do not identify the context within which the politics of monetary union will be made. Once the context is identified, strategies which start within it, but may have the purpose of transforming it, can be devised. Instead they again show a voluntaristic attitude towards European politics. They present alternatives (a slower process with wider looser targets or a 'two-speed' union) on monetary union as if they were options from which 'we' have a free choice. They seem to rule out the two-speed option, because of its 'dangers', in particular the likelihood that it would create two semi-permanent tiers (1996:161–2). However, it is fairly clear that the Maastricht Treaty was designed to create two tiers, and no measures equal to the task of bringing states from the 'second' tier into the union were specified. Most important, the conditions and agents which shaped the form of the monetary union remain strong, making it difficult to see how it might be changed, and who would change it.

Not only do Hirst and Thompson criticize the deflationary character of the monetary union and the neo-liberal form of the institutions created to regulate it, they also canvass the possibility of a wholesale reversal of the monetarist logic underpinning it. Europe, they argue, could adopt a strategy of continental Keynesianism. To be fair, Hirst and Thompson take care explicitly to argue that the likelihood of this strategy being adopted is small. It is crucial to their case that something akin to a continental Keynesianism is – in some meaningful sense – possible. As no account is provided of how this possibility might be constructed, it seems to exist mainly in the abstract sense that we can imagine it. It is instructive to note that, although, in this case the authors do suggest that existing structures hinder the Keynesian possibility, again, strong emphasis is placed on the attitudes of political leaders (1996: 163–4).

The general purpose of the Hirst and Thompson argument is to demonstrate that the European Union can be used in order to create economically and socially helpful (re)regulation at the European and international levels. However, in developing this theme there is a strong risk that the authors may concede more than they might otherwise wish to globalization arguments. They certainly assert that national governments have lost crucial capacities to make effective and/or autonomous macro-economic policies. It would be easy to read this argument as suggesting that economic forces have wrought these changes which Euro-politics may be able to resist, by dint of the economic scale of Europe. Moreover, the voluntaristic tone of the argument implies that politics is about choice, whereas the economy is impersonal and structural. It echoes the notion that political agents face impersonal economic structures, often depicted as 'harsh economic realities' (see Hay and Watson 1998). Only a blithe optimism of the will separates this position from the economic determinism of globalization theorists. Perhaps most importantly, the analysis does not identify the important role of European political choices, often of an institution creating kind. It fails to consider the ways in which, and the reasons why, the Community 'itself' is responsible for (some of) the constraints facing European states.

Integration, Globalization and the State

Given the apparent centrality of Europe in globalization, and *vice versa*, as well as the increase in the influence of discourses of globalization, it is striking how rarely notions of globalization appear in the specialist literature on European integration (but see Cowles 1995). Europe is discussed in the globalization literature to some extent, to be sure although in this discussion, Europe can sometimes appear merely as a confirmation of globalization, rather than being discussed adequately in its own terms. The limited discussion of globalization in the specialist literature may be due to the powerful influence of statist (realist and other intergovernmentalist) theories in this context. Indeed, it is not merely discussion of 'globalization' which appears relatively rarely in specialist literature on European integration. There is too little discussion of the 'external', whether understood in terms of 'international' or 'global' factors. The literature is primarily concerned with the 'internal' dynamics of integration. When external issues are considered often they rate little more than a mention, and are treated in the abstract (see, for example, Moravcsik 1993 on economic interdependence). It is not particularly common for 'the external' – whether global or international – to be considered in any extended or systematic manner in the specialist literature, although accounts which do discuss it are among the most important in the literature (particularly Sandholtz and Zysman 1989; Cowles 1995). This point needs to be qualified in the case of historical accounts of the origins of the EEC which do emphasize the influence of external conditions and actors, particularly the Cold War and the US administration, or the degree of economic interdependence which meant that the nation-state needed a European saviour (Milward 1992).

Although, I believe the analysis of integration would be enriched by a more extensive discussion of 'external' influences in the process, on close examination, the fact that a good deal of the literature does not engage with the external is revealing about both the integration process and the literature describing it. On the positive side the existence of several otherwise well-developed and rich accounts of recent integration in Europe which focus primarily on its internal dynamics reveals that these processes are relatively complex and mature. They have some of the features of systems which are capable of generating their own discourses and interpretations of their environment, partially translating and reworking it into their own terms. Much of the literature has been organized around a discussion of the relative importance of the Community institutions and other European 'level' actors on the one hand, and member state governments on the other, which is of more ambiguous value. To give this discussion a theoretical veneer, it has often been presented in terms of a struggle between neo-functionalism and intergovernmentalism. In many, but not all, hands this theoretical discussion has been rather sterile, particularly when the theory has been abstracted from its own roots and been used to push discussion of integration in an ahistorical direction.[3]

If globalization has played a limited role in the specialist literature on European integration, the same cannot be said of the role of the state. Although most of the literature has been concerned with the extent to which states control or influence the integration process, the implication of these developments for the character and form of European state is an important sub-theme in the discussion. A paradox, or at least a puzzle, is thrown up by the intersection of two influential strands of the debate. On the one hand, there is a widespread impression that European integration is undermining sovereignty, contributing to the 'hollowing out of the nation state'. On the other, going beyond the discussion of the role of the state in integration, important and interesting analyses of the manner in which European integration has 'rescued' (Milward 1992) or strengthened the state (Moravcsik 1994; see also Dunleavy 1996).

Milward's version of this approach is primarily historical, focusing on the problem of re-establishing the nation states of continental western Europe during the first couple of decades after the war. Moravcsik's and Dunleavy's accounts share a concern with the potential collective gains which states could achieve through collaboration. This could be presented as a form of reaction to globalizing tendencies by means of pooling sovereignty. Sometimes the gain in autonomy for agents in the state in relation to domestic constituencies is emphasized. This notion has been pioneered in formal public choice (Dunleavy 1996) and game theoretic (Moravcsik 1994) analyses and in general suggests that the state can achieve objectives which would be otherwise unattainable by a strategy of pre-commitment. Moravcsik's argument depends on a etiolated conception of the state in which those holding a few key offices within the central government are identified with the state as a whole. Dunleavy addresses the puzzle of why knowledgeable agents in the apparatus of the various states collaborated in the creation of structures which undermined, or at least strictly constrained, the general institutional form from which they (partly) derived their power and identity. His account attempts to explain the complicity of agents within the states in 'the drift to Brussels' (Dunleavy 1996). Moravcsik's work suffers particularly from the inadequacy of its temporal dimension, rooted in an essentially comparative static approach to change. Dunleavy examines the question of change more directly, and his analysis is free of Moravcsik's rigid statism. Yet, due to its formality, it remains relatively ahistorical and unconcerned with the temporal development of the European Union. This view is somewhat reminiscent of Cerny's conception of the relationship of the state and globalization – in which states are sometimes seen as the authors of their own subjugation and decline (Cerny 1996).

Formal analyses which point to the gains made by states by binding themselves into European structures (which may subsequently undermine the state) are important and suggestive. However, they cannot tell the whole story. They need to be supplemented by or embedded in accounts which highlight the cumulative impact of activity at a European level. As more and more activity occurs in Brussels a process of institutionalization may occur, a path dependency may be generated, which eventually binds the state within a web of commitments and rules which it has helped to spin. Moreover, the question of why and how state agents are able credibly to pre-commit themselves to activity at a European level needs to be considered. Although it introduces a particularistic element which formal analysts committed to general theory may not welcome, the 'path' of development of the European Community may be important here as well. During earlier episodes institutions were created, particularly the ECJ, which provide relatively strong mechanisms for enforcing commitments. Finally, formal analyses generally assume the state to be unitary, partly for methodological reasons (although Dunleavy emphasizes that this assumption might be usefully relaxed in subsequent work). However, the institutions of the Community, and particularly the Council of Ministers as it operated in the 1970s and '80s, provide a forum within which fragmentive tendencies within the state can be played out. Rather viewing the Community simply as providing an opportunity for unitary states to gain autonomy from society, the opportunity for functional ministers can pursue particular projects relatively autonomously from other agents within the government as well.

The view of the European integration as a difficult process of political construction, in which contingent decisions and events running partly beyond the control of political actors eventually solidify into determinate and partially determining institutional forms gains some support from those specialists in the analysis of integration who *do* consider external factors – even globalization – in some detail. I will discuss two important examples here. In ground-breaking work on the role of big business in the development of the internal market, Maria Green Cowles has argued that 'events *external* to the bureaucratic functioning of the Community' (1995: 522) were important. Central developments within 'Europe' were 'in response ... to the challenge of a globalizing world economy and growing international competition' (523). Nevertheless, the burden of the story Cowles wants to tell concerns not the overweening constraints of the external, but the political activity of particular business leaders, especially as organized into the European Round Table of Industrialists (ERT). Strategic action by the leaders of major European business has contributed to the creation of new institutions. These new structures have their own biases. The emphasis is on the political choices made by business leaders in a process of constructing a particular form of European market. Most general analyses of business and politics strongly emphasize the structural. Although the structural position of business does feature in Cowles' analysis of the ERT, she strongly stresses that 'the ERT became a political actor in its own right' and that certain business leaders were 'active political actors that shaped EC . . . agendas' (522).

Sandholtz and Zysman present a clear and interesting account of shifts in the international economic structure which 'triggered' the 1992 process. However, these shifts are conceived of as necessary rather than sufficient for the development of '1992'. They are analysed mainly in the geo-strategic terms of a decline in US and a rise in Japanese economic power, rather than in terms of the nature of the productive processes involved, although the latter element seems in places to lurk below the surface of the account. It should be emphasized that this analysis does not rely upon a conception of the shifts in the economy in terms of a notion of globalization, as Zysman has made clear in a recent critique of globalism (1996). Alongside these changes in the economy, the shift towards a market orientation among the politicians in control of national executives is also important. Shifts in the international economy provide the conditions within which the European Commission, aided by the ERT, constructed the European market. The Commission is depicted as a 'policy entrepreneur' (Sandholtz and Zysman 1989: 95–6). Crucially, as with Cowles' analysis, Sandholtz and Zysman place emphasis on the politics of constructing Europe (and European integration). This construction is conceived of as essentially open, 'dependent on the timing and dynamics of a long series of contingent decisions' (1989: 128). Analysis of this sort contradicts the deterministic thrust of simple globalization theory and qualifies the complex globalization approach.

An Account of European Integration

If European integration is best viewed as a political construction then the question of its substantive character becomes centrally important.

Too little of the 'political' analysis of integration has directly drawn attention either to its substantive political implications[4] or to the options and strategies of agents situated in particular institutional and temporal situations. The apolitical and formalistic bent of much integration theory has resulted in analyses which treat certain (economic or political) structures as determining the form of the European Community. Even more, 'political' analysis has all too often developed on the basis of a voluntaristic and therefore misplaced and misleading view of the history of integration and political possibilities that the Community faces. We have seen the social democratic potential of the Union exaggerated in Hirst and Thompson's analysis. Similar, although not identical, points can be made about the gender and environmental implications of the Community. In each of these two areas, a significant body of European law and policy exists which do provide resources for political actors of various sorts, which are sometimes used by them in conflicts with branches of particular European states. However, it is also possible to tell a persuasive story about the limitations of each of these bodies of law and policy. Most important of all, is the (enormous) question of the overall impact of the Community/Union in each of these areas. In other words, whatever the value of its specific gender or environmental policy, the overall impact of the Community/Union point strongly in the other direction as far as the position of women or the condition of the environment is concerned. For example, on balance men are likely to gain more than women from the operation of a big European market as it is likely to strengthen those already in a powerful position, who are generally men. European gender policy is not strong enough effectively to counteract this impact.

During the late 1970s and early 1980s states, and particularly knowledgeable agents in the most senior positions within them, used the particular pre-existing institutions of the Community to make a series of commitments which altered rechannelled domestic social pressures and restructured the overall pattern of relationships within individual governments in various ways. The form of integration which was achieved was based on, and strongly entrenched, a particular (market strengthening) understanding of the economic. The Single European Market illustrates and strengthens the idea of a society organized around the market. It also provides a context within which many (big) businesses can behave in ways which bear more than a passing resemblance to the visions of globalization theorists, both in terms of capital movement within, and foreign investment into, Europe . It has proven to be extremely difficult to develop European rules and norms which bolster the institutions and forces which embed alternative conceptions of capitalism within member states. The creation of European level alternatives is still more problematic. Those countertendencies are massively outweighed by the original market-oriented thrust. The conception of the European Union as a political construction is helpful, in my view. However, there is a risk that such a view conjures an image of a (few) powerful and instrumentally rational actor(s) in control of the process, successfully realizing a 'project'. The outcome of the integration process is a (probably contradictory) product of the interaction of competing projects for integration carried by institutionally located actors in an environment they do not wholly control (or, for that matter, fully comprehend). While the outcome has been the construction of a significantly (not wholly) neo-liberal market in Europe, rather fewer actors sought to realize a neo-liberal project. Even many of the actors who sought to strengthen the role of the market, or of capital (relative to workers) operated with a conception of the market as requiring some regulation. The outcome of the process has been to increase the importance of market freedoms and even, notwithstanding the innovative nature of some EU regulation, to undercut some market supportive national regulation.

The market strengthening tendency of the integration process can be seen in the two most important 'history making' (Peterson 1995) episodes which occurred during this period: the Single European Act (SEA) and the Treaty on European Union (TEU). The dominant consequence of both these revisions has been neo-liberal, strengthening owners and weakening workers, and although this consequence is clearer in the SEA, it is potentially more devastating in the case of the TEU. It is crucial to recognize that the significance of major Treaty revisions is not unambiguously written into their legal texts, for at least two reasons. First, the documents themselves are political compromises. Secondly, their full significance unfolds through subsequent political action. These documents provide resources for actors, but other aspects of the conditions within which these actors attempt to make use of the resources, and the ingenuity of the actors themselves also have an influence. The evaluation of the character of a particular Treaty is usually made retrospectively (or anachronistically depending on your preference) and depends on the position in time from which it is viewed. The TEU is a complex even contradictory document. At the time of writing, its significance depends substantially on whether a monetary union is created, and the form it takes if it is. This still seems to me to be a genuinely open question. Certainly, when the Treaty itself was signed, a number of different paths to the future were possible. However, if the meaning of the TEU is open, it is not unconstrained. We can talk sensibly about the implications of the various forms which monetary union may take, and about what may transpire if it does not come into being. If a monetary union is achieved, and particularly if it includes both Germany and France, then it is likely to have a strongly deflationary bias. Moreover, from today's perspective, it is quite clear that in order to attempt to qualify for monetary union, a number of states have drastically altered their public, and particularly social, policy provision.

Compared to the TEU, at the moment it was written, the SEA was relatively simple. Its dominant tendency was much more clearly neo-liberal. Also the SEA was embedded within the broader single market programme. Overall, this programme was constructed around the market-oriented notion of freeing up the movement of factors of production. Even within this orientation, it was much more concerned with the free movement of goods and capital than that of individuals. To the extent that the free movement of individuals was encouraged, it was first, of individuals setting up (especially service) businesses, and secondly of highly qualified professionals, rather than workers generally.

European integration since the mid 1970s, then, has been characterized by a mixture of the legacy of the institutions and policies formed in the earlier episodes of integration, with various new initiatives and projects. The most important of the new initiatives and projects have mainly been (at least partially) constructed as responses and resolutions to a perceived crisis in Europe and the perception of the catastrophic condition of the institutions of the European Community itself. However, although it is a commonplace to refer to the significance of the 'oil price rise' and related stagflation in Europe (and beyond) in the 1970s as the backdrop to, and in contrast with the dynamism of Europe in the 1980s, it should be clear that the later dynamism was not an automatic response to the earlier crisis. Indeed, it is only after other projects had been pursued, and failed in several states, that the European project took off. The 'failure' of Mitterrand's experiment with socialism and subsequent turn to Europe is the key here. In other words a time lag existed between the crisis and the European 'response', which itself needed to be constructed.

Two questions arise about this process of construction who was most centrally involved in it, and from what material, under which conditions, was it made. To some extent the first of these questions takes us back to the terrain of debate about national versus European level actors. Here, all it seems relevant to say is that clearly various nationally based actors can and have exercised leadership in the development of the Community and members of national executives have held a veto over the development of the Community. However, it seems equally clear that European level actors, particularly in EC institutions and big business (Cowles 1995) have also played a leadership role at times. Work by Cram and others has suggested that the crucial issue is to identify what allows these different sorts of actors to be influential (see Cram 1993, 1997a; see also Pollack 1995). If it is important to sort out which actors have been influential, it is also crucial to identify the resources that have selected from the context(s) in which they find themselves, and the conditions which allowed them to be successful. In this context, it is worth pointing out that various actors in the European Union constructed narratives of crisis in order to motivate political projects. The language of crisis is very widely used in the politics of integration. Indeed, the crisis of the 1970s and the perception of the catastrophic condition of the Community during this period are ritual incantations of those involved in the construction of Europe.

The 'external' and latterly sometimes even 'globalization' itself have been used by actors in Europe as elements in their crisis narratives, motivations for their corrective political projects. Financial, and particularly currency, markets stand out as a key 'external' influence on developments in Europe, from the turbulence of the 1970s, out of which the European Monetary System grew, by way of the enormous significance of Mitterrand's abandonment of Keynesian reflation and nationalization in favour of a 'European strategy' in the face of pressure from financial markets, which served as a symbol of the crisis of the so-called 'Keynesian Welfare State', to the complex, even contradictory, reactions of the financial markets to Monetary Union. External economic threats, and particularly that posed by Japanese manufacturing, from high technology to automobiles proved particularly potent in the construction of the Internal Market. The debate about the future of Europe is most likely to be taken forward fruitfully by rigorous and detailed analysis of these episodes.

Conclusion

Unless used very carefully, the concept of globalization hinders the analysis of European (Welfare) States and of European integration. Promiscuous use of the notion of 'globalization', particularly where it succumbs to the temptation of reifying the concept and treating it as a causal force, separate from the various trends and tendencies which *might* bring 'the global' into reality, is obfuscatory. Equally, however, many critics of globalization have misused the European experience in order to make their arguments. A debate between 'globalization' and 'internationalization', while it might make a handy topic for the student syllabus, is not likely to help to clarify matters. Indeed, Hirst and Thompson's view, where they make it clear that emphasis ought to be placed on the role of finance, for example, in constraining political choice, comes rather close to the approach of complex globalization theorists, if stripped of some of its baggage.

Moreover, a comparison of Cerny and Hirst and Thompson on the role of the state in internationalization/globalization shows both accounts depicting the state – or states – as pursuing policies which undermine themselves (Cerny 1996: 634–5; Hirst and Thompson 1996: 15). This form of analysis focuses on key moments of change, or, more effectively on episodes within which particular moments have the potential for precipitating change. The episode with which we are concerned begins during the 1970s. The main point at issue between these two approaches becomes one of interpretation. The key question which separates Cerny from Hirst and Thompson is whether the erosion of state power which occurred during this episode can be reversed. Both see important changes in remarkably similar terms as 'conjunctural' and 'important in their effects and scale, and at least in part policy driven' (as the sceptical Hirst and Thompson put it 1996: 15). But for Hirst and Thompson, this makes the change reversible, while for Cerny 'conjunctural shifts can have long-term structural consequences' (1996: 635). As such Cerny seems to identify the episode as continuing into the 1980s and strengthening, while Hirst and Thompson see it as starting and ending in the 1970s (although they do acknowledge that conjunctural change can have structural consequences; see 1996: 206).

There is strong risk that both integration and globalization (as we have seen) can be abstracted and reified. The episodes around which many analyses of globalization turn, which began in the 1970s, do not concern 'globalization' in the abstract. Instead, while the actions of those in positions of power in European states during the 1970s can be considered from the angle of globalization or internationalization, these same actions also shaped or constituted European developments. As the overwhelming majority of liberal democratic and industrial societies are European, it is all too easy to read the pattern of constraints and opportunities within which these stages operate in a generalizing manner, as manifestations of globalization. If the generalizations of globalization are not helpful neither is the voluntarism of its opponents.

Instead, the debate is likely to be moved forward fruitfully by focusing on the episodes which *both* sides of the debate agree are key, and examine in detail the intersection of structures and interplay of actors, an examination in which states, the European Union (into which some states are partly fused), (particularly transnational) business/business organizations and financial markets are likely to be particularly important.

Acknowledgments

I would like to thank those who attended the conference on which this book is based for their sharply perceptive comments on my original paper on this subject, and Colin Hay for helping me to make the final version much better than earlier ones. The usual disclaimers apply, of course.

Notes

1. As are a good many social democratic analyses of European integration and unlike some of the same authors' other work on the subject. See for instance Hirst 1995.
2. This contrast may suggest that the optimism about integration present in this book is engendered more by the requirements of the critique of globalization than it is by any more dispassionate assessment of political and economic opportunities.
3. For a coruscating critique of contemporary accounts of integration which parade a deracinated stylization of neofunctionalist theory see the work of Laura Cram 1996; 1997a; 1997b.
4. But see, among others, Grahl and Teague 1989 for an analysis which focuses on the substantive political and economic character and consequence of the internal market.

Bibliography

Baldwin, P. (1990) *The Politics of Social Solidarity: Class Bases of the European Welfare State 1875–1975*, Cambridge: Cambridge University Press.

Bernard, M. (1996) 'Regions in the Global Political Economy: Beyond the Local-Global Divide in the Formation of the Eastern Asian Region', *New Political Economy*, 1 (3), 335–53.

Castles, F. (1985) *The Working Class and Welfare: Reflections on the Political Development of Welfare States in Australia and New Zealand, 1890–1980*, Sydney: Allen and Unwin.

Castles, F. and D. Mitchell (1993) 'Worlds of Welfare and Families of Nations', in F. Castles (ed.) *Families of Nations: Patterns of Public Policy in Western Democracies*, Aldershot: Dartmouth.

Castles, F. and C. Pierson (1996) 'A New Convergence? Recent Policy Developments in the United Kingdom, Australia and New Zealand', *Policy and Politics*, 24 (3), 233–45.

Cerny, P. G. (1990) *The Changing Architecture of Politics: Structure, Agency and the Future of the State*, London: Sage.

Cerny, P. G. (1995) 'Globalization and the Changing Logic of Collective Action', *International Organization*, 49, 595–625.

Cerny, P. G. (1996) 'Globalization and other stories: The search for a new paradigm for international relations', *International Journal*, 51 (4), 617–37.

Coleman, W. D. and G. R. D. Underhill (1995) (eds) *The Single Market and global economic integration*, special edition of the *Journal of European Public Policy*, 2 (3), 331–534.

Cowles, M. G. (1995) 'Setting the Agenda for a New Europe: The ERT and EC 1992', *Journal of Common Market Studies*, 33 (4), 501–26.

Cram, L. (1993) 'Calling the Tune without Paying the Piper: The Role of the Commission in European Community Social Policy', *Policy and Politics*, 21 (2), 135–46.

Cram, L. (1996) 'Integration theory and the study of the European policy process' in J. J. Richardson (ed.) *European Union: Power and Policy-Making*, London: Routledge.

Cram, L. (1997a) *Policymaking in the European Union: Conceptual Lenses and the Integration Process*, London: Routledge.

Cram, L. (1997b) 'The European Commission and the 'European Interest': Institutions, Interaction and Preference Formation in the EU Context' Paper presented at the European Community Studies Association Meeting, 29 May–1 June, Seattle, USA.

Dolowitz, D. and D. Marsh (1996) 'Who Learns What from Whom', *Political Studies*, 44 (2), 343–57.

Dunleavy, P. (1996) 'The Allocation of Governance Functions in the European Union: Explaining the 'Drift to Brussels' Paper to the Forschungsgesprach at the University of St Gallen, Switzerland 11–13 September 1996 'Creating Countervailing Institutions in Europe'.

Esping-Andersen, G. (1990) *The Three Worlds of Welfare Capitalism*, Cambridge: Polity.

Grahl, J. and P. Teague (1989) *1992: The Big Market*, London: Lawrence and Wishart.

Hay, C. (1996) *Re-Stating Social and Political Change*, Buckingham: Open University Press.

Hirst, P. Q. (1995) 'The European Union at the Crossroads: Integration or Decline?' in Bellamy, R., V. Bufacchi and D. Castiglione *Democracy and Constitutional Culture in Europe*, London: Lothian Foundation.

Hirst, P. and G. Thompson (1996) *Globalization in Question*, Cambridge: Polity.

Hutton, W. (1996) *The State We're In*, New and Revised Edition London: Vintage.

Ludlam, S. (1996) 'The Spectre Haunting Conservatism: Europe and Backbench Rebellion', in S. Ludlam and M. J. Smith (eds) *Contemporary British Conservatism*. London: Macmillan.

MacNamara, K. (1997) 'Globalization Is What We Make of It?' Paper presented at the European Community Studies Association Meeting, 29 May–1 June, Seattle, USA.

Milward, A. S. (1992) *The European Rescue of the Nation-State*, London: Routledge.

Mount, F. (1992) *The British Constitution Now*, London: Heinemann.

Moravcsik, A. (1993) 'Preferences and Power in the European Community: A Liberal Intergovernmentalist Approach', *Journal of Common Market Studies*, 31 (4), 473–524.

Moravcsik, A. (1994) 'Why the European Community Strengthens the State: Domestic Politics and International Cooperation' Paper presented to the Conference of Europeanists, Chicago April 1994.

Ohmae, K. (1990) *The Borderless World*, London: Collins.

Ohmae, K. (1996) *The End of the Nation State*, London: Collins.

Orloff, A. S. (1993) 'Gender and the Social Rights of Citizenship: The Comparative Analysis of Gender Relations and Welfare States', *American Sociological Review*, 58 (3), 303–28.

Peterson, J. (1995) 'Decision-making in the European Union: Towards a framework for analysis', *Journal of European Public Policy*, 2 (1), 69–93.

Pollack, M. (1995) 'Creeping Competence: The Expanding Agenda of the European Community', *Journal of Public Policy*, 14 (2), 97–143.

Pollack, M. (1996) 'The New Institutionalism and EC Governance: The Promise and Limits of Institutional Analysis', *Governance*, 9 (4), 429–58.

Robertson, R. (1992) *Globalization: Social Theory and Global Culture*, London: Sage.

Sandholtz, W. and J. Zysman (1989) '1992: Recasting the European Bargain', *World Politics* , 42 (1), 5–28.

Watson, M. (1999) 'Globalisation and British Political Development' in D. Marsh, J. Buller, C. Hay, P. Kerr, J. Johnston, S. McAnulla and M. Watson, *Postwar British Politics in Perspective*. Combridge: Polity.

Watson, M. and Hay, C. (1998) 'In the Dedicated Pursuit of Dedicated Capital: Restoring an Indigenous Investment Ethic to British Capitalism', *New Political Economy*, forthcoming.

Wincott, D. (1996) 'Federalism and European Union: The Scope and Limits of the Treaty of Maastricht', *International Political Science Review*, 17 (4), 403–15.

Wincott, D., Buller, J. and Hay, C. (1999) 'Strategic Errors and/or Structural Binds? John Major and Europe', in P. Dorey (ed.) *The Major Premiership: Politics and Policies under John Major*. London: Macmillan.

Zysman, J. (1996) 'The Myth of a 'Global' Economy: Enduring National Foundations and Emerging Regional Realities', *New Political Economy*, 1 (2), 157–84.

Index

194 *Index*